Glorious Gifts from Your Kitchen

By the Same Author

THE EFFICIENT EPICURE

Lisa Yockelson

Glorious Gifts from Your Kitchen

E. P. Dutton, Inc.   New York

Published in the United States by E. P. Dutton, Inc.,
2 Park Avenue, New York, N.Y. 10016

Library of Congress Cataloging in Publication Data

Yockelson, Lisa.
    Glorious gifts from your kitchen.

    1. Cookery.   2. Gifts.   I. Title.
TX652.Y63   1984   641.5   84-4210

ISBN: 0-525-24255-4

Published simultaneously in Canada by
Fitzhenry & Whiteside Limited, Toronto
COBE

10 9 8 7 6 5 4 3 2 1
First Edition

For Steven F. Madeoy
forever and always

Contents

Acknowledgments

Two women, Diane Harris and Susan Lescher, have followed this project to completion with absolute dedication. Diane Harris's keen editorial eye and good taste are evident on each and every page, and Susan Lescher's enthusiasm and support never failed to be a mainstay.

Glorious Gifts from Your Kitchen

1

On
Food Gifts

Food gifts are the sum of a cook's abundance, the outpouring of a special kind of sharing. My hall pantry bulges with all kinds of baskets, tins, and assorted containers, and the sweet and savory things to fill them up. For me, the pleasures of making and giving presents that are edible began one summer many years ago, when I found several nests of beautiful old baskets at an arts and antiques fair. For Christmas of that year, I baked and preserved things for filling the baskets to give as gifts, adding charming frills for decoration. Ever since, I have taken pleasure in cooking up things like unusual jams, setting to mellow simple extracts, or turning out several batches of homey drop cookies, all for filling the odd and numerous containers I have in my collection. To achieve exceptional gifts, I've found you have to be equally dedicated to the goodness of the food and to a handsomely designed package.

So this is a sensuous cookbook, one which emphasizes not only the taste of unusually good foods but the visual appeal of just the right jar, basket, or some such vessel. Those of you who enjoy cooking, crafting, and gift-giving of a personal nature will find this book packed with festive recipes and equally merry ways for creating arrangements. There are recipes for a whole range of food projects—steamed puddings in anticipation of the holidays, brandied fruit mixtures, the very simple flavoring of vinegar with fresh berries, an easy and elegant chocolate spread. But in the main, I see the cook as a designer, cleverly juggling form and color and food.

Home-cooked food gifts should follow a practical and delicious seasonal orientation. That way, you will have the right gift at the right time: a load of jars holding brandied fruit at the end of summer, and other assorted fruit, nut, and vegetable concoctions for the purpose of indulging others; a pantry that boasts a rich assortment of Christmas cookies by mid-December, or some mellowing fruitcakes. Choose simple, cool presents in the summer months (such as any of my suave, luxurious spreads) or more complex, hearty gifts in the winter. Bake a down-to-earth country kind of cookie to give the hostess of a picnic in the woods, or put up showpiece jars of Blueberries in Black Currant Liqueur to take along for feasting at a stylish summer house.

Mainly, I turn to antique cookware, modern baskets and wireware containers, and tins of all sorts for filling with what's homemade. The combination of my own avid interest in collecting antique pottery, baskets, and glassware and a certain intense domestic involvement have combined to create my interest for joining food with novel containers. While traveling, I love to browse through small out-of-the-way stores and look over the sometimes tumultuous assortment of old pieces of kitchenware, with thoughts for filling them with something delectable at other times of the year. Sometimes, you will make an investment in a container because the gift is a special one and the container will endure as a piece of creative work while the food that's held within is to be enjoyed for the moment. At other times, you can buy a handful of small and not too expensive old cookie stamps or cutters and afix those to the sides of a jar of preserves—in that way, you're still contributing to the unity of giving something lasting with something good to eat.

Both my paternal grandmother and mother were lovers of all things beautiful and they introduced me at an early age to an appreciation of such treasures as bowls, jars, and all the gaily decorated folk arts of other cultures. My pleasure in these inspires, supports, and most emphatically touches whatever gifts come from my kitchen.

Food Gifts with Style

Food gifts have an unfailingly distinctive character to them because they can be tailored to fit almost any occasion—family picnics, boating parties, alfresco luncheons and dinners, holiday suppers. I love to keep a variety of delectable presents on hand for those times when I'm invited to a beach picnic or a country barbecue or some other impromptu occasion. And when friends come by with a gift of a big basket of home-grown tomatoes, I want to reciprocate with something from my kitchen, perhaps a few jars of spicy chutney or liqueur-steeped fruits.

Apart from making delightful presents, many of the recipes in this book would be ideal for creating a storehouse of good things to add richness and variety to your own meals. So don't hesitate to set aside for yourself a few jars of anything you prepare. Connie's Hot Pepper Jelly is terribly good whisked into the pan juices of sautéed chicken or pork and also makes a delicious tangy spread on its own on crackers; Brandied Cherries may enhance a holiday bird or pound cake, or you can puree a quarter cupful to create an intriguing pan sauce for pork or chicken; Red Onion and Currant Marmalade is a delightful tart-sweet condiment to accompany grilled beef or chicken. And any of the nine recipes for cooked cranberries will serve you well for your Thanksgiving table as well as being an opulent addition to a buffet lunch, open house, or supper of roasted or smoked meats or poultry.

The best part about preparing food gifts is that it brings a variety of different, satisfying experiences into your life. First, there is the pleasure of the planning and shopping stage, then the down-to-earth rewards of a quiet afternoon presiding over a mixing bowl or canning kettle. And throughout the year there is the heightened awareness that comes with being on the lookout for unusual containers and other packaging materials. Finally, making up food gifts is a special opportunity to imprint your own style of hospitality.

As I'm hooked on crisp butter cookies, I bake and pack up at least fifteen tins of them a season; they look lovely wrapped and mounded in old metal cake molds, or, to splurge, in deep copper molds. Large old funnel-shaped dippers are great to fill with any kind of cookie, as are shiny black lacquered flour sifters, cake tins, and cheese boxes. Old footed colanders with ear handles in tin, stamped tin, or gray graniteware are capacious, strong looking, and very handy for filling with small cakes and candies. So are spouted kugelhof molds and oval and oblong rimmed jelly molds; just invert and fill up. Antique butter molds, shortbread molds, and breadboards are expensive but still exquisite bases for a heap of cookies held in place with clear cellophane. Pewter ice cream molds and classically styled heart-shaped cream cheese molds are fine treasures for containing cookies and small dainty cakes.

A blue stoneware cookie jar is a fine old collectible piece (filled with Cinnamon-Chocolate Crisps and Chocolate-Walnut Shortbread) to give the cook who has everything. I have just such a jar with the somewhat baffling words "Cookie Jar Bricker" on the front. Bricks, it turns out, are hard Pennsylvania tea cookies. I keep plushy and soft date mounds, chewy chocolate cookies, or macaroons in it because I don't bake bricks. Following is what I do bake, and I hope you enjoy baking and giving such bounty as much as I have each season.

The Versatility of Food Gifts

Homemade sweets, snacks, cookies and cakes, condiments, flavored nuts and fruits, and pâté-type spreads—these, alone, or in combination with other food, make striking gifts for any occasion. Whether the gift is intended for your dinner party host or hostess, the couple that invites you to their summer house or winter ski condominium, or if you find yourself frequently asked to impromptu picnics or covered-dish suppers, food gifts are always a welcome addition to any event. The gift may be used right on the spot, or may be saved for future good eating. Either way, no good cook can have too many assorted jars of sauce, jams, compotes, or other preserved goodies for gracing the pantries and tables of friends.

Preserved fruits make a beautiful gift to take along to a brunch, or if you are a weekend guest, to your host or hostess. I find that my butter cakes, fruitcakes, and cookies are heartily received at Sunday suppers, buffet dinners, and open houses; these, wrapped up on beautiful breadboards or gracefully laid out on flat baskets lined with fresh leaves and ringed with fragrant bundles of spices, make a smashing gift.

Mincemeat, Nesselrode, and any of the specialties from the Rum Pot in chapter 3, I find make the best gifts during the months of September and October, when cooks think about including them in their holiday cooking. Even so, I keep these put-up things year-round because I am likely to incorporate them into desserts not traditionally linked to the holidays.

Simple Yet Special Gifts of Food

Some of the simplest recipes I know make the liveliest and handsomest food gifts. For the cooks on your gift list, you might want to give delicacies that are used to enhance other foods—a superlatively rich vanilla-brandy extract to spoon over a compote of fruits, to stir into an eggnog, or to flavor a mousse; preserved chestnuts to embellish simple ice cream or to garnish cakes and custards; seasoned pecans and walnuts for nibbling or to scatter over ice cream, cookies, and cake icing; a luscious chestnut and chocolate spread to serve paired with plain cookies or to ice a pound cake. It's no trouble at all to put up Flavored Honey and Herb Sugars and both add a distinctive taste to drinks, baked goods, and fruit desserts. I like to make these up in fairly large batches to keep them on hand. All that's needed is an attractive jar, perhaps covered

4

with a checked napkin or fresh leaves and topped with any one of my edible trimmings (see chapter 2).

The Sweet and Hot Mustard is another easy-to-prepare but unusually delicious treat. A piquant, smooth-textured mustard, it looks appealing when parceled out in small glass pots or straight-sided cylinders secured with corks.

Apricots in Rum Pot, Currants or Yellow Raisins in Rum Pot, or Dates in Brandy Pot, are all easy, fragrant possibilities for gift-giving. These recipes produce a delectable rum-steeped fruit without the somewhat more elaborate steps involved in the Summer and Autumn Rum Pot. Any of these crocked fruits make luscious toppings for a plain cake or ice cream or for use in hot or cold puddings.

The Chocolate-Chestnut Spread with Rum, a chocolate lover's delight with an intriguing richness of chestnuts and rum, couldn't be simpler to make yet is a happy marriage of good ingredients. And it makes an alluring gift when packed in small crocks. Suggest to the fortunate recipient that it's ideal as a quick icing for one small layer cake or loaf, or to spread on butter biscuits or with fresh fruit.

Twice-Cooked Crispy Walnuts, Toasted Texas Pecans, Cinnamoned and Sugared Pecans, Whole Chestnuts in Rum-Spice Syrup, Whole Chestnuts in Maple Liqueur Syrup, Apple Mincemeat with Almonds and Dates, Pear Mincemeat, or Fruit and Nut Rum Fantasia are good nut and fruit ideas to make as gifts—though none involve intricate canning procedures and look professional when jarred. Besides, they are such fun to make. Pack them in clear glass jars and decorate the tops with edible treats and keep them on hand over a period of weeks. I find such gifts are most welcome because people generally do not take the time to cook and flavor nuts, make a special kind of mincemeat, or prepare jars of sweet chestnuts.

Tuna Spread with Walnuts, Savory Cream Cheese Spread, Roquefort Cream, Goat Cheese and Crème Fraiche Spread with Herbs, and Smoked Whitefish Spread with Dill are delectable gifts that can be made in a hurry yet are truly elegant. For a close friend choose a handsome terrine or crock for holding one of these mixtures and the container becomes a valuable serving piece when the contents have been gobbled up.

These special super-easy recipes require no more than prime ingredients, a bit of time, and the enthusiasm of the cook. They are especially well suited to the cook who takes pleasure in making interesting gifts that are essentially undemanding. Because they have a cheerful homemade goodness and a dash of luxury, they are exactly the kind of little flourishes that capture the spirit of the season.

The Comfort of a Full Larder

Good cooking is all about having a steady seasonal supply of delicious things to enjoy. Making food gifts is an especially satisfying way of keeping the larder stocked. As you create gifts for special friends you can also set aside a few jars of all the good things for yourself.

To maintain a pantry of delectable foods, I encourage you to follow nature's clock. Quality-minded cooks know the value of working with all the glorious produce when it is plentiful and prime. Come the end of summer your cupboard may hold glistening jars of blueberry chutney; in fall an array of cranberry relishes; during Christmas an assortment of cookies in many flavors, seasoned nuts, containers of candied peels, tins of mellowing fruitcakes. Throughout the year, you will then have various kinds of food that make great gifts. You'll find that the mix of recipes in this book have a range of storage capability. With a little economy of time and practicality you can also think ahead and plan out several interrelated cooking sessions; this is especially helpful during the winter holidays when baking goodies for presents in the calm of your own kitchen is a wonderful experience.

STORING YOUR GIFTS

My fruitcakes, steamed pudding, canned brandied fruit, conserves, chutneys, jams, and specialties of the Rum Pot are all enticing food that need not be eaten immediately, but may be prepared months ahead for storage. Fruitcakes may be made up to six full months ahead of time (I've even aged a fruitcake for one year, basting it now and again with a little brandy) sealed in an airtight container; the shelf life of canned food is one year, as long as it is held in a cool, dark pantry. Butter cakes, tea breads, and most cookies (with the exception of the cookies in Chapter 5's Christmas Cookie Tin) should be baked, wrapped, and presented as a gift within a day of baking. Cookies from the Christmas Cookie Tin may be baked several weeks ahead and stored airtight on a cool cupboard shelf. All of the pound cakes in Summer Feasting should age a bit, overnight or up to two days to mellow, which means that you may bake the pound cake ahead and wrap it up a day later. This is a good cake to have around in the summer to serve with fresh fruit, but you will also appreciate the do-ahead quality of the cakes around Christmas when a pound cake is so handy to serve with eggnog, mulled wine, and other drinks. Fruitcakes, of course, love to linger about, with or without additional anointments of liqueur; then I glaze and decorate them at the last moment.

Whenever I need a food gift and there's no time to bake or can, I turn to recipes such as Toasted Texas Pecans, Twice-Cooked Crispy Walnuts, Cinnamoned and Sugared Pecans, Fruit and Nut Rum Fantasia, Flavored Honey, Herb Sugars, Whole Chestnuts in Rum-Spice Syrup, or Whole Chestnuts in Maple Liqueur Syrup. Other possibilities are such ongoing treats as the Rum Pot fruits, marinated olives, and it's always nice to have a few dozen cookies on hand to wrap up for guests that drop by.

When food gifts are presented, magically wrapped, it's always a nice idea to include serving suggestions. And friends who cook do seem to appreciate a handwritten recipe attached to the present.

Planning for the Cooking Sessions

Part of the pleasure of cooking up a batch of food gifts is in the planning—looking out for beautiful containers, choosing ingredients that are ripe and plentiful, and letting the seasons inspire and coordinate the many kinds of food you can prepare for gift-giving. Gorgeous vegetables and fruits, the products of a warm and bountiful summer, inspire jams, jellies, relishes, and the like, and the cold, blustery, stay-at-home early fall and winter months encourage us to stay by a warm oven and remove sheet after sheet of cookies or deep pans of fruitcake.

It's a good idea to begin gathering fruits and nuts as early as the end of summer, start marinating them beginning mid-September, and actually cooking the recipes shortly thereafter. I like to organize special cooking sessions for food gifts alone—to make several fruitcakes (which takes the better part of one whole day), several batches of cookies (a long afternoon), or a few jars of flavored honey or sugar (just under an hour's preparation time). Since I am as concerned with the good looks of the food as I am with the taste of it, I like to set up separate sessions—small or large—in two areas: assembling the raw ingredients and selecting the complementary containers and accessories.

Selecting Containers and Accessories

Canning jars must be thoroughly cleaned before food is turned into them, but other packaging containers need be assembled only after the food is cooked and ready for presentation. Lay out the food and the containers on an open working surface, preferably in the kitchen, along with any accessories you are using to complete the package. After the food is wrapped, store it on an open shelf until it is given away; baked goods should be carefully stored lest they tumble out of their containers and get crushed. You can give things such as puddings or tea loaves in the containers in which they were made along with the recipe, a particularly nice gift as the recipient already has the appropriate baking vessel at hand to re-create the recipe. Make sure that you wipe loaves clean with a damp sponge to take off any crumbs; then wrap the food in clear cellophane and nest it in a beautiful basket or tray of some depth.

Achieving the Golden Cupboard

Special Guidelines on Canning Food Gifts

Veteran canners already know the pleasures of a pantry glowing and groaning with neat rows of tasty jams, preserves, chutneys, and like things, and are familiar with the procedures for putting up a batch of this or that. And even casual cooks, who would only make up a few jars of a favorite seasonal preserve, know the glories of having sparkling jars on hand.

The following information outlines all you need to know about canning the recipes in this book: the simple techniques for choosing ingredients and equipment, filling the jars, and preparing them for safekeeping on the cupboard shelf by treating them to a boiling-water bath—the method that preserves the food. When a recipe suggests that you use the boiling-water bath technique, it is here that you turn for directions; if you scrupulously attend to all of the details covered below, you will have perfectly canned food. Many of the preserved things in this book do not have to be canned, however, and can be safely stored in the refrigerator until you parcel out the contents for gift-giving. Each recipe will advise you of the length of time the goods may be stored.

Preparing the Ingredients and Equipment

Always choose fruits and vegetables that are fine, fresh, and completely unblemished. Quite simply, I am a stickler for having at hand quality ingredients. You just cannot beat their lovely sweet scent and taste, and as a gift-giver, you should want to use only the best materials.

Scrupulously pick, smell, and prod *everything* at the greengrocer or farm market to establish age. Any produce that is bruised, dented, or oozing juicy droplets is not fit for canning. While picking, select whole fruit for their even size so that cooking and canning heat is able to penetrate the goods evenly. Carefully and gently remove cores, skins, seeds, pits, and like parts as each recipe directs. Sometimes the skin of the fruit is left on, and after washing, is pierced with a skewer (as in my recipe for Kumquats in White Wine Syrup) in order that the fruit does not burst open when introduced into the hot liquid. Other times, fruit is peeled to preserve its shape whole before being submerged in some type of syrup, and a very sharp swivel-bladed peeler takes care of the irregular surface lumps and bumps while smoothing out the figure of the fruit.

I depend upon the following collection of items, a small list, and house them together in one cabinet section of my kitchen. With the exception of jars, these need not be replaced on a yearly basis, so when purchasing canning equipment, look out for solidly built pieces that look and feel strong in and out of the hand.

Glass jars, commonly referred to as "Ball jars" (a most reliable brand name), are available in sizes ranging from half pint (1 cup) to pint (2 cups) to quart (4 cups). Jars of 1-cup and 2-cup capacity are preferable for filling up with food intended as gifts. I look for "wide-mouth tapered pints" when buying the pint jars; the wide mouths make filling effortless. Check over the rims of the glass jars to detect any nicks or cracks. The jars will be accompanied by a package of dome lids, really two separate units—a flat vacuum lid with sealant running about ⅛ inch wide on the inside, and a screw band that holds the lid in place. Wash the jars and two-piece lids in hot soapy water using a soft sponge (a bristly scrubber could damage the glass or sealing compound), then rinse well. On preserving day, keep the clean lids in a saucepan of water set asimmering (about 180° F.) and the jars in a pot of hot water, off the heat, or in a warm (170° F.) oven on a cookie sheet.

A water-bath canner is essentially a large kettle deep enough to hold a series of jars and enough bubbling water to cover them by 2 inches. I own two canners, both made of speckled blue and white graniteware, both bought at my local hardware store (but I see them in drugstores, and most large supermarkets). The shorter one holds half pints and pints; the larger one is for big-load quarts. Each canner comes with a rack or "basket" that sits inside and holds the jars upright so that they are not able to touch the bottom of the canner or bump into each other. The boiling water circulates properly around the filled jars when they are so positioned. The lid to the canner should fit comfortably; on buying your canner, make sure that the lid sits level and does not wobble. All fruits and similarly acidic food, as well as jams, preserves, chutneys, fruit sauces, butters, conserves, and certain pickles and relishes, need to be canned by the boiling-water bath method if they are to be held on the cupboard shelf, so microorganisms never get a chance to develop.

I know of no other quick and efficient way to remove a hot, hot jar from a canning kettle than to use a jar lifter. This looks like a wide set of tongs that opens into two curved, plastic-coated sides that latch onto the top of a jar.

Now, this just-processed jar does not like to be placed in a draft (just like when *you* emerge from a bath or shower, all warm and content, you don't sit in a chilly or breezy room), or suffer any extremes of temperature. So, to provide a neutral, cozy surface on which to cool newly canned food, keep two or three very thick and cushiony terry cloth towels. Use the towels to line the top of a wooden board and set the hot jars right side up on the towels.

Filling the Jars

The jars are filled in two ways: either all hot and bothered, having been syruped and spiced and cooked down and thickened (this is known as a "hot pack"), or cool-as-a-cucumber cold, when food is placed in raw, and after that packing, a hot syrup is added (this is known as "raw pack" or "cold pack"). The alcoholic fruit (Brandied Cherries, Brandied Plums, Brandied Grapes, Blueberries in Black Currant Liqueur) is an example of the "cold pack"—these fruits are delicate and most easily handled when raw, especially since overcooking would damage the texture and contour of the fruit.

But before you ladle or arrange anything in jars, have the canner on the burner with the rack in place. For hot-packed foods, fill the canner two-thirds full with *boiling* water; for cold-packed food, fill it two-thirds full with *hot* water. Jarred cold-packed food should never be immersed in boiling water, lest the glass break.

Whether you are positioning bright sweet cherries in jars, soon to be covered with a hot brandy mixture, or spooning in a heady spiced chutney, it is important to do so with an eye toward beauty. Jewel-like sweets and savories are even more delectable when they are packed cleanly and compactly, in a neat pattern. For whole fruit, fill up jars with the prepared pieces and pour on enough syrup to cover the fruit to ½ inch of the top; thick jams, chutneys, marmalades, and so on should be poured in to ¼ inch of the top. This is called "headspace allowance," a rather clinical term, I think, but an important one to practice, as crowded, too tightly packed jars never process correctly. They do not vent out and the seals never complete themselves.

After each jar is filled up (again, make sure all jars are clean, dry, and hot), slip a very thin and narrow spatula or palette knife down the insides of the jar in two or three places, right between the food and the glass, to expel any air bubbles that may have developed during filling. Clean the top of the jar with a hot, damp cloth or paper towel. Press on a *dry, hot* lid and firmly screw on a dry band.

The Processing Procedure: Boiling-Water Bath

Place the jars in the rack, one in each slot. For hot-packed foods, add enough boiling water to rise up at least 1 inch, or preferably 2 inches, over the top of the jars. Pour the water to the sides, not on top of, the jars. For cold-packed food, fill up the canner with extra hot water.

For both packs, the process continues in the same manner. Bring the water to a furious boil. As the bubbles break the surface, and the water boils steadily, cover the canner and begin timing as required by each recipe. From time to time, check the level of the water and add more water if necessary to maintain the 1- to 2-inch level. When processing time is up, carefully remove each jar with a jar lifter to the towel-padded wooden board. Place the jars at least 3 inches apart so that the air can freely circulate around them. Allow the jars to cool undisturbed.

When the jars have cooled down, in about 3 hours, test for a good seal: with the pad of your index finger, press down on the center of the flat lid. If the seal has taken, it will look and remain slightly concave and *it will not pop back up*. If the lid springs up again, the seal has not been completed, and the food cannot be stored in a pantry.

After 12 hours, or the next day, label the jars and store them in a cool, dark cabinet. Light speeds up oxidation, so pretty as the jars are, keep them under cover.

In all actuality, this shower of information may indeed take longer to read than to practice. Once each procedure is accomplished, the next one turns into the most natural thing to do. Enter into this little exercise with a loving spirit and you'll find each movement rhythmic and easy.

2

All Sorts of Packages

A single open-weave mushroom crate, a scalloped ice cream mold, an antique Chinese basket, a wide glass pharmaceutical beaker with measurement lines etched on one side, an old stoneware batter pail with a basket-weave design, and a plain white Chinese take-out carton of heavy cardboard all have one thing in common—they are handsome possibilities for housing food gifts.

From a recycled berry basket to a moderately priced stoneware bowl to a fancy pewter ice cream mold in the design of an apple or an Eskimo there is an exceptional range for seeking out food containers based on both your pocketbook and imagination. In the end, no matter what vessel you choose, the food and its container must be a harmonious whole.

With the willingness to experiment, the cook now becomes the designer; and, the food having been made, the next consideration is the marriage between food and packaging. Therefore, in choosing containers, I first look to the shape and size. This is most important if, for example, you know that you'll be baking a lot of cookies, cakes, or breads as food gifts. It is particularly useful to buy containers at least one size or two larger than you *think* you'll need, as much of the baked goods, once wrapped in clear cellophane, takes up a lot of space. Anyway, the areas that are not filled up with food may be stuffed with clumps of Spanish moss, several cascades of freshly picked leaves, or partially dried autumnal just-turning-color leaves, or anything that is lightweight and decorative.

All Sorts of Packages

Flat trays, old lacquered or new bamboo, may be lined with fresh flat leaves, live ti leaves, or a batik napkin, making a solid base for tea breads and tea cakes, fruitcakes, pound cakes, and butter cakes. Colanders are large enough to hold wrapped cookies and even several jars of preserved fruit. For other containers to hold cookies, I look for both highly ornamented bowls and plain bowls with more subtle patterns. Wireware egg baskets or cabbage washers or early American herb-gathering and flower-gathering baskets make exceptional containers for baked teatime goodies.

Clasps of garlic, ginger, or cinnamon stick are easy to make, as are traditional pomanders—those citrus fruits punctuated with a mess of cloves and rolled in spice powder. For these projects, herbs and spices may be purchased in bulk from mail order sources, which are listed in the Appendix. The attachments look charming on all kinds of packages, whether the packaging material is slatted wood, ceramic, basketry, pewter, tin, wire, or copper. Ginger bundles are good for both sweet and savory packages of food, but I use the garlic bundle for savory food only. My recipes for aromatic add-ons to packages, Edible Trimmings and Festive Baubles, appear later on in this chapter.

Antique attachments to packages are lovely accents, too. Individual madeleine molds (some unusual ones may be found in the shape of a horse's head or a large cluster of grapes), a rosewood pie crimper with a porcelain wheel, a tin and wire doughnut cutter, or small, carefully carved butter-print molds are wonderful and highly individual objects for decorating containers. These are not inexpensive, however, so you must weigh their suitability accordingly. I find them interesting additions when ribboned to the side of a plain jar of something preserved.

The taste and style of the food gift often dictates the type of container to be used. During the Christmas holidays, I turn into a never-to-be-changed traditionalist and insist on yards of wide red and green satin ribbon, cookies and cake tins with miniature sleighs and holly branches printed on them, and dozens of cookie cutters bound together with silver and gold cording (to be used when pomanders and cinnamon sticks are not being pressed into service). In summer, I cherish the design of wood and straw, highly polished metal, and neutral whites and beiges for a cool, easy-flowing feeling to food gifts. I also rely on strong, natural materials and work with moss, hay, and rail-thin elegant branches to decorate food packages, and use bright and bold fabrics to cover and line containers.

I believe in a stable, studied relationship between the color and texture of the food and the color and texture of the container. A delicate fruit butter looks just wonderful in a graceful wireware canning rack or a slender woven basket tube. New wide, low baskets are perfect for any of my big fruitcakes, pound cakes, or butter cakes; late-nineteenth-century field baskets that are oval and wide make pleasing containers for a mixture of sweet and savory jarred gifts. A late-nineteenth- or early-twentieth-century half basket, literally half of a whole basket (oftentimes constructed with smooth hickory handles) is expensive but makes an unusual gift loaded with bar cookies or drop cookies, or better yet, gingerbread people. Most old baskets were originally designed with specific purposes in mind—for use in the orchard or herb patch (these baskets were wide and rectangular for storing herbs; or hexagonal and loosely woven for drying herbs)—but we can make them branch out from their fixed function into a contemporary setting.

Improvising containers when you are not relying on some antique beauty to do the job is satisfying, creative work. Some food gifts beg for a one-of-a-kind presentation, and I know two dramatic ways for crafting containers and one method for sprucing up single jars of anything put up. Both the Spanish moss basket and the leaf container are shapely and unforgettable constructions that are welcome and warm looking. The Spanish moss basket is a loose and casual-appearing basket that is covered in fluffy, squiggly Spanish moss, a lively environment for holding most any kind of food. And the leafy container, also, can hold just about anything. Then a playful way to decorate a preserving jar, in addition to tying a square of fabric to the lid, is to cover the bottom third with shiny galax leaves; it's a quick 10-minute project. Here are my directions for making these containers—a fresh and appealing collection!

A SPANISH MOSS BASKET

A large basket covered with Spanish moss at once looks homey and stylish, and will elicit sighs of pleasure with a bounty of individually wrapped Vanilla Shortbread or dozens of anything small and baked heaped within. Twice-Cooked Walnuts and Toasted Texas Pecans are perfectly suited to smaller mossy baskets; the nuts seem most welcome in this natural, woodsy environment.

To make this container, you'll need:

a long length of glossy freezer wrap or   *rubber cement*
   parchment paper   *Spanish moss*
a finely woven, inexpensive, unvar-
   nished basket, with ample sides

Spread out the freezer wrap or parchment paper shiny side up on an open work space; the basket will be constructed on this. At all costs, avoid using newspaper, which smudges the moss, the basket, your fingers, the whole project. Moss does like to fly about—it is stringy and frail—so if you are bothered about finding it in crevices around you, take everything outside on a sunny, *wind-free,* day.

14

Invert the basket on the paper. Apply a layer of rubber cement all over the sides, not too thin, not too thick. Leave the bottom completely unglued. When the cement has dried to tacky, about 1 minute, begin pressing down clumps of Spanish moss to the sides of the basket a section at a time.

The basket looks refined and elegant if the curly moss is kept even with the top of the basket. If it extends over the top, it will begin to resemble fly-away hair; trim the moss flush when it has dried thoroughly.

It is a waste of time and energy to stick big, thick clumps of moss to the basket; 4-inch patties about ⅓ inch thick settle quite perfectly on the sticky sides. Work quickly, so that the cement does not dry to a firmness; if it does, just brush on a little more.

Soon you will have established a steady pace and then it is possible to put together several baskets in the course of an hour or two. If you are working outdoors, bring the finished baskets indoors and let them dry in a relatively cool, draft-free room for a day or two.

Store each basket in a plastic bag and secure with a twist-tie. For safekeeping, place the basket on an open, flat shelf where other things cannot topple on top of your work.

A LEAFY CONTAINER

Unlike the Spanish moss basket, this vessel stays lush and beautiful for a few days only. But it is spectacular. The fresh leaves that adorn the outside of a straight glass cylinder must be emphatically green, supple (lightly so), and perfect. Magnolia leaves, being pliant yet firm, and not lacy, are my first choice. Whatever type of leaf you select, check it against the side of the chosen container. That is, leaves must be in proportion to the container—a very deep one needs leaves that are tall enough to extend fully top to bottom, without leaving a short space uncovered at the bottom.

Relatively thin, round, and smooth glass soufflé dishes are ideal to transform into a leafy container, although any plain, round wide-mouth type works as long as it is 4 inches high. You'll need:

*a sheet of freezer wrap or parchment
   paper*
a straight-sided glass container
*florist's adhesive clay, available wher-
   ever fresh flowers are sold (it
   comes coiled up on paper strips)*

fresh, firm leaves
a spool of enameled green florist's wire
raffia; or plain, sturdy ribbon
Spanish moss

(*continued*)

In your mind's eye, divide the container into thirds; place it on the sheet of freezer wrap or parchment paper. Press on an uninterrupted length of florist's clay around the top and bottom thirds of the container, leaving the center third bare.

To begin the application of leaves, take the widest leaf and place it at a slight diagonal angle on the bottom third of the container. Position the remaining leaves, one overlapping the next, *straight not slanted*, pressing firmly into the clay to hold them fast. Place leaves of the same length at the top of the container, making an even top edge. The leaves may certainly be at odd lengths on the bottom because they get trimmed off later on. Continue pressing on leaves, thus covering the entire container, rolling it along the sides as you go.

With a pair of very sharp scissors, cut off the leaves at the base so that the container can sit upright. Place the container right side up on a tabletop and check that it stands correctly. Retrim the base as necessary.

To finish the leafy container with ribbon, first run a length of florist's wire two times around the container just above the center. Hold out about 2 inches at the beginning, wrap around the wire, and twist both ends together as economically as possible. Press the twisted ends close to the container. Draw the ribbon around the wire and fashion the ends into a bow.

Otherwise, tie a triple-ply cord of raffia right above the middle of the container, knot it tightly twice, then tie the ends into a bow. With truly good raffia you can fluff out the bow by gently pulling apart each section with your thumbnails.

When you are ready to fill the container, prop up enough Spanish moss along the inside of it to conceal the outer florist's clay.

Fill and admire.

GALAX-LEAFED PRESERVING JARS

Glossy galax leaves secured to the bottom half of a filled jar is a fresh and simple approach to festooning relish and chutney, and other fruity mixtures. The strong leaves cling well to the sides of the jar (with a little help from florist's clay), making a delicate and witty sort of partial covering. Some of the contents of the jar still shows, which is pleasing to the eye. You'll need:

florist's clay
about 6 galax leaves for a half-pint pre-
    serving jar, about 9 leaves for a
    pint preserving jar
raffia

Afix a thin band (both in width and thickness) of florist's clay around the preserving jar, about 2 inches from the base.

Overlap the leaves at relatively wide spacing, shiny-side up, and press them firmly against the clay. Let the curved edges make their own free-form, almost rufflelike, design border around the sides of the jar. Arrange the leaves to keep the bottom even; but do snip off any thready stems at the base of the jar.

Encircle the leaves at the halfway point with a double band of raffia tied in a bow or just a plain knot.

Edible Trimmings and Festive Baubles

What makes a package of food so enticing, so special, are the little enhancements prettily attached to the sides of containers—a beautiful old cookie stamp or a small tin candy mold tucked to the side of a basket of cookies; a bunch of fragrant dried herb tied to the handle of a wire box of miniature cakes, fruited loaves, or steamed puddings; a bundle of dried gourds (available in the fall) joined with raffia and fastened to the side of preserved food.

Mostly these trimmings, or attachments, have a use all their own after the gift is opened and eaten up. Herbs and spices are useful in cooking year round; a homemade pomander hung in the closet or pantry makes the air smell clean and spicy-bright. And remember that all garnishes for packages need not be consumable: kitchen gadgets also add a provocative touch to the finished gift—aspic cutters, small graters (for nutmeg, ginger), individual melon ball scoops, an attractive candy thermometer (old or new), a handcrafted wooden ravioli wheel, a butter knife or spreader, or a honey dipper. Attach these with silky cord or ribbon or use a little flexible florist's wire or clay (or both) to secure the decoration to the container, then make sure that it is covered by the ribbon.

BOUQUETS OF CINNAMON STICKS

Pungent red-brown cinnamon sticks, the curled bark of a small tree native to Ceylon, are at home tucked into a country basket of cookies; tied in a bundle and added to an array of jams, fruit breads, and other treats; or combined with holly to create a bold wreath around a festive fruitcake. Garland them, too, around my Apricot Holiday

Pudding for an altogether spectacular gift. (Note: At holiday time make the air fragrant and sweet by simmering cinnamon sticks in a small pot of water on a back burner.)

For each bouquet, you'll need:

8 4-inch cinnamon sticks*
florist's wire
satiny or ribbed ribbon

Place the cinnamon sticks on a cookie sheet and pop them into a preheated 275° F. oven for 10 minutes (use the middle shelf). With a pair of tongs, remove the sticks to a wire cooling rack. This brief heating helps the spice to weather all sorts of climates.

When the cinnamon sticks have reached room temperature, pack them into taut parcels by encircling a length of florist's wire eight or ten times around the center of the bouquet.

Hide the wire by wrapping a piece of colorful ribbon around the wire fastening, then draw both ends together into a graceful bow.

ORANGE OR LEMON POMANDERS

Pomanders provide such a classic, Decemberish holiday scent that having them around the house in spring or summer constantly reminds me of jingle bells, snow, and pine branches. I don't mind at all. The purity of the cinnamon-allspice-clove mixture that the pomanders are rolled around in is held fast and powerful by orrisroot (*Iris florentina*), a fixative available powdered and chopped at pharmacies and herbalists. Orrisroot is characterized by a light violetlike fragrance; it mingles so well with the bolder, more seductive spices.

For 4 firm, small oranges or lemons, you'll need:

8 ounces whole cloves (about 2 ounces	*¼ cup ground allspice*
for each piece of fruit)	*¼ cup ground cloves*
¼ cup ground cinnamon	*¼ cup orrisroot powder*

Stick each impeccably dry piece of fruit full of cloves by inserting each clove individually into the flesh ⅛ inch apart. Cloves resemble nailheads, so the elongated

---

* Cinnamon sticks in a variety of lengths up to 12 inches can be ordered from the spice shops listed in the Resources for Spices in the Appendix.

"nail" section is to be pressed into the fruit, leaving the head to decorate the surface of the fruit.

Ordinarily the rind of the fruit is easily pierced by the cloves, but if the surface resists slightly or is the least bit tough, you can use the pointed end of a thin skewer to begin the process and then insert the cloves. Place cloves so that the color of the fruit is barely visible. This will give the full look required and produces a pomander that will last almost indefinitely. Making these holiday specialties is a worthy but time-consuming project, which happily can be picked up and put down at will.

Sometime during the studding of the fruit, or right after you have finished, measure out the spices and orrisroot powder into a large jar. Shake vigorously to blend before storing in a cool place.

To finish the pomander, spread out the spice mixture in a deep plate or shallow soup bowl. Roll the fruit around and around in the powdery concoction. Then set the fruit on a screened tray or on a cooling rack set over a cookie sheet for a few days to dry out. At least once a day reroll the fruit in the spice mixture. After 1 week, the pomander is ready to attach to the handle of a basket as a garnish; for this, crisscross with ribbon, then loop onto a handle.

BUNDLES OF GARLIC, BUNDLES OF GINGER

Ginger, still knobby all over when dried, and ivory-skinned garlic (American) or purple-skinned garlic (Mexican or Italian) make lively clusters for topping off packages. The dried ginger has a remarkably clean kind of air about it, and that makes it a highly versatile accompaniment to any food present, a garnish that can be used in another form by grinding it finely on one of those tiny nutmeg graters (spice cakes and cookies will benefit from this ground spice). If bottled dried Jamaican ginger is difficult for you to locate, a clasp of fresh ginger is just as enticing a creation—firm-fleshed ginger, young and hard, peaks in the United States in early autumn. Also, fresh ginger does form a somewhat bulky mass when you tie together a few pieces, so for the best effect, pair it with a square oversized tin or a round wooden box.

You'll need:

3 whole, fat bulbs of garlic, or 5 large pieces of dried Jamaican ginger	*green florist's wire* *decorative ribbon or raffia*

For each bundle, choose plump, even-size bulbs of garlic with thin papery extensions. The paper segments must join to a point for this garnish to work; for the papery topknots to be the joining point, you need to find bulbs that have not been cut or otherwise robbed of them.

Wind a 12-inch length of florist's wire several times on one topknot, leaving about 2 inches free at one side. Add the second garlic bulb, drawing the wire around several times, and finish by fastening with the third bulb and wrapping the wire around it several times. Complete the unit by twisting the free ends together firmly. Trim off any long ends with a pair of wire clippers or sturdy scissors, and press any outstanding wire close in to the other wound-up wire to secure it.

Circle the wire several times with a length of raffia, leaving about 4 inches free on one side. Finish the bundle by joining two free ends of raffia into a knot, leaving about a 1- to 2-inch loop for sliding onto a basket handle, or onto a piece of ribbon for decorating a package.

Three garlic bundles, I must tell you, tied up at the three topknots, make a smashing looking "ball" for attaching to a box or basket.

To bundle up the ginger, heap it together in a clump, find a common center section, and tightly wind florist's wire around the middle. Since dried ginger is squiggly looking, you will get a rather free-form decorative chunk that is beautiful in its own rustic way. Knot up the wire by twisting the ends together, then bind with raffia as described above.

To keep the mood, dried ginger bundles are especially appropriate garnishes for any cookie or cake featuring the root spice. The garlic garnish is best used around savory things, since its potency somehow clashes with sweet bakery specialties.

Packing Food Gifts

One important consideration for all the delicious baked or otherwise prepared food you'll give as gifts is keeping it fresh and lovely tasting from the time it is baked to the time it is delivered. For packing cookies, I am fond of wrapping them individually, or in the case of very large yields wrapping two cookies back to back in clear (not colored) heavy cellophane wrap. Cakes may also be wrapped in cellophane before packing into a container. The cellophane keeps the baked goods moist, but cakes and cookies should be removed from airtight containers and wrapped just before assembling and giving to keep things fresh. Big round cakes and fruitcakes may be wrapped in a large square of cellophane, the ends gathered up into a topknot, clasped with a ribbon, and garnished with sprigs of fresh leaves, herbs, or spices. Occasionally, I'll put a piece of solid-colored tissue paper between the container and the cellophane-wrapped goody for a sparkling, crisp effect (the tissue paper is particularly convenient if you haven't any fabric on hand).

Vessels that come in direct contact with the food, such as bottles for holding homemade extract, wire-hinged preserving jars, or standard preserving jars with lids and bands, need to be impeccably clean before filling with food. A wash in warm sudsy water followed by a rinsing and full dishwasher cycle of washing and drying produces a sterile jar. If you are corking bottles of vinegar, extract, or fruit syrup, take care to check the corks for smooth bottoms and sides—this is essential for a proper seal. Likewise, round rubber gaskets for sealing hinged preserving jars should be free of any cracks or breaks.

For cushioning a combination of jarred gifts in one large basket, or a nest of cookies, a large clump of Spanish moss looks pretty and works quite well. If moss isn't available, either cedar or juniper sprigs can be used. Place a rather thick layer of moss on the bottom of the container, then set in one jar and tuck moss around it. Continue to set in more jars and protect the sides with moss until you have filled up the basket and the jars sit snugly. Cookies and loaf cakes won't move around when set in a bed of moss, and if you are traveling with food gifts, the moss is especially good protection against filled containers losing their shape.

Labeling Food Gifts

As mentioned earlier, when it comes to labeling some wonderful homemade creation, a note about what its appropriate uses are or a special suggestion on how the gift should be served or stored (especially once opened) is a considerate addition to a name tag that accompanies each gift.

Blank, solid-colored tags, with a hole punched out to one side for sliding a length of ribbon or cord through is the best surface on which to identify a food gift. If you don't mind parting with it, the neatly handwritten recipe for the gift, tied together with a ribbon, is a splendid touch—and is designed to avoid the almost inevitable telephone call for the recipe once the gift has been eaten. Oftentimes, if I do include the recipe and there's some ingredient listed that's hard to find, I'll add a little note on the source for obtaining the specialty, or even include the ingredient in the packaging of the gift.

3

Summer Feasting and Harvesting

DIPS, SPREADS, AND SAVORY SNACKS

CHICK-PEA–YOGURT DIP
RED PEPPER AND HERB DIP
SAVORY CREAM CHEESE SPREAD
HERBED CREAM CHEESE SPREAD
ROQUEFORT CREAM
GOAT CHEESE AND CRÈME FRAICHE SPREAD WITH HERBS
TUNA SPREAD WITH WALNUTS
TUNA SPREAD WITH SUMMER SAVORY
SMOKED WHITEFISH SPREAD WITH DILL
OLIVE AND ANCHOVY SPREAD
HERRING WITH LEMON AND SPICES
HERRING AND POTATO VINAIGRETTE WITH DILL
SWEET AND SOUR HERRING WITH SPICES

SPECIAL CONDIMENTS AND PICKLES

BLACK RASPBERRY VINEGAR
BLUEBERRY VINEGAR
CONNIE'S HOT PEPPER JELLY

YELLOW TOMATO JAM
LEMON-TOMATO JAM
TOMATO, RED PEPPER, AND ONION RELISH
CUCUMBER AND ONION PICKLES
SWEET SPICED DILL PICKLES
ALICE'S "Z" RELISH
PICKLED OKRA
RED TOMATO AND CUCUMBER CHUTNEY
TOMATO AND RED PEPPER CHILI SAUCE
CHILI BARBECUE SAUCE
CHILI-ONION BARBECUE SAUCE

THE BRANDIED FRUIT OF SUMMER

BRANDIED CHERRIES
SPICED CHERRIES
BRANDIED PLUMS
BRANDIED PEACHES
APRICOTS IN APRICOT LIQUEUR
BRANDIED GRAPES
BLUEBERRIES IN BLACK CURRANT LIQUEUR
SAVORY PAPAYA AND RED PLUM COMPOTE

SWEET SAUCES AND PRESERVES

BLUEBERRY SYRUP
SPICY APRICOT GLAZE
RED PLUM SAUCE
FRESH APRICOT SAUCE
NECTARINE AND GINGER CHUTNEY
RED PLUM CHUTNEY
SPICED BLUEBERRY CONSERVE
ORANGE-PLUM CONSERVE WITH WALNUTS
PEACH BUTTER
CANTALOUPE BUTTER
BLACKBERRY JAM WITH CASSIS
CINNAMON-LEMON PRUNE PLUMS

POUND CAKES AND MUFFINS

> VANILLA POUND CAKE
> CREAM CHEESE POUND CAKE
> RUM POUND CAKE
> CINNAMON-SOUR CREAM POUND CAKE
> DELICATE ALMOND POUND CAKE
> LEMON POUND CAKE
> WHOLE-WHEAT MUFFINS WITH CURRANTS
> BRAN MUFFINS

AFTER SUMMER HERB GATHERING

> DRIED MIXED HERB BOUQUETS
> DRIED HERB BUNDLES
> SAVORY PACKETS

THE RUM POT

> SUMMER AND AUTUMN RUM POT
> APRICOTS IN RUM POT
> CURRANTS OR YELLOW RAISINS IN RUM POT
> DATES IN BRANDY POT
> FRUIT AND NUT RUM FANTASIA

Summer—summer—summer! The soundless footsteps on the grass.

—JOHN GALSWORTHY
The Indian Summer of a Forsyte, 1918

Footsteps are muted by the thick, even tufts of cool grass in the open expanse of the lawn. A picnic in the park heralds the new lingering warmth. The simple, fresh taste of the season's first blueberries, nectarines, peaches, and plums is set against the rich goodness of velvety pound cake. Summer is a stimulating pleasure of contrasts.

Food gifts of the months of June, July, and August should be really "summer-proof"—eminently packable and crisp and cool—a happy contrast of bright and pungent with smooth and mellow. Visually, I like food at this time of year to reflect the kaleidoscope of color found in a vegetable garden. To guarantee your host or hostess's pleasure at any summer gathering, combine several of these delights and eliminate much of their work. Pound cake and fruit sauces are natural companions. The dips and spreads, too, have an easy affinity for each other and look elegant when several are jarred and arranged in a natural wooden basket; choose a container that is finely woven and make a bottom layer of dried beans to set the crocks and jars into. The layer of beans will anchor everything while forming a nifty base. Any small dried legume will do (as long as your basket is not full of gaping open patches), but I have found that Great Northern white beans or pinto beans work best.

For garnishing jars of savory food gifts, such as my Red Plum Chutney, Cucumber and Onion Pickles, or Nectarine and Ginger Chutney, small fresh hot peppers—like red cayenne or green serrano chile—are great for binding together in a tiny bundle: attach the peppers to the top side of the jar with a ribbon. The peppers will look just beautiful and give off a fiery, warm feeling. On the same principle, use a fresh clump of a sturdy herb like summer savory or thyme to tie onto the side of a jar. Tarragon, basil, or sage gets all weepy looking; what you want is a strong herb that still flourishes after an hour or two. Wind thin kitchen string around a fresh green bunch of sprigs, cover the string with ribbon, and hook onto the side of the jar.

In this the season of undiminished delights, canning good things and filling the pantry with them becomes my special passion. One friend of mine regularly makes beach plum chutney and jam—that's her traditional summer project—and friends greedily look forward to a jar, which is judiciously given out during the Christmas season. Luckily, for those of us who care, preserving food has become a more finely tuned art, strengthened more and more by regional food styles and some down-to-earth food sense. For example, I take great pleasure in giving shape and style to the likes of Jersey corn, tomatoes, and melon. Preserving them is a skillful way of keeping the vibrant flavors of the raw ingredients when they are at their peak.

Since summer preserving projects are often turned to winter gifts, don't forget to look through the recipes in other sections for ways to put up summer fruits in spirits, such as Brandied Cherries, Brandied Plums, Apricots in Apricot Liqueur, Blueberries in Black Currant Liqueur, and the luscious recipe for fruit as a savory, the Savory Papaya and Red Plum Compote. Likewise, a brilliant Rum Pot can (indeed must) be initiated with summer fruit, and now is the time to start.

Dips, Spreads, and Savory Snacks

Here is an array of easy-to-make distinctive dips, spreads, and herring dishes. Most take only minutes to prepare and all acquire a particular depth when made up ahead of time and refrigerated. It's important to use good-looking, clean crocks with tight-fitting lids for the handsomest looks when putting up these gifts. Pack dips, spreads, and herring layerings into crocks or jars most carefully; mostly the top layer of a spread is visible, but herring mixtures set up in clear glass jars are best. Really attend to the looks of the food—meticulously smooth the tops of spreads with a narrow flexible spatula, and make sure that nut halves or herb leaves used to decorate them are arranged in handsome patterns. The taste on the tongue and the taste to the eye are inseparable parts of any food gift, but savory things seem to need an extra little bit of attention.

CHICK-PEA–YOGURT DIP

Season this flavored dip with young, tender mint leaves, those that detach easily from the stem—then, the minty taste is subtle and sweet.

1½ cups dried chick-peas, picked over,
* or 4½ cups canned chick-peas*
* (see Note)*
2 cups plain yogurt
4 tablespoons freshly squeezed lemon
* juice*

¼ cup chopped fresh spearmint leaves
4 small garlic cloves, minced
¾ teaspoon sweet or hot paprika
salt and freshly ground white pepper,
* to taste*

Soak the chick-peas in a large bowl in cold water to cover by at least 3 inches. Let stand overnight.

The next day, drain the chick-peas in a colander. Dump the chick-peas in a 4-quart casserole or saucepan and cover with 3 inches of cold water. Bring the water to a boil over moderately high heat, then cover the pot and reduce the heat so that the water simmers very gently. Cook the chick-peas until they are positively and absolutely tender, about 2½ hours.

Drain the chick-peas and discard any of the loose skins that may be floating around. Puree them in the bowl of a food processor fitted with a steel blade. Press the puree through a medium-meshed stainless-steel sieve or through a food mill into a mixing bowl.

To the puree, add in the remaining ingredients. Pour the dip into good-looking decorative jars to ¼ inch of the top and close with the lids. Refrigerate for up to 3 days.

NOTE: If you use canned chick-peas, drain very well and rinse several times in cold water in a colander. Begin the recipe by pureeing and straining them, just as you would with the freshly cooked chick-peas.

RED PEPPER AND HERB DIP

What makes this red pepper dip so captivating is that when the peppers are roasted and pureed, the flavor turns intense and delicate at once.

3 pounds (about 5 medium-large) red
  peppers, firm and meaty
1½ cups sour cream
⅓ cup crème fraiche
⅓ cup plain yogurt
2 tablespoons freshly squeezed lemon
  juice
2 tablespoons finely snipped fresh
  chives

2 tablespoons finely chopped fresh
  parsley
2 teaspoons finely chopped fresh basil
  leaves (pick small, tender leaves)
2 teaspoons finely chopped fresh
  thyme leaves
2 small garlic cloves, minced
salt and freshly ground white pepper,
  to taste

Broil the red peppers until the skins are blistery and dark, turning them several times to evenly char them. Remove the peppers from the broiler and wrap them in a large sheet of aluminum foil; let stand for 45 minutes. Unwrap the foil; skin, core, and deseed the peppers.

Place the peppers in the bowl of a food processor fitted with a steel blade; puree.

Transfer the puree to a large mixing bowl. Stir in all remaining ingredients except the last. Mix well. Season with salt and pepper.

Pour the dip into jars to ¼ inch of the top. Cover with lids. Refrigerate for up to 3 days.

SAVORY CREAM CHEESE SPREAD   MAKES ABOUT 2¼ CUPS

The following three recipes require nothing more than a hand mixer to blend together the ingredients. And a smooth crock of either of the three makes for zesty spreading on triple-grain peasant bread served with other cold summer delicacies. (Incidentally, very young cooks could be happily introduced to the measuring–beating–mixing–filling containers process by putting together any one of these recipes; but I suggest trying this one first—unless your small cook has an adventurous palate.)

½ pound good-quality cream cheese,
  softened at room temperature
12 tablespoons unsalted sweet butter,
  cool but not cold
1 tablespoon sweet paprika
¼ teaspoon lightly crushed caraway
  seed

2 teaspoons finely chopped tiny nonpareil capers
5 anchovy fillets, drained and chopped
1 teaspoon Worcestershire sauce
1 tablespoon finely snipped fresh
  chives
freshly ground white pepper, to taste

In the large bowl of an electric mixer or in the bowl of a food processor fitted with a steel blade, beat together the cream cheese and butter until well combined.

Beat in the paprika, caraway seed, and capers. Mix for 1 minute; then add in the anchovies and Worcestershire sauce.

If blended in a food processor, turn the cream cheese mixture into a large mixing bowl. By hand, stir in the snipped chives. Grind in white pepper to taste.

Pack the spread into crocks and cover with lids. Store the spread in the refrigerator for up to 2 weeks.

HERBED CREAM CHEESE SPREAD   MAKES ABOUT 4 CUPS

This spread is completely untemperamental and flexible, one that can move happily from one group of savory herbs to the next, depending on what you are growing, or what's on hand in bunches at the greengrocer. For an outdoor event, put out a crock of the spread alongside a cool chicken and veal pâté, a platter of steamed vegetables shiny with a mustard–olive oil–vinegar–honey dressing poured over at the last minute, a big loaf of peasant bread to pull apart, and berries and cookies to finish off the meal. This is a restorative country sort of supper, and this spread makes it even more refreshing. As a guest, you'll be adored if you bring a terrine of Herbed Cream Cheese Spread along.

1½ pounds fresh preservative-free
*   cream cheese*
¼ cup crème fraiche
2 tablespoons minced fresh oregano
2 tablespoons minced fresh summer
*   savory*
1 tablespoon minced fresh tarragon

1 tablespoon minced fresh parsley
*   (preferably the Italian flat-leafed*
*   variety)*
salt and freshly ground white pepper,
*   to taste*
1 garlic clove, finely chopped

In the bowl of an electric mixer, cream the cream cheese and crème fraiche together on moderately high speed for 3 to 4 minutes, or until the cheese turns quite light and fluffy. On low speed, blend in the herbs. Season the mixture with salt and pepper. Stir in the garlic.

Pack the spread into a crock, bowl, or terrine. Level the top with a flexible rubber spatula, then run a thin palette knife over it to smooth the surface.

Cover the spread and chill it until serving time, or up to 3 days ahead of serving. Serve the spread cool, having removed it from the refrigerator about 15 minutes before serving to let it soften up slightly.

ROQUEFORT CREAM

MAKES ABOUT 3¾ CUPS

This "cream" has a depth and intensity of flavor only Roquefort cheese could contribute. It stores well, and I like to slide a circle of brown paper moistened with a little extra cognac onto the top layer of the spread before sealing up the crocks.

¾ pound best-quality Roquefort
    cheese, at room temperature
½ pound preservative-free cream
    cheese, at room temperature
1 cup unsalted sweet butter, cool but
    not cold

2 teaspoons Worcestershire sauce
¼ cup cognac
a few sprinkles of cayenne pepper, or a
    few drops of hot pepper sauce,
    such as Tabasco

In the large bowl of an electric mixer (or in the bowl of a food processor fitted with a steel blade) cream the Roquefort cheese with the cream cheese until well combined.

Beat in the butter, 2 tablespoons at a time, blending thoroughly after each addition.

Slowly beat in the Worcestershire sauce and cognac. Season to taste with the cayenne pepper or Tabasco; scrape down the sides of the bowl and beat for 1 minute longer to blend all of the ingredients completely.

Pack the "cream" into crocks or other containers. Cover securely with a lid.

Store the spread in the refrigerator for up to 1 month. Serve cool but not cold.

GOAT CHEESE AND CRÈME FRAICHE WITH HERBS

MAKES ABOUT 4 CUPS

I have found that the goat cheese called *Montrachet Bûche* (available in 11-ounce cylinders) has the perfect mild smoothness for this spread.

2 pounds goat cheese (preferably Mon-
    trachet Bûche), cool but not cold
½ cup crème fraiche, cool but not
    cold
2 tablespoons finely chopped fresh
    tarragon
1 tablespoon finely snipped fresh
    chives

2 teaspoons finely chopped fresh
    thyme leaves
2 garlic cloves, coarsely chopped, then
    mashed to a paste with ¼ tea-
    spoon salt
freshly ground white pepper, to taste
freshly ground coarse sea salt, to taste

In the large bowl of an electric mixer, cream the goat cheese with the crème fraiche until well combined, about 5 minutes on moderate speed.

By hand, stir in the tarragon, chives, thyme, mashed garlic-salt, and season to taste with white pepper and sea salt.

Pack the spread into crocks and level the top with a spatula or palette knife. Close the containers with the lids.

Refrigerate the spread for up to 1 week; serve cool but not cold.

TUNA SPREAD WITH WALNUTS   MAKES ABOUT 3 CUPS

A marvelous savory spread that can serve as a fast (and fashionable) first course when presented with crusty bread. To double this recipe (give one away, and squirrel away the other for yourself), prepare the spread in two separate batches.

10 pitted oil-cured black olives
1 tablespoon tiny nonpareil capers
4 anchovy fillets
2 garlic cloves, peeled and halved
2 tablespoons cognac
2 tablespoons freshly squeezed lemon
  juice

1 tablespoon fresh thyme leaves
9 ounces tuna packed in olive oil, un-
  drained
10 tablespoons unsalted sweet butter,
  softened but still cool
freshly ground white pepper, to taste
¼ cup finely chopped walnuts

In the bowl of a food processor fitted with a steel blade, place the first 7 ingredients. Process until everything is very finely chopped.

Add tuna in oil and process until it's pureed. Scrape down the sides of the processor with a spatula; process for a few seconds longer.

With the processor on, add the butter, 2 tablespoons at a time, allowing each chunk to be incorporated before adding the next amount.

Turn the tuna mixture into a mixing bowl. Season with the white pepper and fold in the chopped walnuts.

Pour and scrape the spread into a 3-cup terrine; I use a plain oval white one that has a lid. Level the top with a spatula or palette knife. Refrigerate the spread, uncovered, for 30 minutes to set the top slightly. Then cover the container with plastic wrap (but don't let the wrap touch the top of the spread) and gently set the lid on top.

Refrigerate the spread until needed, or up to 5 days. For gift-giving, transport the spread from your refrigerator to the recipient's refrigerator as quickly as possible. Before giving, decorate the top of the spread with some pretty fresh Italian parsley leaves and a few perfect walnut halves, if you like. Spread should be served cool but not cold.

TUNA SPREAD WITH SUMMER SAVORY   MAKES ABOUT 1½ CUPS

This tuna spread is good to have on hand during the summer months not only because it stores well but the mixture is simplicity itself to put together. The spread makes for an informal first course, and any hostess will appreciate receiving it.

7 ounces tuna packed in olive oil, undrained
4 anchovy fillets
3 tablespoons sour cream
1 teaspoon Dijon mustard
1 medium garlic clove, minced
½ cup unsalted sweet butter, softened but still cool

¼ cup coarsely chopped pitted oil-cured olives
2 tablespoons finely minced summer savory
1 tablespoon freshly squeezed lemon juice
several drops of hot pepper sauce, such as Tabasco

In the bowl of a food processor fitted with a steel blade, puree the first 5 ingredients. Scrape down the sides of the bowl with a rubber spatula and process a few seconds longer.

With the motor running, add the cool butter, processing a tablespoon at a time. Pour and scrape the mixture into a large mixing bowl.

Stir in the olives, savory, and lemon juice. Season with a few drops of hot pepper sauce.

Turn the spread into a 1½-cup crock or small terrine. Level the top with a spatula or palette knife. Refrigerate the spread, uncovered, for 30 minutes to set the top. Then cover the container with plastic wrap (but do not let the wrap touch the top of the spread); gently close with the lid.

Refrigerate the spread until needed, or up to 5 days. Serve the spread cool but not cold.

SMOKED WHITEFISH SPREAD WITH DILL   MAKES ABOUT 3 CUPS

An herb-flecked bread, such as crunchy loaf of rye with dillseed winding through the batter, is a fine addition to this spread.

9 ounces boneless and skinless smoked
   whitefish
2 teaspoons tiny nonpareil capers
½ cup plus 2 tablespoons sour cream
4 ounces cream cheese, cool but not
   cold
1 tablespoon freshly squeezed lemon
   juice

10 tablespoons (½ cup plus 2 tablespoons) unsalted sweet butter,
   cool but not cold
2 tablespoons finely snipped fresh dill
2 tablespoons finely minced scallions
   (use only the white part)
salt and freshly ground white pepper,
   to taste

In the container of a food processor fitted with a steel blade, puree the first 5 in-gredients. Scrape down the sides of the bowl and process again for a few seconds.

With the motor running, add the butter, processing only a tablespoon at a time. Transfer the mixture to a large mixing bowl.

Beat in the dill and scallions. Season to taste with salt and pepper.

Pour the mixture into a 3-cup terrine or crock and level the top with a spatula or palette knife. Place the spread in the refrigerator for 30 minutes to set the top. Cover the container with plastic wrap (but do not let the plastic touch the top of the spread) and cover with the lid. Refrigerate the spread up to 2 days.

OLIVE AND ANCHOVY SPREAD   MAKES ABOUT 1½ CUPS

My favorite use for this lovely puree is to spread it on thin toasted rounds of French bread, place a pat of goat cheese on top, broil it briefly, then set it above some sharp salad greens tossed with a vibrant vinaigrette dressing. (A little whisked into a plain oil and vinegar-based dressing is delicious, too.)

15 anchovy fillets
2 small garlic cloves, coarsely chopped
freshly ground black pepper, to taste
3 tablespoons tiny nonpareil capers,
   rinsed briefly in cool water and
   drained well on a thickness of
   paper toweling

1¼ pounds pitted oil-cured black
   olives
⅓ cup light virgin olive oil (preferably
   French)
extra light olive oil, for packing

Place the anchovies, garlic, and several grindings of black pepper in the container of a food processor fitted with a steel blade. Process until coarsely chopped.

Add the capers, black olives, and virgin olive oil; process until everything is coarsely chopped, then scrape down the sides of the bowl with a spatula; process for a few seconds longer until everything is finely chopped but not pureed.

Pour and scrape the spread into small (½-cup) glass jars; cover with a thin film of oil. Place on the lids. Refrigerate the spread for up to 1 year.

HERRING WITH LEMON AND SPICES　　　MAKES ABOUT 4 CUPS

To be blunt, I am a fanatic about any kind of herring. A layered or mixed herring salad is a delectable thing to have on hand, especially when matched with a grainy loaf of bread. These three high-flavored herring arrangements are considerably addictive with a caraway rye bread (crunchy of crust, chewy within) or flat, waferlike crackers.

10 ounces skinless and boneless schmaltz herring fillets, cut into 2-inch pieces
2 medium-size red onions, thinly sliced
1 small lemon, thinly sliced and seeds removed
2 small imported Turkish bay leaves
4 whole allspice berries

4 whole cloves
½ teaspoon yellow mustard seed
2 tablespoons firmly packed light brown sugar
¼ cup apple cider vinegar
1 tablespoon water
2 teaspoons Dijon mustard
½ cup safflower oil

In two 2-cup glass jars—a sleek, not heavily patterned jar is best for this—layer the herring pieces with the red onions, lemon slices, bay leaves, allspice, cloves, and mustard seed. Let stand for 15 minutes while you prepare the dressing.

In a medium-size nonmetallic bowl, whisk together the brown sugar and cider vinegar. Beat in the water and Dijon mustard. Gradually whisk in the safflower oil, adding it in a very thin stream.

Pour the dressing over the herring layers, making sure that it reaches all around the sides.

Cover the herring and refrigerate for up to 1 week.

HERRING AND POTATO VINAIGRETTE WITH DILL　　MAKES 4 TO 5 CUPS

The potatoes are the ideal foil for the herring, and the two combined make this dish terribly good all on its own as a summery first course, or as part of a multi-dish first course tray during the winter holidays. Put this salad together in a wide-mouthed jar, layering everything as you go.

10 ounces skinless and boneless
  schmaltz herring fillets, cut into
  2-inch pieces
1 pound small firm "boiling" potatoes
  (in the summer use Red Bliss),
  steamed until tender, and sliced
  ½ inch thick
1 medium red onion, thinly sliced into
  rings

4 tablespoons red wine vinegar
2 teaspoons Dijon mustard
6 tablespoons safflower oil
6 tablespoons light fruity olive oil
freshly ground black pepper, to taste
3 tablespoons finely snipped fresh dill
¼ teaspoon yellow mustard seed

In a clean, straight, wide-mouthed glass jar, layer the herring pieces with the potatoes and red onion; I use two plain 2-cup Mason jars or one 5-cup (approximately) crock.

In a medium-size nonmetallic bowl, whisk together the red wine vinegar and mustard. Beat in the safflower oil a tablespoon at a time; then beat in the olive oil a tablespoon at a time.

Season the dressing with freshly ground black pepper. Whisk in the dill and the mustard seed.

Pour the dressing over the herring, dividing it equally among the two jars as necessary, and close the jars with the lids. Refrigerate the herring up to 1 week.

SWEET AND SOUR HERRING WITH SPICES   MAKES ABOUT 3 CUPS

I have found that this piquant herring is a good overture to a summer meal. It calls the taste buds to attention, tastes marvelous with other spiced and smoked foods, and is a fine thing to transport to someone's alfresco dinner as a gift.

1½ pounds skinless and boneless
  schmaltz herring fillets, cut into
  2-inch pieces
1 large red onion, thinly sliced
6 slender fresh carrots, peeled and
  sliced into thin rounds
5 whole allspice berries
5 whole cloves

1 small imported Turkish bay leaf
8 whole black peppercorns, lightly
  crushed with a rolling pin or in a
  mortar and pestle
¾ cup apple cider vinegar
⅓ cup water
¼ cup plus 2 tablespoons granulated
  sugar

Layer the herring pieces with the onion slices, carrot coins, allspice, cloves, and bay leaf in a wide-mouthed glass jar (about 3½-cup capacity) or use 2 smaller jars.

In a small (1-quart) nonmetallic saucepan—preferably of enameled cast iron—place the remaining ingredients. Cook over a low heat to dissolve the sugar completely. Bring to a boil over moderately high heat, boil for 3 minutes, and cool thoroughly.

Pour the vinegar solution over the herring, tilting the jar from side to side so that the solution permeates all of the layers.

Cover the jar(s) and refrigerate the herring up to 2 weeks.

Special Condiments and Pickles

What a gorgeous landscape it is to have glimmering jars of bright-colored vegetables—the pickles and preserves of summer—decorating your pantry shelf. Though I like to give these to summer hosts and hostesses, from the moment the first chill of autumn sets in, I begin thinking about who will receive what during the holidays, and how I'll decorate the jars for a full, rich effect.

What's inside the jars generally suggests plenty of ideas for decoration. Standard preserving jars need a boost of fabric caps snugly fitted to the tops of the jars. Cover the bottom of the jars with galax leaves (see chapter 2 for instructions). Antique individual wire canning racks, originally made for water-bath canning, are worth keeping an eye out for. For a special gift, combine a jar or two of preserves with the rack and the recipient can enjoy the good things immediately and use the rack over and again, either at table as a novel serving vessel or decoratively mounted on a kitchen pegboard.

Most recipes in this section will keep for up to a year unless otherwise noted.

BLACK RASPBERRY VINEGAR   MAKES 4 CUPS

I love this vinegar for its refreshing, sharp taste; it is a recipe I make "on the side" right after picking black raspberries at a nearby Maryland farm. Arriving home with my customary treasure load of quarts of these gems, I pour a tangy champagne vinegar over a sizable quantity of these berries, then go about turning the rest of them into deep-colored jam and conserve.

4 cups plump, fresh black raspberries,   *4 cups good-quality champagne*
   picked over   *vinegar*

Place the black raspberries in a 6-cup jar that has been washed in hot soapy water, rinsed well, and dried thoroughly. Pour in the vinegar. Cover the jar.

Let the berries stand in the vinegar for about 4 days, tipping the jar from time to time.

Strain the vinegar through 3 or 4 thicknesses of clean cheesecloth cradled in a stainless steel strainer that you have placed atop a large measuring cup. Now, pour the vinegar into small bottles and cap.

VARIATION: Blueberry Vinegar can be made the same way, but be sure that the blueberries are very ripe. Mash them with the back of a spoon and let them stand in the vinegar at least 4 days.

CONNIE'S HOT PEPPER JELLY   MAKES ABOUT 7 CUPS

I have the recipe for this partially transparent, sweet, tart, and not strongly hot jelly from Connie Kurz—good friend, occasional comrade in the kitchen, and highly versatile food editor.

At frequent intervals during the summer, Connie is known to take on a canning project based upon when the ample supply of produce her home garden (and her mother's Richmond, Virginia, garden) spills out. Once she gave me a scrumptious jar of Royal Fruit—blueberries and other juicy seasonal fruit floating in a bold brandy concoction and so named because the blueberries turned the liquid in the jar a bluish-purple, a highly royal color. Delicious! Then Connie brought a jar of Hot Pepper Jelly to one of my cooking lectures as a gift. On tasting the jelly, I knew I had to have the recipe. With a certain modesty I attribute directly to southern gentility, Connie forwarded the recipe to me but hesitated to have it printed in this volume. I pressed. She agreed.

Note Connie says both sweet and hot red peppers may be exchanged for the green ones (decrease the sugar to 5½ cups, for the red peppers are sweeter), but don't mix red and green peppers, to keep the jelly from turning muddy looking.

1½ cups apple cider vinegar
1 cup coarsely chopped green bell
*   peppers*
⅓ to ½ cup coarsely chopped, de-
*   seeded jalapeño peppers*

1 medium onion, chopped
6 cups granulated sugar
1 6-ounce bottle liquid fruit pectin

Place ½ cup apple cider vinegar with the peppers and onion in the container of a blender or a food processor (fitted with a steel blade). Puree the mixture finely.

Pour the contents of the container into a stainless-steel sieve lined with a double thickness of cheesecloth; mash the solids with the back of a wooden spoon so that all of the good juices are extracted. Discard the solids.

In a 6-quart casserole or preserving kettle, pour in the strained liquid mixture, the remaining vinegar, and all of the granulated sugar. Bring the contents to a rolling boil, stirring constantly for 3 minutes. Remove from the heat and allow the mixture to sit for 5 minutes. Skim off any foam that rises to the top. Stir in the liquid pectin.

Pour the jelly into hot, sterilized half-pint jars to ⅛ inch of the top. Cover immediately with hot lids and bands. Cool, then store.

YELLOW TOMATO JAM

MAKES ABOUT 7 CUPS

This is a glorious-colored sweet jam with a marvelously seductive taste. Yellow tomatoes should smell sweet and slightly perfumed; insist on hand-picking each one of the 5 pounds. And do make it a point to cook up the tomatoes within a day of purchasing them (leave the tomatoes set out in 1 layer on a cutting board at room temperature). This jam beautifully matches all kinds of herb breads—yeasted, batter, and savory muffins and rolls—as a spread. I even swirl a bit of the jam with a splash of vinegar into the pan juices of sautéed chicken.

5 pounds yellow tomatoes, peeled, cored, seeded, and cut into 1-inch cubes	*4 4-inch cinnamon sticks*
	4 whole allspice berries
	4 whole cloves
juice of 3 lemons	*⅓ cup apple cider vinegar*
4 cups granulated sugar	*1 cup water*

Combine the first 6 ingredients in a nonmetallic 12-quart kettle. Stir well and let the mixture stand for 1 hour.

Add the vinegar and water; let stand for 30 minutes, stirring occasionally.

Place the kettle over a low heat and cook slowly until the sugar has dissolved completely. When every granule of sugar has melted down, raise the heat to moderately high and boil the mixture slowly for about 50 minutes, or until a spoonful holds its shape on a cold plate. Pick out and discard the cloves and allspice berries.

Ladle the boiling-hot jam into 3 or 4 hot pint jars (include a cinnamon stick in each jar) to ⅛ inch of the top; seal immediately with hot lids and bands. You may also use half-pint jars, when extra cinnamon sticks should be set out at jar-filling time; fill and seal as described for the pint jars.

Alternately, pour the jam into a sturdy storage container, cool to room temperature, then cover and refrigerate for up to 3 months.

LEMON-TOMATO JAM MAKES ABOUT 5 CUPS

This is a simple and bright jam made from scarlet home-grown tomatoes—there is no place for forlorn, aged tomatoes, or any tomato that is not smooth, full, and burstingly ripe. Sometimes I sprinkle a little coarse salt and about ¼ cup granulated sugar (from the 3 cups below) over the tomato cubes and let them marinate for a while; this quick procedure makes the tomato nuggets cook down rich and glazed-over looking.

3½ pounds red, ripe tomatoes, peeled, seeded, and cut into 1½-inch cubes
3 cups granulated sugar

2 small lemons, thinly sliced and seeded
2 tablespoons finely grated fresh ginger
1 cup water

Combine the tomatoes, sugar, and lemons in a nonmetallic 12-quart kettle. Stir well. Let the tomato mixture stand for 4 hours, stirring several times each hour.

Add the ginger and water to the pot; stir them in. Set the pot over a low heat and cook slowly until the sugar dissolves completely. Raise the heat to moderately high and cook the mixture until thick, about 35 minutes, when a blob of jam will hold its shape lightly on a chilled plate. The jam will need to be stirred frequently, lest it stick and burn on the bottom of the kettle.

Ladle the boiling-hot jam into hot pint or half-pint jars to ⅛ inch of the top; seal immediately with hot lids and bands.

Alternately, pour the jam into a sturdy storage container, cool to room temperature, cover and refrigerate for up to 3 months.

TOMATO, RED PEPPER, AND ONION RELISH MAKES ABOUT 10 CUPS

Simple ingredients at their peak make this a favorite of mine. It is essential that the tomatoes be invitingly ripe for the relish to work out. It takes a little energy to arrive at seeded wedges from 6 pounds of tomatoes, but the rest of the recipe is simple work of boiling and simmering. The longer the relish sits, the more enjoyable it becomes; I prefer to keep it in the refrigerator for end of the summer and early fall enjoyment.

6 pounds red, ripe tomatoes, peeled,
    seeded, and cut into 1-inch
    wedges
5 meaty, firm red peppers, cored,
    seeded, and cut into ⅓-inch-thick
    strips
4 sweet white onions, halved and cut
    into thin half rings

⅓ cup chopped, deseeded jalapeño
    peppers
1 tablespoon finely chopped garlic
1 tablespoon coarse (kosher) salt
⅔ cup granulated sugar
2 cups apple cider vinegar

Combine all the ingredients except vinegar in a nonmetallic 12-quart kettle; stir. Let the tomato mixture sit for 1 hour, stirring occasionally.

Pour in the apple cider vinegar; stir. Place the pot over a moderately low heat and cook the mixture until the sugar has dissolved. Raise the heat and bring the contents of the pot to a boil. Adjust the heat so that the mixture simmers slowly, for about 25 minutes (or until lightly thickened).

Spoon the mixture into a sturdy container or clean glass jars. Cool to room temperature, then cover and refrigerate for up to 3 months.

CUCUMBER AND ONION PICKLES   MAKES ABOUT 6 QUARTS

Jars of Cucumber and Onion Pickles are the satisfying reward for hand-picking the smallest cucumbers you can locate. All in all, this is a delicious relish that is in the homey category of chowchow, piccalilli, and mustard pickles—to be eaten up with sandwiches, grilled food, meat loaves, and the like. Seeing a row of these pickles on your pantry shelf will elicit a great sense of self-satisfaction, and in a small way, you'll have restored the appealing art of pickling.

5 quarts pickling cucumber slices cut
    ⅓ inch thick, sliced from the
    smallest cucumbers you can find
    (about 20 cups)
3 quarts thinly sliced sweet cooking
    onions (about 12 cups)
1 cup coarse (kosher) salt
4½ cups granulated sugar

3¾ cups apple cider vinegar
2 teaspoons all-purpose flour (prefera-
    bly unbleached)
1 tablespoon yellow mustard seed
2 teaspoons ground turmeric
1 teaspoon ground ginger
2 teaspoons celery seed

Place the cucumbers, onions, and salt in a large nonmetallic bowl; stir. Let the mixture stand overnight, loosely covered with a sheet of plastic wrap.

The next day, drain the cucumbers and onions very well; reserve.

In the largest nonmetallic kettle you can find, preferably of at least 16-quart capacity, pour in the granulated sugar and vinegar. Then stir in the remaining listed ingredients.

Cook the mixture over a low heat to dissolve the sugar completely. Raise the heat to high and bring the liquid to a boil; boil for 5 minutes.

Add the cucumber slices and onions, bring everything to a boil, and boil for 3 minutes.

Ladle the cucumbers and onions with liquid into hot, sterilized pint jars to ¼ inch of the top; seal with lids and bands. Cool, then store.

SWEET SPICED DILL PICKLES   MAKES ABOUT 3½ QUARTS

This I like to call "cheaters' sweet pickles," a phenomenal recipe for those who like to play at preserving by exerting only a minimal amount of effort. You start out with jarred dill pickles and stimulate them with sugar and spices for 6 days, after which time they come out very crisp with a slightly crystal quality to each slice. Once crocked for just under a week, you pack up the bouncy pickles in jars and store them in the refrigerator for up to 6 months. Then, at Christmas, astonish your friends with a jar of these pickles you have worked magic on, and whether or not you let them in on the secret of the recipe is entirely up to you.

4 quarts processed dill pickles, sliced   *1 cup apple cider vinegar*
⅓ inch thick (about 16 cups)   *2 medium-size garlic cloves, peeled*
5 pounds granulated sugar   *and halved*
2 ounces mixed pickling spice

Combine the pickles and sugar in a large, deep crock of about 30-quart capacity; the crock I use measures 11 inches across the top and 11½ inches high.

Secure the pickling spice in a triple-layered square of cheesecloth and tie up the bundle with a piece of kitchen string.

Add the spice package to the pickles and sugar with the vinegar and garlic. Carefully stir up everything. Loosely cover the crock with a sheet of plastic wrap and let the pickles stand for 6 days, stirring twice a day. Discard the spice bundle and garlic cloves.

Pack the pickles with the liquid into clean half-pint jars to ½ inch of the top; close with lids. Refrigerate the jars for up to 6 months.

ALICE'S "Z" RELISH

MAKES ABOUT 12 CUPS

Z is for zucchini, of course, and Z is for "Z Relish"—that's what my friend Alice Romejko calls this—and it is so very good. Relish sold so dearly in food emporiums is not as delicious as this one you make at home; and what most home gardeners wouldn't give to have this recipe for taking care of several armloads of zucchini. Make up a double batch, and stockpile the jars for gift-giving year-round, but especially during Christmas, when the green (zucchini) and red (pimento) color echoes the holiday.

5 pounds small, firm zucchini, well
    scrubbed and finely chopped
2½ pounds sweet white onions, very
    finely chopped
½ cup coarse (kosher) salt
2 cups apple cider vinegar
1¼ cups granulated sugar
2 teaspoons yellow mustard seed

2 teaspoons celery seed
1 teaspoon ground cinnamon
½ teaspoon freshly ground nutmeg
½ teaspoon freshly ground white
    pepper
½ cup finely chopped canned
    pimentos

Place the chopped zucchini and onions in a large nonmetallic bowl, preferably of glazed pottery. Sprinkle with coarse salt and mix well. Pour on enough cold water to cover, stir, and loosely cover the bowl with a sheet of plastic wrap. Let stand overnight in a cool place, but do not refrigerate.

The next day, drain the vegetables very well. Cover with cold water, let stand 15 minutes, then drain again.

Turn the vegetables into a nonmetallic 12-quart kettle. Add all the remaining ingredients and stir.

Place the kettle over a low heat and cook slowly to dissolve the sugar completely. Raise the heat to high and bring the contents of the kettle to a hard boil; reduce the heat and simmer the mixture for 15 minutes, stirring occasionally.

Ladle the hot relish into 6 boiling-hot pint jars to ¼ inch of the top; seal with hot lids and bands. Process pint jars in a boiling-water bath (see pp. 8–11) for 15 minutes; cool.

Alternately, spoon the relish into a sturdy storage container, cool to room temperature, then cover and refrigerate for up to 2 months. (I prefer to can the relish and process the jars in a boiling-water bath; it produces the easiest and tastiest results.)

NOTE: This relish holds well in the refrigerator but even longer once it is canned in a boiling-water bath. The color of the relish remains intact and the flavor stays crisp and clear.

PICKLED OKRA

This is a summertime specialty of Virginia caterer and ambitious canner Liz Taylor. My friend Liz got the recipe from her sister Pam Seaman. Liz calls these pickles "cornichonlike" and so serves them with homemade pâté (I add traditional American meat loaf to the go-with list). I like to select pods no more than 3 inches long—the younger pods are more tender and less fibrous. Note that thin sprigs of fresh tarragon may be substituted for the dillseed; you would use a healthy leafy length of about 4 inches.

SOLUTION:

1 quart distilled white vinegar
1 cup water

⅓ cup plus 2 tablespoons pickling
(uniodized) salt

EACH PINT JAR:

15, approximately, okra pods, the stem
end slit ⅓ inch into the pod with
a sharp paring knife

1 garlic clove, peeled
1 small fresh cayenne pepper
1 teaspoon dillseed

Place the solution ingredients in a 2-quart saucepan and bring to a boil. Simmer for 5 minutes; keep warm.

In the bottom of 5 hot jars, place the okra pods pointed side down, stem side up. Edge in the garlic clove and pepper. Sprinkle on the dillseed.

Pour the hot vinegar brine over the okra to cover by ½ inch. Seal jars with lids and bands. Cool. Okra turns into pickles in a week.

Liz keeps the jars in the pantry, but I store mine in the refrigerator when cool. The jars do not spoil in the pantry, but having tried it both ways, I seem to think that the pickled taste is more vibrant when the jars are kept cold.

RED TOMATO AND CUCUMBER CHUTNEY

Only beautiful, ripe, summer-harvested tomatoes need apply for this recipe. Plain food—grilled, roasted, or smoked meats or poultry—is the best match here.

3 *sweet white onions, chopped*
2 *cups firmly packed light brown sugar*
3 *cups apple cider vinegar*
3 *small jalapeño peppers, cored,*
  seeded, and chopped (use rubber
  gloves to protect your hands)
2 *tablespoons ground ginger*

2 *teaspoons ground cinnamon*
1 *tablespoon coarse (kosher) salt*
30 *medium-size (about 10 pounds)*
  ripe and juicy tomatoes
2 *"European" burpless cucumbers,*
  cubed

In a 10-quart kettle, place the first 7 ingredients. Cover the pot and cook the mixture over a low heat to dissolve the sugar. When the sugar has dissolved, adjust the heat so that the contents simmer; simmer for 15 to 20 minutes or until the onions are very soft.

Meanwhile, drop the tomatoes, 2 at a time, in a pot of boiling water for about 10 seconds, then cool them down in a spray of cold water. Slip off the skins with the aid of a small sharp paring knife, then seed them and cut them into 1-inch cubes.

Uncover the kettle, bring the onion-syrup to a boil, and boil for 5 to 10 minutes or until lightly thickened. Add the tomatoes and cucumbers and simmer them in the syrup until cooked through but not mushy. The cucumbers will retain a just-firm crunch and the tomatoes will not break down.

Ladle the boiling-hot chutney into hot pint jars to ¼ inch of the top; seal with hot lids and bands. Process pint jars in a boiling-water bath (see pp. 8–11) for 10 minutes; cool.

Alternately, ladle the chutney into containers and cool to room temperature. Cover the containers and refrigerate for up to 2 months.

TOMATO AND RED PEPPER CHILI SAUCE MAKES ABOUT 10 CUPS

Chili Barbecue Sauce and Chili-Onion Barbecue Sauce, which follow, are spectacular if you start out with Tomato and Red Pepper Chili Sauce as a base. It turns either barbecue sauce into a doubly fruitful project, one I recommend highly when you find a heap of tomatoes innocently taking over the countertops of your kitchen. Each summer I fall prey to bringing home half bushels of the juicy specimens from farm markets not too far away from where I live.

The proprietor of each market (who has by now caught on to my passion for the red beauties) regularly asks what each half bushel of tomatoes will end up to be, how they'll be treated, with a concern similar to that of a parent who reluctantly releases a child to his or her very first day of kindergarten class. Most times, I return in a few days with a jar of sauce, jam, or chutney, beautifully done up, to remind the owner that the tomatoes have been treated with respect.

Summer Feasting and Harvesting

If you are a spicy sensualist, you will love to paint any of these three sauces on country spareribs that are relatively lean and meaty. Or can a sauce to give as a gift later. (See pp. 8–11 for instructions on boiling-water bath.)

24 large, red, and ripe summer tomatoes, peeled, cored, seeded, and
  cut into rough cubes
4 red peppers, cored, seeded, and
  finely chopped
4 onions, finely chopped
4 garlic cloves, finely chopped
½ cup apple cider vinegar

1 cup granulated sugar
1 cup water
2 tablespoons coarse (kosher) salt
2 teaspoons mustard seed
2 teaspoons celery seed
1½ teaspoons ground cinnamon
1 teaspoon ground ginger

Place the first 8 ingredients in an 8-quart pot, preferably of enameled cast iron. Cover and cook slowly until the sugar has melted down completely.

Uncover the pot, and add the remaining ingredients. Raise the heat to moderately high, stir the pot once or twice, then let the contents come to a boil. Boil slowly for about 50 minutes, or until the sauce coats a spoon lightly; it will thicken somewhat on standing.

Process the sauce by pouring into 5 boiling-hot pint jars to ¼ inch of the top, and can in a boiling-water bath for 10 minutes.

Alternately, cool the sauce to room temperature, then refrigerate in tightly sealed jars up to 2 weeks.

CHILI BARBECUE SAUCE

MAKES 3 CUPS

Sharp and oniony!

¼ cup vegetable oil
¼ cup peanut oil
2 onions, chopped
1¾ cups chili sauce (such as Tomato
  and Red Pepper Chili Sauce, see
  p. 44)
¾ cup water
⅓ cup strained, freshly squeezed
  lemon juice
⅓ cup apple cider vinegar
2 tablespoons granulated sugar

2 tablespoons firmly packed light
  brown sugar
2 tablespoons light molasses
1 tablespoon good-quality Dijon mustard
¼ cup Worcestershire sauce
coarse (kosher) salt, to taste
freshly ground white pepper, to taste
drops of hot pepper sauce, such as
  Tabasco, to taste

(continued)

45

In a 4-quart enameled cast-iron casserole, pour in the vegetable oil and peanut oil. Set the casserole over moderate heat, stir in the onions, and cook them until they begin to turn translucent, about 4 to 5 minutes.

Add the remaining ingredients, bringing the contents of the casserole to a rapid simmer. Simmer for about 25 minutes, or until lightly thickened.

Pour the sauce into hot pint jars to ¼ inch of the top, close with lids and bands; process the jars in a boiling-water bath for 10 minutes.

Alternately, cool the sauce to room temperature, pack into containers, and refrigerate for up to 2 weeks.

CHILI-ONION BARBECUE SAUCE

MAKES ABOUT 3 CUPS

2 medium-size onions, finely chopped
⅓ cup vegetable oil
2 cups chili sauce, such as Tomato and Red Pepper Chili Sauce (see p. 44)
¼ cup firmly packed dark brown sugar
¾ cup water

⅓ cup apple cider vinegar
¼ cup Worcestershire sauce
2 teaspoons dry mustard (preferably imported)
1 teaspoon hot pepper sauce, such as Tabasco, or to taste

In a 4-quart casserole, cook the onions in the vegetable oil over moderately low heat until it has softened completely, about 5 minutes. The onions should not color at all.

Pour in the chili sauce; stir in the remaining ingredients. Bring the contents of the casserole to a fast bubble, then simmer for about 25 minutes, partially covered. Puree the sauce in a blender, return it to the rinsed-out casserole, and bring to a boil.

Pour the sauce into hot pint jars to ¼ inch of the top, close with lids and bands. Process in a boiling-water bath (see pp. 8–11) for 10 minutes.

Alternately, do not return the pureed sauce to the casserole for a final boiling. Simply cool the pureed sauce, pour it into containers, cover, and refrigerate for up to 2 weeks.

The Brandied Fruit of Summer

If I'm invited as a weekend guest, it is likely that I'll add a big jar of fruit preserved in some kind of brandy or a savory compote to my canvas tote. Most brandied fruit available commercially has nothing in common with the ambrosia you can put together at home, and brandied fruit has a practical kind of beauty, one that makes an exceptional gift.

The most casual cook can turn out jars of brandied fruit with no trouble at all as long as a few canning watchpoints are followed. I prefer to process all spirited fruits (and various other kinds of jarred food, as appropriate) in a boiling-water bath. Veteran canners will have a practical knowledge of this already. The method is described on pp. 8–11 in chapter 1, and whatever is treated by the boiling-water bath procedure may be stored safely in the pantry. Some of the fruit and alcohol combinations may be put together and stored in the refrigerator; others will not benefit from refrigerator storage. Throughout this book, many recipes include instructions on the timing and other various details you should know about using the boiling-water bath method for a particular recipe.

Canning by the boiling-water bath method—both cold and hot pack—is an easy process which involves a small expenditure in equipment (a large kettle, canning jars) and only a little time on your part to go over the method.

BRANDIED CHERRIES

MAKES ABOUT 12 CUPS

When you come upon really firm, sweet cherries, it's time to break open a bottle of clear cherry brandy and set to boil a sugar syrup—the two liquids in brandied cherries. The aesthetic fanatic in me picks out each individual cherry with a stem attached (it does require a certain temperament to get 5 pounds of cherries with stems). The cherries will be just as delicious, however, if you make up this recipe and not include the stems, just not as fancy looking. Try the cherries as a side dish to holiday turkey, goose, or duck. Or turn a spoonful over ice cream or pound cake.

1½ cups granulated sugar
2 cups water
1½ cups cherry brandy (kirschwasser)

5 pounds sweet Bing or Lambert
    cherries
18 whole cloves

In a 4-cup saucepan, place the sugar and water. Cover the pan, place it over a low heat, and cook slowly to dissolve the sugar. When the sugar has melted down completely (dip a metal spoon into the bottom to detect any gritty sugar grains that may not have dissolved), bring the liquid to a boil; boil for 1 minute. Keep warm. In another saucepan, warm the brandy.

While the sugar syrup is cooking, thoroughly wash and dry the cherries. With the point of a small trussing needle or skewer, prick each cherry in 2 or 3 places (so the fruit will not burst).

47

Using the cold-pack method, place the cherries in 6 hot pint jars. Add 4 tablespoons brandy to each jar, then cover to ½ inch of the top with the warm sugar syrup. Drop 3 cloves in each jar; cover with lids and bands.

Process pint jars in a boiling-water bath for 20 minutes; cool.

Alternately, dump all of the cherries into a large container or 2 large glass jars. If using 1 large container, pour on the brandy and syrup and add the cloves. If using glass jars, divide the brandy and syrup in half, pour into each jar, and distribute the cloves between the 2 jars. Cool, cover, and refrigerate for up to 2 months.

SPICED CHERRIES   MAKES 2 POUNDS, ABOUT 5 CUPS

If you are of the mind that cherries are marvelous in savory dishes, and do not think of them in terms of cobbler or pie alone, this spicy condiment is a resourceful way to treat them when they have peaked in summer. You might try canning some in anticipation of the November and December holidays (they cut the richness of meat quite nicely).

1½ cups water
1½ cups granulated sugar
1½ cups apple cider vinegar
2 cinnamon sticks
9 whole cloves

6 whole allspice berries
12 white peppercorns
2 pounds dark, firm cherries (preferably with stems)

For refrigerator storage, prepare the cherries in the following way: Place all the ingredients except cherries in a 6-quart casserole or kettle. Cover the pot and heat the sugar and spice mixture over a low heat until the sugar dissolves completely. Uncover the pot, raise the heat to moderately high, and bring the liquid to a boil; boil for 3 minutes.

Add the cherries to the liquid, regulating the heat so that the liquid simmers at a gentle bubble. Poach the cherries in the syrup for about 5 minutes, or until they lose some of their initial firmness, but still retain their shape.

Carefully remove the cherries with a slotted spoon to a large container, then strain over the liquid. Pick out the spices from the strainer and put them back into the cherries and liquid. Cool to room temperature, then cover the container; refrigerate. The cherries will keep up to 1 month.

For canning: place all ingredients except cherries in a 2-quart saucepan. Cover and cook the mixture over a moderately low heat to dissolve the sugar. Uncover the pot, raise the heat to moderately high, and boil the syrup for 4 minutes.

Fill 2 pint jars with the cherries to 1 inch of the top of each jar, then fill to ½ inch of the top with the hot syrup. Seal the jars with lids and bands, and process the jars in a boiling-water bath for 20 minutes; cool.

BRANDIED PLUMS   MAKES ABOUT 12 CUPS

To have brandied plums on hand is to have an exquisite bright jar of fruit that inspires other preparations. Very small cubes of the fruit may be added to the sauce for a dish of wild game, Cornish hen, or medallions of pork. For a striking fall fruit compote that tastes homey and good, add some halves of these drunken plums to a dish of lightly poached apples and pears.

1½ cups granulated sugar
1¾ cups water
18 whole allspice berries
6 pounds small Italian blue prune
  plums, halved and pitted

6 4-inch cinnamon sticks
1½ cups warmed plum brandy
  (mirabelle)

In a 4-cup saucepan, place the sugar and water. Cover and cook over moderately low heat to dissolve the sugar. Uncover the pan, add the allspice, and bring the liquid to a boil; boil 2 minutes. Keep warm.

Pack 6 pint jars with the plums, firmly, but do not squish the plums against one another so that they look mashed. Sit a piece of cinnamon in each jar, preferably up against the side of the jar.

Spoon 4 tablespoons brandy in each jar of fruit and fill the jar with the warm syrup, including some allspice in each container. Fill the jars using the cold-pack method, leaving ½ inch headspace. Close with lids and bands.

Process pint jars in a boiling-water bath for 20 minutes; cool.

Alternately, place all of the plum halves in a big container, pour on the syrup and brandy, and add the cinnamon sticks. Stir well; let the mixture sit for 2 hours. Pour the contents of the container into a 10- or 12-quart pot (preferably of enameled cast iron) and bring to a boil; then simmer 5 minutes. Cool. Refrigerate the plums in the syrup, tightly covered, for 3 weeks. (I prefer to use the cold-pack method for canning and preserving these plums, rather than refrigerator storage.)

VARIATION: For Brandied Peaches, use the same amounts of sugar, water, and

49

spice but use peach brandy instead of plum brandy. Also, to the sugar and water add three tablespoons granular fresh fruit preserver, and continue making syrup as directed.

APRICOTS IN APRICOT LIQUEUR   MAKES ABOUT 12 CUPS

If I could have only one preserved fresh fruit, it would be apricots, sealed up in an easily made but ornate-tasting blend of apricot liqueur and dense sugar syrup. Choose apricots that are petite since they are usually more flavorful, and small apricot halves look better in the jar. On a more technical note, I am not advising refrigerator storage for these apricots; their fresh, clean taste keeps best when they are canned. Use the apricots in mixed fruit compotes, or as a sweet side dish to the big bird at Thanksgiving.

2 cups granulated sugar
2¾ cups water
2 tablespoons granular Fresh Fruit
    Preserver

5½–6 pounds fresh, ripe apricots,
    halved and pitted
30 whole allspice berries
1½ cups warmed apricot liqueur

In a 5- or 6-cup saucepan, place the sugar, water, and Fresh Fruit Preserver. Cover the pan and cook the mixture over a moderately low heat to dissolve all of the sugar. Uncover the pan, raise the heat to high, and bring the liquid to a boil; boil 2 minutes. Keep warm.

Arrange the apricot halves in a delightful pattern in 6 pint jars, adding 5 whole allspice berries to each jar as you go. Spoon 4 tablespoons apricot liqueur into each jar and fill up to ½ inch of the top with the warm sugar syrup. Close the jars with lids and bands.

Using the cold-pack method, process the pint jars in a boiling-water bath for 20 minutes; cool.

BRANDIED GRAPES   MAKES ABOUT 12 CUPS

It is reasonable to assume that plump green grapes might turn dreary if marinated. Well, that just isn't so—at least in this recipe. These grapes take on a lyrical quality when the fresh ginger pieces make the syrup taste decisively pungent. They make a fresh-tasting sweet adjunct to grilled duck or Cornish hen. Or use them whole in fruit compotes and chopped in a fruit mousse or a Bavarian cream.

1½ cups granulated sugar

2 cups water

18 dime-size pieces of fresh ginger, lightly mangled with the flat blade of a knife or cleaver

5½–6 pounds Thompson seedless grapes, plucked from the stems

1½ cups grape brandy (grappa)

In a 4- to 5-cup saucepan, place the sugar, water, and ginger. Cover the pan and set it over a low heat until the sugar dissolves completely. Uncover the saucepan, raise the heat to high, and boil the syrup for 2 minutes; keep warm.

Pack the grapes in 6 pint jars to 1 inch of the top. Pour in 4 tablespoons grape brandy, fill up the rest of the jar with the warm syrup (including some ginger pieces in each jar) to ½ inch of the top. Close the jars with lids and bands.

Process the jars in a boiling-water bath for 20 minutes; cool. Refrigerator storage of the grapes is not recommended.

NOTE: An added touch is to remove the fresh ginger after the syrup has been cooked and, on packing the fruit, replace it with chopped ginger preserved in syrup. This treatment dresses the grapes in party clothes.

BLUEBERRIES IN BLACK CURRANT LIQUEUR MAKES ABOUT 12 CUPS

My unabashed love for blueberries sometimes makes me want to treat them in an understated, elegant fashion. These blueberries can be used in creations in the appetizer, main course, or dessert category with equal grace when you want to get a sweet-savory tilt of flavors. In this recipe, the granular Fresh Fruit Preserver helps to stop the blueberries from turning too pale; a very little color will leech out, nevertheless, but that is all right.

1½ cups granulated sugar

2 cups water

2 tablespoons granular Fresh Fruit Preserver

1 cup black currant liqueur (crème de cassis)

6 pounds firm, sweet blueberries, picked over, washed, and drained well

6 3-inch cinnamon sticks

In a 5- to 6-cup saucepan, place the granulated sugar, water, and Fresh Fruit Preserver. Cover the pan and set over a low heat until the sugar dissolves completely. Uncover the pot, raise the heat to high, and boil the syrup for 2 minutes. Add the black currant liqueur and bring everything to a boil; keep warm.

Carefully scoop the blueberries into 6 pint jars, being careful not to smash or bruise any of them. While you are adding the blueberries, stick a piece of cinnamon in each jar, straight up against the side. Arrange the blueberries so that the top level is an even ½ inch from the top of the jar. Pour in enough of the hot syrup to cover the berries, still maintaining the ½ inch headspace. Close the jars with lids and bands.

Process the jars in a boiling-water bath for 10 minutes; cool. Preparing these berries for refrigerator storage is not recommended.

SAVORY PAPAYA AND RED PLUM COMPOTE   MAKES ABOUT 12½ CUPS

In the classic sense of the word, this is not your traditional dessert compote. It is, though, a completely tasty mingling of fruit and spices, something between a relish, chutney, and pickle—a brilliant partner for grilled meat, chicken salad, beef salad, cold roasted pork, and like food.

2 cups apple cider vinegar
⅓ cup freshly squeezed lemon juice
1 cup water
2¼ cups granulated sugar
1 tablespoon granular Fresh Fruit
   Preserver
2 teaspoons coarse (kosher) salt
2 teaspoons yellow mustard seed
1 teaspoon whole allspice berries
3 pounds barely ripe papaya, peeled,
   seeded, and cut into 2-inch cubes

3 pounds firm red plums, halved, pitted, and quartered
½ teaspoon cayenne pepper, or to
   taste
1 cup golden raisins
½ cup currants
3 tablespoons grated fresh ginger
6 3-inch cinnamon sticks

In a large 6-quart casserole, preferably of enameled cast iron, pour in the vinegar, lemon juice, and water. Add the sugar, fruit preserver, salt, mustard seed, and allspice. Cover the pot, place it over a moderately low heat, and cook until the sugar has dissolved completely. Uncover the casserole, raise the heat to moderately high, and bring the mixture to a boil; boil hard for 2 minutes.

Add the remaining ingredients to the syrup and bring to a boil. Reduce the heat and boil the mixture slowly for 4 to 5 minutes, or until the fruit is cooked but not softened down into mush.

With a stainless-steel slotted spoon, remove all of the solids to a bowl. Boil down the syrup for 5 to 6 minutes or until it has thickened. Pour the syrup over the fruit.

Pour the compote into 6 boiling-hot pint jars to ½ inch of the top; seal with lids and bands. Process the jars in a boiling-water bath for 10 minutes. As you pack the compote, include the cinnamon sticks in the jar, set up against the sides for an attractive effect.

Alternately, let the compote cool to room temperature, and refrigerate in a large covered container for up to 2 months. Repack before giving.

Sweet Sauces and Preserves

BLUEBERRY SYRUP   MAKES ABOUT 2½ CUPS

This is a bit like bottling summer. It captures the rich, assertive taste of blueberries for other seasons. I've used sweet cultivated berries to make it, but if you should discover wild blueberries on a country walk, by all means use them for this syrup. Just bear in mind that wild berries are spicily tart, so you should omit the lemon juice. Spoon over pancakes, French toast, waffles, and ice cream or ladle a few spoonfuls onto individual dessert plates and then center on them a mound of lemon mousse, a small dome of orange custard, or chunks of cantaloupe or honeydew.

For gift-giving, funnel the syrup into slim-necked clear glass bottles with porcelain caps, and then top with neat squares of country calico. Use a silky ribbon to hold these fabric caps in place.

4 pints fresh blueberries, picked over   *3 cups granulated sugar*
(about 6 cups)   *1 teaspoon ground allspice*
¼ cup strained, freshly squeezed
lemon juice

Puree the blueberries in several batches in the container of a food processor fitted with a steel blade. Turn the puree into a 10-quart nonmetallic kettle as it is processed. Stir in the lemon juice, sugar, and ground allspice.

Place the kettle over a low heat and cook the mixture until the sugar dissolves completely. Raise the heat so that the mixture simmers steadily and gently; simmer for 12 to 15 minutes, or until very lightly thickened. Let stand for 10 minutes.

Place a large stainless-steel fine-meshed sieve over a large nonmetallic bowl. In several batches, pour in the blueberry mixture and press down on the solids to extract the juice with the back of a wooden spoon. Discard the pulpy remains before adding a new batch to be strained.

Pour the syrup into bottles or jars, then close tightly with the covers or caps. Cool to room temperature, then store in the refrigerator for up to 8 months.

SPICY APRICOT GLAZE

MAKES ABOUT 1¾ CUPS

For glazing lamb riblets, country spareribs, chicken pieces, and pork roasts.

4 tablespoons peanut oil
1 onion, finely chopped
2 jalapeño peppers, stemmed, seeded,
and roughly chopped (using rub-
ber gloves to protect your hands)
1½ tablespoons grated fresh ginger
and ½ teaspoon ground ginger
2 tablespoons Worcestershire sauce
¼ cup apple cider vinegar

¼ teaspoon ground allspice
pinch of ground cloves
1½ cups preservative-free chunky apri-
cot preserves
2 tablespoons Dijon mustard
½ cup unsweetened apricot juice
(available at health-food stores)
blended with ¼ cup water

In a 4-quart nonmetallic casserole, heat the peanut oil over a low heat. Stir in the onion and sauté slowly until the onion is soft and translucent.

Stir in the next 6 ingredients. Cook-stir over a moderate heat for 2 minutes.

Blend in the remaining ingredients and simmer for 6 minutes.

Cool the glaze for 5 minutes, then puree it in the bowl of a food processor fitted with a steel blade. Pour the glaze into a clean glass jar. Cool to room temperature, cover, and refrigerate for up to 5 months.

NOTE: This recipe may be doubled or tripled without problem.

RED PLUM SAUCE

MAKES ABOUT 4 CUPS

This glowing plum sauce and the apricot one that follows are sweet-tart, sumptuous, and visually gorgeous—such a nice contrast to simple poached apples or pears, or to a plain vanilla soufflé or mousse. For me, fruit sauces have become an essential luxury to keep on my refrigerator shelf because they are such a wonderfully easy way to add another taste, another hint of flavor to a dessert.

3 cups granulated sugar
3 cups water
juice of 2 lemons, strained
6 cups peeled red plum slices
½ teaspoon ground cinnamon

¼ teaspoon freshly ground nutmeg
¼ teaspoon ground allspice
¼ teaspoon ground ginger
2 tablespoons plum brandy (mirabelle)

Combine the sugar, water, and lemon juice in a nonmetallic 8- to 10-quart kettle or casserole. Cover and cook over a low heat to dissolve the sugar. Uncover the pot, raise the heat to high, and boil the liquid for 5 minutes.

Add the plum slices, cinnamon, nutmeg, allspice, and ginger. Bring to a boil. Simmer the plum slices until they are falling-apart tender, stirring the pot from time to time (depending upon the age of the fruit, this will take about 15 to 25 minutes). Halfway during the cooking time, or after 8 minutes or so, add the plum brandy.

Cool the plum mixture for 10 minutes, then remove the slices to a bowl with a stainless-steel slotted spoon. After 15 minutes, puree the slices in the bowl of a food processor fitted with a steel blade.

Assemble a stainless-steel sieve on top of a large nonmetallic bowl. Combine the plum puree with cooking syrup, then strain it through the sieve. Press down on the solids with a wooden spoon to push out every last drop of fruit sauce.

Cool the sauce to room temperature, then stir it and pour it into clean jars. Cover and refrigerate for up to 5 months.

NOTE: Depending upon the sweetness of the plums, you may need to add more lemon juice to the cooked sauce; blend in the juice as the sauce cools down.

FRESH APRICOT SAUCE
MAKES ABOUT 4 CUPS

Pair this sauce with a warm apricot bread pudding (or other custardy, nursery-type dessert), for a dramatic and wonderful contrast. Or spoon a little of it over pecan buttermilk waffles. A thin layer of this amber-rich sauce on a dessert plate *before* you spoon out soufflé or mousse adds a pleasing visual effect and a citric sweetness. (I use a 60-proof French apricot liqueur to make this.)

30 *(about 2 pounds) plump, soft, and*
utterly ripe fresh apricots
juice of 2 lemons, strained
1 *cup granulated sugar*
2 *3-inch cinnamon sticks*

1 *vanilla bean, split down the center to*
show the tiny seeds
2 *cups water*
2 *tablespoons fine apricot liqueur*

Peel and pit the apricots, and reserve the peel and pits in a small bowl. Cut up the apricots (using a stainless-steel serrated knife) into rough chunks.

Turn the apricot chunks into a bowl, add the lemon juice and granulated sugar, and stir to combine all. Let the apricots stand for 2 hours, turning them around in the sugar now and again.

After 2 hours, place the apricot-sugar mixture into an 8-quart nonmetallic casserole or kettle. Add the pits and skins, cinnamon sticks, vanilla bean, and water. Bring to a boil over a moderately high heat. Stir in the apricot liqueur. Cover and simmer for 10 minutes. Uncover and bring to a boil again.

Partially cover the pot and cook the mixture until the apricots are quite tender, about 12 minutes. Cool the mixture for 5 minutes. Carefully pick out all of the pits and discard them. Remove the cinnamon sticks and vanilla bean.

Set a food mill over a large nonmetallic bowl, and puree the apricots and liquid through the mill in small batches..

Cool the sauce to room temperature; stir it up once before pouring it into clean glass jars to ¼ inch of the top. Cover with lids. Store the sauce in the refrigerator for up to 5 months.

NOTE: This recipe doubles easily; simply cook the sauce in a roomy 12-quart pot.

NECTARINE AND GINGER CHUTNEY   MAKES ABOUT 8 CUPS

The nectarines in this recipe produce an exceptionally flavorful chutney that is dandy with roast lamb, pork, or game. Freestone peaches or red plums may be substituted for the nectarines, with more than admirable results.

5 pounds sweet, ripe but firm nectarines, peeled, pitted, and cut into
   1½-inch cubes
finely grated rind and juice of 2
   lemons
2 cups granulated sugar
¼ cup firmly packed dark brown sugar
¼ cup firmly packed light brown
   sugar
2 teaspoons coarse (kosher) salt

1 teaspoon celery seed
1 teaspoon hot pepper sauce, such as
   Tabasco
1 cup water
2 3-inch cinnamon sticks
1⅓ cups apple cider vinegar
½ cup drained, coarsely chopped ginger preserved in syrup
½ cup dried, but moist, currants

In a large nonmetallic 12-quart kettle, combine all but the last 3 ingredients. Stir well and let stand in a cool place (but not in the refrigerator) for 2 hours, stirring several times each hour.

Pour in the apple cider vinegar and place the pot over a moderate heat. Cook the mixture until the sugars dissolve completely. Raise the heat to high and boil the mixture for about 6 minutes or until the nectarines are just tender.

With a stainless-steel slotted spoon, remove the nectarine chunks to a large side bowl; add the ginger and currants. Stir.

Boil the syrup until it has condensed and reduced in volume by about one third, approximately 7 minutes. Add the nectarines and bring everything to a boil.

Ladle the boiling-hot chutney into 4 hot pint jars to ¼ inch of the top (discard the cinnamon sticks as you go); seal with hot lids and bands. Process the chutney in a boiling-water bath (see pp. 8–11) for 10 minutes; cool.

Alternately, ladle the chutney into a sturdy storage container, cool to room temperature, then cover and refrigerate for up to 3 months.

RED PLUM CHUTNEY   MAKES ABOUT 6 CUPS

Among stone-fruit chutneys, this is my very favorite. Serve with grilled chicken or pork, turkey, spareribs, or any meat with a special succulence that needs a bright note, a lift, a spark.

1 cup apple cider vinegar
¼ cup strained, freshly squeezed
  lemon juice
⅓ cup water
1¾ cups granulated sugar blended
  with 2 teaspoons granular Fresh
  Fruit Preserver and 1½ teaspoons
  coarse salt
1 teaspoon yellow mustard seed
3¼ pounds just-ripe plums, halved,
  stones removed, and cut into
  1-inch cubes

¼ cup dark seedless raisins
4 jalapeño peppers, stemmed, seeded,
  and coarsely chopped (using rub-
  ber gloves to protect your hands)
6 pieces coarsely chopped ginger pre-
  served in syrup
2 tablespoons syrup from the preserved
  ginger
2 tablespoons finely grated fresh ginger

Combine the first 5 ingredients in a nonmetallic 10-quart kettle or casserole. Cover and cook slowly until the sugar dissolves completely. Uncover the pot and bring the contents to a boil over a high heat; boil for 2 minutes.

Add the remaining ingredients to the boiling syrup. Boil the plums slowly until they are just tender, about 5 minutes.

Remove the plums to a side bowl with a stainless-steel slotted spoon; boil the syrup until lightly thickened and condensed, about 4 minutes. Pour the hot syrup over the fruit.

Ladle the boiling-hot chutney into 3 hot pint jars to ½ inch of the top; seal with hot lids and bands. Process the pint jars in a boiling-water bath for 10 minutes; cool.

Alternately, pour the chutney into a sturdy storage container, cool to room temperature, then cover and refrigerate for up to 3 months.

SPICED BLUEBERRY CONSERVE   MAKES ABOUT 5 CUPS

Mildly flavored with freshly grated ginger, cinnamon, cloves, mace, and nutmeg, this piquant conserve is a grand accompaniment to savory meat turnovers, cold cuts, grilled pork, and chicken.

1½ cups blueberry vinegar (available in specialty food shops or make your own—see recipe for Black Raspberry Vinegar, p. 36)
1 cup water
3 cups granulated sugar
3½ pints fresh blueberries, picked over

1½ teaspoons ground cinnamon
½ teaspoon ground cloves
½ teaspoon ground mace
¼ teaspoon freshly ground nutmeg
⅓ cup black currant liqueur (crème de cassis)

Place the vinegar, water, ginger, and sugar in a heavy 12-quart kettle. Place the pot over a low heat and slowly cook the mixture to dissolve the sugar. Raise the heat to high, bring the liquid to a boil, and boil for 10 minutes.

Add the blueberries and spices; bring to a boil. Boil for 3 minutes, then remove the blueberries to a bowl with a slotted spoon.

Continue boiling the syrup for about 40 minutes, or until it is thick and reduced by half. Return the blueberries to the pot, and add the black currant liqueur. Boil until thick, about 7 minutes longer.

Ladle the conserve into 2 or 3 hot pint jars to ¼ inch of the top; seal with hot lids and bands.

Process pint jars in a boiling-water bath for 15 minutes; cool.

Alternately, pour the conserve into a sturdy container, cool, cover, and store in the refrigerator for up to 4 months.

ORANGE-PLUM CONSERVE WITH WALNUTS   MAKES ABOUT 5 CUPS

Summer! And its succulent berries, dark cherries, ruddy plums, and shore melons. When I'm not concocting fools, grunts, slumps, pandowdies, and reasonably *haute* compotes out of nature's finest, I preserve them into an excellent litany of conserves, butter, jams, and so on. Plums, especially, get more delicious when you cook them, I think, as their assertive juiciness comes forward well in things like this conserve, and don't overlook them as pie fruit or as material for plain old jam. As a surprise, I give winter dinner guests a beautiful jar of this conserve, in part to remind them of sun-soaked summer days, in part to add energy to the more substantial meals on cold days.

4 pounds ripe red plums, preferably
  Santa Rosas, halved, pitted, then
  quartered
4 medium-size sweet oranges, peeled,
  seeds removed, and flesh coarsely
  chopped

3 cups granulated sugar blended with
  2 teaspoons ground cinnamon
  and ½ teaspoon ground cloves
juice of 2 lemons
1 cup chopped walnuts
½ cup dark seedless raisins

In a nonmetallic 12-quart kettle stir together all but last 2 ingredients. Let stand for 1 hour, stirring occasionally, to melt down the sugar.

Place the kettle over a low heat and cook slowly to dissolve every last granule of sugar. Raise the heat to moderately high and cook the mixture steadily until almost jamlike, about 15 minutes; it will barely hold its shape in a spoon. Add the walnuts and raisins, and continue to cook the mixture until thick enough to hold its shape in a spoon, about 5 to 7 minutes longer.

Ladle the conserve into 2 or 3 boiling-hot pint jars to ¼ inch of the top; seal with hot lids and bands. Process the pint jars in a boiling-water bath for 15 minutes; cool.

Alternately, pour the conserve into a sturdy storage container, cool to room temperature, then cover and refrigerate for up to 3 months.

PEACH BUTTER
MAKES ABOUT 8 CUPS

One summer not long ago, I spent the weekend at a cottage located smack in the middle of a peach orchard. While I was there the large freestones ripened at such an alarming rate you could hardly eat, preserve, or give away the fruit. On leaving, my host and hostess loaded up my car with peaches—six bags full. Hence this recipe for peach butter, a disarmingly luxurious spread made from an utterly commonplace fruit. It's first-rate on homemade yeast bread and quick batter bread, and on muffins and buttermilk biscuits. Whip a little of it into a custard to go under glazed peach slices for a tart, or churn a cup into vanilla ice cream and treat it like a princely puree.

8 pounds juicy ripe freestone peaches,
   peeled, pitted, and cut into small
   chunks
1½ cups water
juice of 3 lemons

about 3 cups granulated sugar
2 teaspoons ground cinnamon
½ teaspoon ground allspice
½ teaspoon freshly ground nutmeg
¼ teaspoon ground cloves

Combine the peaches, water, and lemon juice in a heavy nonmetallic 12-quart kettle. Cover the kettle and cook the peaches over a low heat until they are very soft, about 35 minutes.

Pass the peaches and liquid through the fine disk of a food mill, or puree, a batch at a time, in the bowl of a food processor fitted with a steel blade.

For each 2 cups puree, measure out ¾ cup granulated sugar. Pour the puree into the rinsed-out kettle; add the granulated sugar and spices. Cook the mixture over a low heat to dissolve the sugar, then raise the heat to moderate and cook the mixture at a steady bubble until just thick enough to hold its shape in a spoon, about 40 minutes.

Ladle the butter into 4 hot, sterilized pint jars to ¼ inch of the top; seal with hot lids and bands. Process the butter in a boiling-water bath for 15 minutes; cool.

Alternately, pour the butter into a sturdy storage container, cool to room temperature, then cover and refrigerate for up to 3 months.

CANTALOUPE BUTTER

MAKES ABOUT 10 CUPS

A fruit butter that tastes faintly tropical. Mix a little of it into vanilla pastry cream for spreading in the bottom of a tart shell topped with fresh melon. Use it as a spread for toasted pound cake at breakfast, or blend a few tablespoons into mayonnaise to be folded into curried salads. Stir a generous cupful into a big recipe of creamy vanilla custard ice cream about 20 minutes before churning time is up.

6 large, ripe cantaloupes, peeled,
   halved, seeded, and cubed

2 cups water

FOR EACH 4 CUPS PUREED CANTALOUPE:

1½ cups granulated sugar
juice of 1 lemon
⅛ teaspoon freshly ground nutmeg

⅛ teaspoon ground ginger
⅛ teaspoon ground cinnamon

Place the cubed cantaloupe in a nonmetallic 12-quart kettle and pour in water. Cover and cook over a low heat until the cantaloupe has softened completely, about

15 minutes, or longer, depending upon the ripeness of the fruit. Stir up the cantaloupe from time to time.

Puree the cantaloupe in several batches in the bowl of a food processor fitted with a steel blade, including all of the juices as you go along. Rinse out the kettle and add the fruit puree to it, measuring it before you pour in each batch.

For each 4 cups puree, add the ingredients in the proportions given above. Cover the pot and cook the fruit and sugar until the sugar has completely melted down. Uncover the pot, bring the contents to a boil, stirring. Continue cooking the puree at a slow boil until silky and thick, but not pastelike, about 40 minutes.

Ladle the hot butter into 10 boiling-hot half-pint or 5 pint jars to ⅛ inch of the top; seal the jars immediately with hot lids and bands. Cool.

BLACKBERRY JAM WITH CASSIS   MAKES ABOUT 7 CUPS

I love blackberries cooked by themselves (I tend to leave them out of mixed fruit combinations), so that the exquisite flavor of the fruit may be enjoyed in all its glory. Sometimes I am lucky enough to pick wild blackberries for this jam—these are earthy and aromatic. Blackberry jam goes with all kinds of hot breads, but my favorite place to use it is between rounds of buttery nut cookies, like Linzer cookies, in place of the usual raspberry jam.

2 quarts smallish blackberries, carefully picked over
3 pounds granulated sugar blended with 2 teaspoons ground cinnamon, 1 teaspoon ground allspice, and ½ teaspoon ground cloves

juice of 2 lemons, strained
⅓ cup black currant liqueur (crème de cassis)
3 ounces liquid pectin (not powdered pectin)

In a heavy nonmetallic 12-quart kettle, stir together the blackberries and sugar-spice blend. Place over a low heat and cook slowly until the sugar dissolves completely. Stir in the lemon juice. On high heat, bring the mixture to a boil; boil 2 minutes.

Stir in the black currant liqueur and bring the contents of the kettle to a hard, rolling boil that doesn't break down when you stir the pot. Boil hard for 1 minute.

Immediately remove the pot from the heat source and stir in the liquid pectin. Continue stirring for 1 minute, then ladle the boiling-hot jam into 7 hot, sterilized half-pint jars to ⅛ inch of the top. Seal immediately with lids and bands. Cool the jars to room temperature (this takes about 6 to 7 hours), then store them in a cool pantry.

CINNAMON-LEMON PRUNE PLUMS   MAKES 4 POUNDS, ABOUT 8 CUPS

These plums are a late summer–early fall treat; I use them as part of a mixed fruit compote when I poach other fruit separately and arrange them together on individual plates with some kind of fruit sauce underneath it all. But eaten plain and by themselves, these plums are good with a rich eggy custard sauce.

3½ cups water
2¾ cups granulated sugar
¼ cup liquid brown sugar
juice of 1 lemon, strained

1 4-inch cinnamon stick
4 whole allspice berries
4 whole cloves
4 pounds small purple prune plums

Place all the ingredients except plums in a heavy nonmetallic 10-quart pot. Cover and cook slowly over a low heat to dissolve the granulated sugar completely.

Uncover the pot, raise the heat to high, and boil the liquid for 5 minutes. Reduce the heat to moderate, add the plums, and adjust the heat so that the liquid simmers gently. Simmer the plums until they are just tender, about 7 minutes, then remove the plums to a side bowl with a stainless-steel slotted spoon.

Reduce the syrup over a high heat until it is lightly thickened, about 4 minutes. Pour the syrup over the plums and cool to room temperature.

Transfer the plums and liquid to a storage container, cover, and refrigerate for up to 6 weeks.

Pound Cakes and Muffins

A basket or round wooden pantry box filled with muffins is a lovely gift to receive, as is an extremely good pound cake, nestled in a deep colorful box. And the rewards for the giver are many. There is nothing quite so pleasurable as the process of baking, and even the shopping for this kind of cooking is satisfying. In one shopping expedition you can have at hand all the butter, spices, flour, and flavorings you'll need for several forays into the kitchen.

To amplify the gift you could tie a small group of cookie cutters or biscuit cutters (scalloped or plain; deep or shallow) and attach them to the boxes or baskets. Other possible additions are assorted small kitchen items, such as a slender goose feather pastry brush, several miniature spatulas, or a nested set of dry measures. Use ribbon that does not fray to wind around these, and bow-tie to the box or basket with another length of ribbon.

VANILLA POUND CAKE

MAKES ONE 10-INCH CAKE

High and rich, this may well be the ultimate vanilla pound cake. The tiny potent seeds from the dark center of the vanilla bean are scraped into a cup of milk, then the bean is sunk into the liquid and left to rest for an hour before the cake is put together. Toasted slices make a fine breakfast treat served with a pot of unusual jam, perhaps a mango or cranberry conserve.

1 vanilla bean, plump and moist
1 cup milk, at room temperature
4 cups sifted all-purpose flour (prefera-
  bly unbleached)
1 tablespoon baking powder
½ teaspoon salt

2 cups unsalted sweet butter, softened
  at room temperature
3 cups granulated sugar
6 jumbo eggs, at room temperature
2 teaspoons pure vanilla extract
confectioners' sugar (optional)

Slit the vanilla bean down the center. Pour the milk into a bowl and scrape out the tiny seeds of the bean into the milk. Plop the bean into the milk and let it stand for 1 hour. Remove the bean.

Lightly butter and flour the inside of a plain 10-inch tube pan; set aside. Preheat the oven to 350° F.

Resift the flour with the baking powder and salt onto a sheet of waxed paper; set aside.

In the large bowl of an electric mixer, cream the butter on moderately high speed until light, about 3 minutes.

Add the granulated sugar in two portions, beating for about 2 minutes after each amount is added. Beat in the eggs, one at a time, and scrape down the sides of the bowl often to ensure an even mixture. Blend in the vanilla extract.

On low speed, add the sifted dry ingredients in three portions alternately with the milk in two portions, beginning and ending with the dry ingredients.

Pour and scrape the batter into the prepared pan. Bake the cake on the lower-level rack of the oven for about 1 hour, or until a toothpick inserted into the cake emerges clean and dry.

Cool the cake in the pan on a rack for 10 minutes, then invert onto a second rack. Invert again to cool the cake right side up.

Store airtight. Dust the top with confectioners' sugar before serving, if you like.

CREAM CHEESE POUND CAKE

MAKES ONE 10-INCH CAKE

This cake has a velvety fine-grained crumb because it is enriched twice, once by a half pound of butter, and again by a half pound of cream cheese. For a wonderful dessert plate, blend a few tablespoons of raspberry syrup into a pint of perfectly ripe raspberries and spoon portions of the fruit to the side of two thin slices of this cake.

3 cups sifted all-purpose flour (preferably unbleached)
1½ teaspoons baking powder
½ teaspoon salt
1 cup unsalted sweet butter, softened at room temperature

½ pound cream cheese, softened at room temperature
3 cups granulated sugar
2 teaspoons pure vanilla extract
6 jumbo eggs, at room temperature
confectioners' sugar (optional)

Lightly butter and flour a fluted 10-inch tube pan and set aside. Preheat oven to 325° F.

Resift the flour with the baking powder and salt onto a sheet of waxed paper; set aside.

In the large bowl of an electric mixer, cream the butter until light on moderately high speed, about 3 minutes.

Add the cream cheese and continue creaming until quite light, about 4 minutes. Add the sugar in three portions, beating on moderately high speed for 2 minutes after each amount is added. Scrape down the sides of the bowl often. The mixture should look extremely light and white. Beat on moderately high speed for an additional 3 minutes. Blend in the vanilla extract.

Beat in the eggs, one at a time, blending well until incorporated before the next egg is added. Scrape down the sides of the bowl often to ensure an even mix. The mixture will look quite thin at this point.

On low speed, add the sifted mixture in three additions, blending just until the flour particles have been absorbed.

Pour and scrape the batter into the prepared pan; gently level the top by shaking the pan from side to side. Bake the cake on the lower-level rack of the oven for 50 to 54 minutes, or until a toothpick inserted in the cake emerges clean and dry.

Cool the cake in the pan on a rack for 10 minutes, then invert onto another rack to cool completely. Store airtight. Dust the top of the cake with confectioners' sugar before serving, if you like.

NOTE: The fluted tube pan I use for this recipe measures 10 inches across the top and a full 4¾ inches high.

RUM POUND CAKE

MAKES ONE 10-INCH CAKE

Dark rum and dark brown sugar turn the batter for this pound cake a beautiful amber color. Large and grand, it has a delicate undertone of nutmeg. Serve it with sturdy winter compotes made from dried figs and apricots or poached apple and pear slices. In the summertime, it is perfect with blackberries and blueberries.

3½ cups sifted all-purpose flour (preferably unbleached)
1½ teaspoons baking powder
½ teaspoon salt
½ teaspoon freshly ground nutmeg
1½ cups unsalted sweet butter, softened at room temperature
about 2⅓ cups firmly packed dark
   brown sugar

1 cup granulated sugar
5 jumbo eggs, at room temperature
¾ cup milk, at room temperature
¼ cup dark rum blended with 2 teaspoons pure vanilla extract
confectioners' sugar

Butter a plain 10-inch tube pan. Line the bottom with a circle of waxed paper, butter the paper, then lightly dust the inside of the pan with flour; set aside. Preheat the oven to 350° F.

Resift the flour with the baking powder, salt, and nutmeg onto a sheet of waxed paper; set aside.

In the large bowl of an electric mixer, cream the butter on moderately high speed until light, about 3 minutes.

Add the dark brown sugar in two additions, creaming on moderately high speed for 3 minutes after each portion is added. Add the granulated sugar and cream for 2 minutes.

Beat in the eggs, one at a time, and blend for 1 minute after each one is added. Scrape down the sides of the bowl after each egg is added to keep the mixture even.

On low speed, add one third of the sifted mixture; blend. Add all of the milk; blend. Add another third of the sifted mixture, mix, and all of the rum-vanilla, and mix again. Add the remaining one third of the sifted flour mixture and blend.

Pour and scrape the batter into the prepared pan. Level the top by gently shaking the pan from side to side. Bake the cake on the lower-level rack of the oven for about 1 hour and 20 minutes, or until a toothpick inserted into the cake emerges clean and dry.

Cool the cake in the pan on a rack for 10 minutes; invert the cake on another rack, then invert again to cool right side up.

Store airtight. Sprinkle the top of the cake with confectioners' sugar just before serving.

CINNAMON–SOUR CREAM POUND CAKE   MAKES ONE 10-INCH CAKE

The cinnamon in this cake gives it a café au lait coloring and an uncommonly appealing flavor. Start with fresh and pungent spice because the impact of this cake depends on its intense aroma and flavor.

3 cups sifted all-purpose flour (prefera-
  bly unbleached)
2 teaspoons baking powder
¼ teaspoon baking soda
½ teaspoon salt
1 tablespoon highly aromatic ground
  cinnamon
1 cup unsalted sweet butter, softened
  at room temperature

3 cups granulated sugar
6 jumbo eggs, at room temperature
1 cup sour cream, at room tempera-
  ture, blended with 1 tablespoon
  pure vanilla extract
confectioners' sugar (optional)

Lightly butter and flour a plain 10-inch tube pan (do not substitute a fluted pan for this recipe); set aside. Preheat oven to 350° F.

Resift the flour with the baking powder, baking soda, salt, and cinnamon onto a sheet of waxed paper; set aside.

In the large bowl of an electric mixer, cream the butter until light on moderately high speed, about 3 minutes. Add the sugar in three additions, beating until light and fluffy before the next portion is added.

Add the eggs, one at a time, beating on moderate speed until each is well incorporated. Scrape down the sides of the bowl often.

On low speed, blend in the sifted dry ingredients in three additions alternately with the sour cream in two additions, beginning and ending with the dry ingredients.

Pour and scrape the batter into the prepared pan; shake the pan gently from side to side to level the top. Bake the cake on the lower-level rack of the oven for about 1 hour and 20 minutes, or until a toothpick inserted in the cake withdraws clean and dry.

Cool the cake in the pan on a rack for 10 minutes, invert it on another rack, and invert again to cool right side up.

When cooled, store airtight. Dust the top of the cake with confectioners' sugar before serving, if you like.

DELICATE ALMOND POUND CAKE   MAKES ONE 10-INCH CAKE

"Beat up the butter until very creamy," wrote my paternal grandmother in her treasured recipe for this delightful pound cake. The results are memorable. Just right as an accompaniment to summer fruit or frosty ice cream.

3 cups cake flour
1½ teaspoons baking powder
½ teaspoon salt
½ teaspoon mace
2 cups unsalted sweet butter, softened
    at room temperature

about 3 cups sifted confectioners'
    sugar
1 tablespoon pure almond extract
8 jumbo eggs, separated, at room tem-
    perature

Lightly butter and flour a plain 10-inch tube pan; set aside. Preheat oven to 350° F.

Sift together the flour, baking powder, salt, and mace onto a sheet of waxed paper; set aside.

In the large bowl of an electric mixer, cream the butter until light, about 5 to 6 minutes on moderately high speed. Add 2⅔ cups confectioners' sugar in two additions, beating well after each amount is added.

Add the egg yolks, one at a time, beating on moderately high speed after each yolk is added. Scrape down the sides of the bowl often to ensure an even mix. Blend in the almond extract.

On low speed, add the sifted flour mixture in three additions, beating just long enough to absorb the flour particles.

In a clean bowl, beat the egg whites until frothy, add a large pinch of salt, and continue beating until the whites form firm, not stiff, peaks. Stir three big spoonfuls of the whites into the cake batter, then fold in the remaining whites.

Gently turn and scrape the batter into the prepared pan; level the top with a spatula. Bake the cake on the lower-level rack of the oven for about 55 minutes, or until a toothpick inserted into the cake emerges clean and dry.

Cool the cake in the pan on a rack for 10 minutes; invert the cake on a rack, then invert again to cool right side up.

When cooled, store airtight. Sprinkle the top with confectioners' sugar before serving.

LEMON POUND CAKE

MAKES ONE 10-INCH CAKE

Well before you preheat the oven and gather the eggs and butter from the refrigerator to bake this cake, blend the lemon extract and lemon rind together in a small ramekin. Allowing the particles of rind to infuse the extract and the extract to soften the bits of rind strengthens the lemon flavor of this fresh-tasting treat.

2 teaspoons pure lemon extract
finely grated rind of 3 large lemons
3¼ cups sifted all-purpose flour (pref-
*   erably unbleached)*
1½ teaspoons baking powder
½ teaspoon salt

1½ cups unsalted sweet butter, soft-
*   ened at room temperature*
2¾ cups granulated sugar
5 jumbo eggs, at room temperature
1 cup milk, at room temperature
confectioners' sugar

One hour before baking time, blend the lemon extract and lemon rind in a small nonmetallic bowl; set aside.

Lightly butter and flour a fluted 10-inch tube pan; set aside.

Resift the flour with the baking powder and salt onto a sheet of waxed paper; set aside. Preheat oven to 325° F.

In the large bowl of an electric mixer, cream the butter until light on moderately high speed, about 3 to 4 minutes. Add the sugar in two additions, beating for 2 minutes on moderate speed after each addition.

Add the eggs, one at a time, beating for 1 minute after each egg is added; scrape down the sides of the bowl often.

On low speed, add the sifted mixture in three additions alternately with the milk in two additions, beginning and ending with the sifted mixture. By hand, stir in the rind-extract blend.

Pour and scrape the batter into the prepared pan; gently level the top with a spatula. Bake the cake on the lower-level rack of the oven for 1 hour and 10 to 15 minutes, or until a toothpick inserted in the cake withdraws without any clinging particles.

Cool the cake in the pan on a rack for 10 minutes. Invert the cake on another rack to cool completely.

Store airtight. Sift confectioners' sugar over the top of the cake before serving.

WHOLE-WHEAT MUFFINS WITH CURRANTS

MAKES 1 DOZEN

These muffins are cakelike and buxom. I have found that chopped dates, finely diced sweet dried apricots, or chopped golden raisins are all tempting substitutes for the currants. Little surprises of dried fruit stirred through the batter compliments the taste of whole wheat, but you could also bake these muffins plain, which is gratifying, too.

1¼ cups sifted all-purpose flour (preferably unbleached)
1¾ cups whole-wheat flour (preferably
  stone-ground)
2 tablespoons plus 1 teaspoon baking
  powder
½ teaspoon salt
¼ teaspoon ground allspice
4 tablespoons unsalted sweet butter,
  softened at room temperature

4 tablespoons solid shortening
⅓ cup granulated sugar
1 jumbo egg, at room temperature
1 cup milk, at room temperature,
  blended with 1 teaspoon pure
  vanilla extract
¼ cup dried currants, plumped in
  boiling water for 10 minutes, then
  drained and dried thoroughly on
  paper toweling

Lightly butter and flour 12 muffin cups measuring 2¾ inches in diameter; set aside. Preheat oven to 450° F.

Resift the flour, baking powder, salt, and allspice onto a sheet of waxed paper; set aside.

In the large bowl of an electric mixer, cream the butter and shortening on moderately high speed for 3 minutes. On moderate speed, beat in the sugar, and cream the fat and sugar together for 3 minutes.

Beat in the egg; scrape down the sides of the bowl to keep the mixture even. Beat on moderately high speed for 1 minute.

On low speed, add the sifted mixture in three additions alternately with the milk-vanilla blend in two additions, beginning and ending with the sifted mixture. Scrape down the sides of the bowl after each addition to keep the batter even. Stir in the currants with a few swift strokes.

Divide the batter evenly among the 12 muffin cups, mounding it in the center of each tin.

Bake the muffins on the middle-level rack of the oven for about 14 minutes, or until spottily golden on the top; a toothpick inserted into the muffin will emerge clean and dry.

Cool the muffins in the pans for 5 minutes, then remove them to a cooling rack. You may serve the muffins immediately, but for gift-giving, cool them to room temperature, bag them, and refrigerate until giving, up to 3 days. The muffins reheat beautifully in aluminum foil in a 350° F. oven for about 12 minutes.

BRAN MUFFINS

MAKES 1 DOZEN

These are a variation on Whole-Wheat Muffins with Currants, with a cup of bran replacing some of the whole-wheat flour. What's special about these muffins is that they are not dense and rough like normal bran muffins but just airy enough to be faintly delicate. For a pleasing small gift combine these with a lusty jam.

1 ¼ cups sifted all-purpose flour (preferably unbleached)
1 cup whole-wheat flour (preferably stone-ground)
2 tablespoons plus 1 teaspoon baking powder
½ teaspoon salt
1 cup raw bran flakes (available in bulk at a health-food store)

8 tablespoons solid shortening
⅓ cup granulated sugar
1 jumbo egg, at room temperature
¾ cup milk, at room temperature, blended with ¼ cup dark molasses and 1 teaspoon pure vanilla extract

Lightly butter and flour the inside of 12 muffin cups measuring 2¾ inches in diameter; set aside. Preheat oven to 450° F.

Resift the flour, baking powder, and salt onto a sheet of waxed paper. Pour the bran on top of the sifted mixture and fold it through with a rubber spatula; set aside.

In the large bowl of an electric mixer, cream the shortening on moderately high speed for 3 minutes. Add the sugar and continue creaming for 2 minutes longer.

On moderate speed, add the egg and beat it in. Scrape down the sides of the bowl to keep the mixture even, then beat for a few moments longer.

On low speed, alternately add the dry ingredients in three additions with the milk-molasses-vanilla in two additions, beginning and ending with the dry ingredients.

Spoon the batter in even amounts into the prepared muffin cups, mounding it in the center. Bake the muffins on the middle-level rack of the oven for 14 minutes, or until a toothpick inserted in the muffin emerges clean and dry.

Cool the muffins in the tin on a rack for 5 minutes, then remove the muffins to cool completely. Bag the muffins and refrigerate them for up to 1 week.

After Summer Herb Gathering

On whatever scale you cultivate your own home-grown herbs, preserve them for use throughout the year to use in soups, warming stews, and savory sauces. The herb bouquets are attractive enough to tie onto the side of a basket, and the aromatic packets look sensational in clear glass cylinders with clamp and rubber gasket fastenings.

DRIED MIXED HERB BOUQUETS   MAKES 24 BOUQUETS

For those of you with access to fresh bay trees, this is a satisfying and unusual way to have them on the spice shelf. A few strands of dried herbs are covered by a pliable bay leaf, tied up into a cigar shape with thin kitchen string, and left out to dry before storing in a covered jar. The herb "packing" outlined below is for mixed herbs, but there is no reason you couldn't play around with other herb arrangements to arrive at your own special "house" formula. Regardless of the filling, one important thing to remember is that the fresh bay leaves must be thoroughly dried before the bouquets are packaged, otherwise they will mildew (it's horrible) if the slightest bit of moisture exists. Home-dried herb sprigs (as detailed in Dried Herb Bundles) are a must here. Use the herb bouquets in soups, ragouts, tomato-based sauces, braised beef, pork, and poultry.

24 fresh, verdant bay leaves
96 short sprigs of dried thyme
48 short sprigs of dried rosemary
48 short sprigs of dried tarragon

48 short sprigs of dried chervil
24 6- to 8-inch lengths of kitchen
*   string, the kind that is slightly*
*   waxen*

Spread out the bay leaves, shiny side down, on a work surface. Group together 24 bundles of herbs, 4 thyme, 2 rosemary, 2 tarragon, 2 chervil each. Wrap a bay leaf around each cluster of herbs and tie it firmly with a piece of string. Wrap and tie the remaining 23 heaps of herbs in this way.

Lay out the bouquets on a large small-meshed cooling rack to dry for 4 to 5 days. Each day, turn over the bouquets to let the air reach all sides evenly.

When the bay leaves are absolutely brittle-dry, pack them loosely into very small apothecary jars with ground glass lids. Store the bouquets airtight.

DRIED HERB BUNDLES

If you are harvesting leafy herbs such as thyme, sage, or savory from your own garden, do so about the middle of the summer when they are bushy and strong. After the early morning dew has settled, on a relatively fair day, cut the herbs with about 5 inches of stem. It is wise to wait for a cutting day that is not sun-drenched as valuable essential oils present in the herbs are driven away by the intense heat of the sun. The bundles are lovely to attach to packages of prepared food or to use in preparation of soups, stews, and grilled meat or poultry.

Choose among these herbs to bundle:

thyme	*oregano*
rosemary	*and*
sage	*kitchen string*
marjoram	*paper bags, as needed*
summer or winter savory	*raffia*
wild fennel	

Bundle together about 15 sprays of lengthy herb sprigs. Collect them in your hand evenly at the stem end and let the leaves arrange themselves at odd points, free-form style, to be naturally decorative.

Tie together the bunches with kitchen string about 2 inches from the middle up the stem, upwards near the beginning of the leaves, leaving a length of string at the beginning. Knot close the stems, and make a hanging loop with the extra string available at both ends.

Slide each bunch of herbs on the hook of a hanger or set up a small line, and hang up the herbs in a dark, yet airy room. Since light robs the herbs of chlorophyll, it is essential to keep the herbs away from it, lest all the glorious flavor and aroma be lost.

You could settle each individual bouquet in a brown paper bag and gather the bag at the opening around the herb stems, tie it up, punch a few holes in the bag, and store it in this lint-free environment if a dark room is hard to come by. Do label the bags.

Herb bouquets generally take about 2 weeks to dry out, when a leaf will crumble readily between your fingertips. Big bouquets make glamorous add-ons to large packages. I love the smaller, daintier ones attached to jars of food that are put up. For presentation, wind a long piece of raffia around the string to beautify the bundle.

SAVORY PACKETS

MAKES 12

The mixed herb packets are great for plucking out of a jar mid-winter when fresh herbs are either too pricy or nowhere to be found. Good cooks traveling to weekend houses will find these and the spice packets handy to take along instead of toting, and keeping, endless bottles of spices whose contents may be of questionable intensity if left over a period of time.

12 3" x 3¾" muslin bags with drawstrings

FOR 12 MIXED HERB PACKETS:

12 dried bay leaves, 1 to a packet
12 3-inch branches of dried rosemary,
   1 to a packet

24 branches dried thyme, 2 to a packet
72 fresh black peppercorns, 6 to a
   packet

FOR 12 MIXED SPICE PACKETS:

48 whole allspice berries, 4 to a bag
24 pieces of dried lemon peel (see
   Dried Orange or Lemon Peels,
   p. 209), 2 to a packet
24 whole cloves, 2 to a packet
12 3-inch cinnamon sticks, broken in
   half, 2 halves to a packet

12 1-inch chunks dried Jamaican ginger, 1 to a packet
12 cardamom pods, 1 to a packet (optional)

The muslin bags are the packets you make warm and savory by filling them with the herb or spice mixtures. They look like large tea bags (and incidentally, you could make your own subtle tea blends and spoon into the bags); the strongest ones are made by Hoan Products and sold in self-seal pouches containing 10 bags.

Having counted out all of the herbs and/or spices, add the given quantities to each bag, and pull the drawstring closed. Tie the string into a bow, if you like, or make a knot close to the bag. That's all there is to it.

Pack the bags in small apothecary jars, stacking them, then put on the lid tightly.

I'm generous and most times give 12 bags to every recipient.

The Rum Pot

A porcelain canister or glazed earthenware pot, filled with fresh fruit (or sometimes dried fruit), layered with granulated sugar and bathed in rum—or occasionally, brandy—is a time-honored custom of putting by fruit. This method of preserving is German in origin, named *rumtopf* and translated as "rum pot." Seasonal fruit is steeped in sugar and brandy and left to mellow in a crock. Some recipes begin with a fruit-juice mixture (simmered crushed fruit and sugar, pureed and strained), but mine just start out with a plain layering of sugar and spirits.

As weeks and months go by, the fruits mature and develop a "crocked" taste. Flawless fresh fruit turns mellow and smooth, and the resulting saturation of liquid and fruit is altogether delightful with plain pound cake, over ice cream, on the sidelines of a scoop of plain mousse or ethereal soufflé. Some people like to eat the mixed fruit variety (see Summer and Autumn Rum Pot) in small bowls with a cascade of lightly whipped cream on top, but I find it too rich.

Some of the preserved fruit may be drained, cut up, and used in fruitcake batters, most notably the Apricots in Rum Pot, Currants or Yellow Raisins in Rum Pot, or Dates in Brandy Pot.

For a stunning gift, pack the finished rum pot compositions in plain jars that seal well. Suggest that the unopened containers be stored in the coolest section of the pantry and in the refrigerator once opened.

A special seasonal note on the rum pot: Summer's bountiful supply of fresh fruit signals that much of it is to be eaten on the spot while you make plans for the remainder to be preserved in many forms for good eating throughout the year. To achieve the perfect rum pot for fresh fruit, you'll need to begin with the first crop of really fresh fruit, which is strawberry season, around late May or early June. But the brandied dried fruit (apricots, currants or raisins, and dates) can be comfortably started late August.

SUMMER AND AUTUMN RUM POT   MAKES ABOUT 12 POUNDS

Here is a rum pot for two seasons, for the ambitious and the patient.

2 pounds fresh, ripe, blemish-free strawberries, hulled
2½ cups granulated sugar
8 cups dark rum plus extra rum, as needed throughout the steeping time

2 pounds fresh, ripe, firm cherries, stemmed
1¾ cups granulated sugar

2 pounds red plums, halved, pitted, and quartered
2 cups granulated sugar

2 pounds firm and ripe blueberries, picked over
1½ cups granulated sugar

1 pound gooseberries, picked over and stemmed
1½ cups granulated sugar

1 pound fresh pineapple chunks
1 cup granulated sugar

2 pounds seedless green grapes, plucked from the stems and halved
1¾ cups granulated sugar

Pour boiling water into a 12-quart glazed stoneware crock that has a lid; let stand for 5 minutes, then pour out the water. Pour boiling water over the lid. Dry the inside of the crock and lid.

74

Starting at the beginning of summer, with strawberries, place the berries in an even layer on the bottom of the crock and sprinkle with the sugar. Carefully pour on the rum. A 1¾-inch level of rum should always cover the fruit. Cover the crock with a double thickness of plastic wrap and let stand in a cool place.

As the sugar melts and the berries begin to pop to the surface, place a lightweight plate on top of the berries to keep them covered; this takes place after the first 12 hours.

After 2 days, gently draw a spatula through the berries, checking to see if all of the sugar has dissolved. Look at the level of rum and add more if the 1¾-inch mark has not been met. Reseal with plastic wrap. Let the fruit continue to stand in a cool place, covered.

When cherries are plentiful and ripe, carefully add a layer of them to the strawberries. Sprinkle on the sugar and check the rum level, adding additional rum to moisten, if necessary (it is likely that there will be enough rum at this point).

When each part of the summer and fall brings the lushest and ripest fruit, add it along with the sugar in the quantities given above. The liquid should always cover the fruit by at least 1 inch at the time when the third type of fruit (red plums) are added. Add more rum to keep the level. Make sure that the sides of the crock are kept clean and the top is covered with plastic wrap, then with the lid, after each fruit is added.

After the last fruit is added, it is traditional to pour on another 2 cups of rum, seal the stoneware vessel for the last time, cover, and let the rum pot mellow out completely until Christmastime. In any case, the rum pot should be left to stand at least 1 month before portioning out into containers as gifts or for use in your own kitchen.

NOTE: This recipe halves successfully; use a 6-quart stoneware vessel.

APRICOTS IN RUM POT   MAKES 4 POUNDS

Chop the apricots and add them to fruitcake batters, or fruit and nut tea breads. Include a half cupful of the diced halves as a special addition to steamed puddings.

2 cups granulated sugar   *about 6 cups dark rum, or enough to*
3 cups water   *cover the fruit*
4 pounds dried apricot halves

Place the sugar and water in a 6-cup saucepan (preferably of enameled cast iron), cover, and cook over a low heat to dissolve the sugar. When every last granule of sugar has dissolved, uncover the pot, bring the liquid to a boil; boil for 2 minutes.

Add the apricot halves and simmer them in the syrup for 2 minutes. Remove from the heat and let cool.

In the meantime, scald a 6-quart stoneware crock and its cover; dry thoroughly. Add the apricots, with all of the sugar syrup, to the crock. Pour on enough rum to cover by at least 1¾ inches. Stir gently. Wipe down the sides of the crock with a hot, damp towel to clean off any splashes of rum or sugar syrup, or both, and seal the crock with a double thickness of plastic wrap. Cover with the lid.

Store the crock in a cool, dry place for 3 to 4 weeks. Check the rum level once or twice, and pour in additional rum to keep the level of 1¾ inches above the fruit.

After about 4 weeks, parcel out the apricots and liquid into clean, dry jars. Cover and keep in a cool pantry or refrigerate.

CURRANTS OR YELLOW RAISINS IN RUM POT   MAKES 3 POUNDS

For enlivening Christmas cakes, all kinds of custard puddings, and nut and spice breads.

3 pounds currants or yellow raisins   *about 6 cups dark rum*

Scald a 4- to 6-quart stoneware or porcelain pot and its lid. Dry the pot with a lint-free towel.

Place the currants or raisins in the pot. Pour on the rum. Seal the pot with a double layer of plastic wrap, then put on the lid.

Store the pot in a cool place, preferably dark, for about 1 month. During the first 4 days, check the level of rum; it should stay 1½ inches above the currants or raisins. And more rum if necessary. Each time you add more rum, reseal the top with a fresh thickness of plastic wrap.

After 4 weeks, divide the rum-soaked currants or raisins among clean, dry jars and seal. Store the crocked fruit in a cool pantry or in the refrigerator.

DATES IN BRANDY POT   MAKES 3 POUNDS

Especially enticing in steamed puddings (chopped up), in date and nut bread (well drained and cut up), and heavenly in bread puddings.

3 pounds dates   *12 whole allspice berries*
2 cinnamon sticks   *about 6 cups dark rum*

Scald a 4- to 6-quart glazed stoneware crock or porcelain crock and its lid. Dry both the crock and lid with a clean tea towel.

Layer the dates with the cinnamon sticks and allspice in the clean crock. Pour on the dark rum; it must cover the fruit by 1¾ inches. Add extra rum if needed.

Cover the crock with a double thickness of plastic wrap, then with the lid to the crock. Hide the crock in a cool, dim place, and let the dates marinate in the rum for up to 1 month. Keep the level of rum at least 1 inch above the fruit after the first week of steeping.

After 4 weeks, divide the date-rum-spice mixture among clean, sterilized jars. Seal the jars. Store in a cool pantry or in the refrigerator.

FRUIT AND NUT RUM FANTASIA   VARIABLE YIELD

This is a medley of familiar things—raisins, dates, walnuts, prunes, currants—all layered up and soaked in light rum. A jar of Fantasia looks gorgeous and is great fun to make up: you simply layer each ingredient in a pattern in a clean, attractive jar and fill up the jar with rum. That's all there is to it. I have held jars of Fantasia for up to a year in the refrigerator and they keep getting better and better. Serve a bit of Fantasia over ice cream, with mousse or soufflé, or pound cake; use the nuts and fruit in puddings and cakes.

Choose 5 of the following fruits and nuts with rum.

perfect walnut halves	*whole dried apricots*
whole dates	*whole dried peaches*
light or dark seedless raisins	*perfect pecan halves*
dried currants	*whole dried mirabelles (plums)*
whole dried prunes	*light rum*

Alternate layers of fruit and nuts in a nice pattern, keeping the layers at about 1 inch thick. This means that you'll probably use a single layer of the thicker fruit, such as dates, prunes, or mirabelles.

Fill the jars with your favorite combination to ⅓ inch of the top. Carefully pour in enough rum to cover the top layer of fruit or nuts. Close the jar(s) tightly and refrigerate.

The Festival of Autumn

MULLED WINE SPICES

SPICE PACKETS

AUTUMN GARDEN ROUNDUP

EGGPLANT RELISH WITH PAPRIKA AND OREGANO
EGGPLANT, TOMATO, AND PEPPER RELISH
RED CABBAGE, APPLE, AND RAISIN SLAW

SPICY FRUITS IN SYRUP AND FRUIT SAUCES

KUMQUATS IN WHITE WINE SYRUP
SPICY PEARS WITH GINGER
SPICY LADY APPLES
PICKLED PRUNE PLUMS
PICKLED SECKEL PEARS
PEAR SAUCE

79

HARVESTTIME COOKIES

PECAN WAFERS
OATMEAL NUGGETS WITH CRANBERRIES
SHREDDED APPLE COOKIES
CRANBERRY-ORANGE DATE COOKIES

SOME GOODIES FROM THE AUTUMN BREADBASKET

CURRANT SCONES
CURRANT-SPICE SCONES
CRANBERRY MUFFINS
APRICOT-NUT MUFFINS
DATE-NUT MUFFINS
THREE-NUT MUFFINS
RAISIN MUFFINS
RAISIN-ORANGE LOAF
RAISIN-ORANGE NUT LOAF
PERSIMMON LOAF

COOL WEATHER FRUIT COMPOTES, PRESERVES, AND CHUTNEYS

CRANBERRY-MAPLE COMPOTE
DRIED APPLE AND CRANBERRY PRESERVE
HONEY-CRANBERRY PRESERVE
CRANBERRY-APPLE PRESERVE
OVEN-COOKED CRANBERRY-ORANGE CONSERVE
CRANBERRY-LEMON CONSERVE WITH ALMONDS
CRANBERRY AND PECAN CONSERVE
SPICY CRANBERRY CHUTNEY
CRANBERRY AND PEAR CHUTNEY
APPLE-CIDERED APPLE BUTTER
PEAR JAM WITH FOUR SPICES AND WALNUTS
LEMON-PEAR BUTTER
PEAR-CRANBERRY BUTTER
PUMPKIN BUTTER
ITALIAN BLUE PLUM CONSERVE
GREEN TOMATO CRISP

Early autumn is the time to celebrate the bounty of the harvest, the overabundance of the vegetable garden and orchard. It signals the arrival of cool weather along with the choicest crisp apples, buttery pears, and tangy cranberries. The pleasures of baking become appealing again. And, of course, this is the time to happily anticipate the holidays to come and to begin planning the gifts you'll want to make and give for both small and big occasions.

Like all enthusiastic cooks, I tend to treasure certain recipes and repeat them every season. I think of it as creating my own tradition. Since many of my favorites are new versions of time-honored recipes, I find that I really do maintain a tie to the past. Every fall when the leaves start changing, and the harvest moon appears, I like to stir up a batch of apple butter deepened with cider, and a lovely variation made with pumpkin. Often I drive out to the country to gather the apples or the pumpkins myself. Picking the raw material adds an extra dimension to the warming and restorative experience of making homemade gifts.

Fall is also the season of entertaining—of dinner parties and Sunday brunches, country weekends and casual suppers. To make your entertaining special or warm the heart of any host or hostess, why not give these gifts before the holidays arrive? They're really too good to wait for, and it's a nice idea to spread a cheery holiday mood to other times of the year.

PACKING YOUR GIFTS

For very special fall food gifts—especially for the baked goods in this section—market baskets, oval egg baskets, and pie baskets made of ash or oak are generous and beautiful-looking containers in which to hold these comestibles. Their capacious quality makes them perfect for filling with my Oatmeal Nuggets with Cranberries, Currant Scones, or any of the fruited and nutted muffins. (And when I'm not filling baskets with cookies or small loaves of bread, I like to heap fresh apples and pomegranates in them to add appeal to kitchen countertops, the dining room, or library.)

Wide pie baskets are just the right depth for holding muffins, loaves, delicate wafers (such as the Pecan Wafers), and assorted kinds of cookies. Pie baskets remain steady during transportation; and best of all, the usual long, carved handle attached to the basket is ample enough to hold a beautiful "garnish" of cinnamon sticks or home-made clove pomanders, or miniature cobs of Indian corn available during the middle of October.

The onset of fall is none too soon to order spices and herbs for baking and for making all sorts of trimmings—especially pomanders, those wonderful clove-studded oranges, lemons, or tiny kumquats (the method for making pomanders is given on p. 18 in chapter 2).

At least a month before Christmas, I gather together containers and begin making lists for the remaining baking and preserving projects I intend to carry forth over the next few weeks. So, count up jars of preserves and locate baskets and trays for presenting a bounty of gifts.

Autumn is the time when families and friends open up their homes to football-watching parties, or migrate into the country to admire the colors of the changing leaves. Among the gifts of preserves, savory relishes, and the variety of baked treats you'll find just the right present to bring to the friends that entertain you.

A *special cooking-ahead note:* Holiday fruitcakes benefit greatly from advance preparation and autumn is the best time to begin the marination of fruits and the baking of cakes so that they turn mellow and rich for Christmas gift-giving. Any of the fruitcakes in chapter 5, Glorious Christmas Gifts, may be baked and stored as early as September. Apple Mincemeat with Almonds and Dates (p. 164) and Pear Mincemeat (p. 165) greatly benefit from being made up well ahead of the holidays, too, for the best flavor.

Mulled Wine Spices

The spicy warmth of mulled wine makes it a great favorite at autumn gatherings. For a great gift, combine 6 packets of spices with a bottle of domestic burgundy or other robust red wine.

SPICE PACKETS   MAKES 6 PACKETS

Use 1 packet of spice for each bottle of wine. To achieve perfect results every time, heat (never boil) the wine in an enamelware saucepan, add ¼ cup sugar and the spices to the hot wine, turn off the stove, and let steep until ready to serve. These spices are also appropriate for making mulled cider, using 2 packets of spices for each gallon of cider. To add a festive touch to the cider, float 6 or so tiny lady apples studded with cloves on the warm mixture.

6 pieces of cheesecloth, or 6 small
    muslin bags with drawstring
    closures
12 4-inch cinnamon sticks

36 whole cloves
36 whole allspice berries
36 pieces of dried lemon peel (see
    p. 209)

Stuff each piece of cheesecloth or bag with 2 cinnamon sticks, broken in half, 6 cloves, 6 allspice berries, and 6 lemon peels. Tie up.

Pack the parcels in a fancy, decorative container, and label as to the use and contents.

NOTE: Generally, I make up about 2 dozen packets at one time; they are nice to have on hand during the winter months.

Autumn Garden Roundup

A graceful way to deal with the season's-end garden deluge of eggplant, tomatoes, and peppers is to turn the harvest into relish. Both Eggplant Relish with Paprika and Oregano, and Eggplant, Tomato, and Pepper Relish have forward, forthcoming flavors and make excellent companions to grilled beef, veal, or chicken, or a substantial warm-weather luncheon dish when good oil-packed tuna is flaked into either mixture. The red cabbage slaw is a glorious color and has a tart peppery taste. People love to get jars of it—often, so I frequently double up on the recipe.

As gifts, these relishes (and the slaw) look and taste country fresh; I always pack them up in simple, clear glass jars. I keep the filled jars in the refrigerator and aim to give the gifts within a few days of cooking them. They are delivered from my refrigerator to the recipient's refrigerator. I don't like to can these vegetable dishes because then the tastes that are so garden sweet tend to blur.

EGGPLANT RELISH WITH PAPRIKA AND OREGANO

MAKES ABOUT 5 CUPS

For this relish it is preferable to use small, firm eggplant. To me, smaller eggplant has a sweeter taste and more compact texture than big, fat eggplant. And the red peppers will back up that sweetness because they are roasted. Ideally, the peppers are best charred over the hot coals of the barbecue; but the fiery heat of a broiler is more than suitable.

*2 pounds eggplant, peeled and cut into
 2-inch cubes
coarse (kosher) salt
3 medium-size sweet cooking onions,
 coarsely chopped
⅓ cup olive oil
6 garlic cloves, chopped
6 red peppers, roasted, peeled, cored,
 seeded, and pulled into narrow
 strips (see Notes)*

*1 tablespoon sweet paprika
3 tablespoons finely chopped fresh
 oregano
3 tablespoons chopped fresh basil
2 teaspoons granulated sugar
juice of 1 lemon
salt and freshly ground black pepper,
 to taste*

Dump the eggplant cubes in a large colander, sprinkle the cubes with coarse salt, toss, and let them stand for about 40 minutes (the bitter juices should begin to drip out of the colander). Drain the eggplant on paper toweling.

In a large skillet, place the onions and olive oil, and cook over moderate heat for 5 minutes. Add the eggplant cubes and continue cooking for another 5 minutes. Add the garlic cloves and cover the skillet. Cook the vegetables over a low heat, stirring frequently, until the eggplant just begins to turn tender, about 15 minutes.

Uncover the pan, stir in the red peppers and paprika, and stir-cook for 1 minute. Add the oregano, basil, sugar, and lemon juice. Cook for 1 minute to dissolve the sugar.

84

Remove the pan from the heat and season lightly with salt and amply with freshly ground pepper; turn into a bowl.

Cool the relish to room temperature, parcel out into containers, cover, and refrigerate for up to 2 weeks.

NOTE: This recipe doubles easily.

To roast the peppers under a broiler, set them on a baking sheet placed about 3 inches from the heat source. As patches of the skin begin to darken and blister, carefully turn the pepper with a pair of tongs to expose another area to the heat. This should happen rather quickly so that the flesh of the peppers will not overcook. Without delay, wrap up the peppers in a large sheet of aluminum foil and set them aside to cool. Steamy moisture will condense between the skin and the flesh and will make them very easy to peel. After about 45 minutes, unwrap the foil package, peel, core, and deseed the peppers. Then tear them into narrow strips with your fingers.

EGGPLANT, TOMATO, AND PEPPER RELISH   MAKES ABOUT 9 CUPS

A delicious not-too-sharp baked relish whose ingredients point up and complement each other.

4 small eggplants, peeled and cut into 2-inch cubes
coarse (kosher) salt
3 onions, coarsely diced
9 ribs of celery heart, cut into 1-inch chunks
3 cups fresh tomato puree (made from peeled, seeded, and pureed red, ripe tomatoes) or an equal amount of pureed canned plum tomatoes
¼ cup sweet red vermouth

2 tablespoons capers, rinsed under cool water, drained and dried
3 tablespoons granulated sugar
½ cup olive oil
3 tablespoons tomato paste
3 tablespoons red wine vinegar
freshly ground black pepper, to taste
2 red peppers, cored, seeded, and cubed
2 green peppers, cored, seeded, and cubed
½ cup oil-cured black olives

Place the eggplant cubes in a large colander, sprinkle with coarse salt, and let them drain out any bitter juices for about 40 minutes, or longer, as necessary. Dry the cubes on several thicknesses of paper toweling.

In a large nonmetallic roasting pan, combine the eggplant, onions, celery, tomato puree, red vermouth, and capers; let stand for 10 minutes, then preheat the oven to 375° F.

In the meantime, combine the sugar, olive oil, tomato paste, and vinegar in a 1-quart saucepan. Bring to a boil; boil 1 minute.

Pour the hot mixture over the vegetables, then stir it in. Season with freshly ground black pepper.

Bake the vegetables, uncovered, on the middle-level rack of the oven for 55 minutes. Stir in the red peppers and green peppers, and continue baking for 20 minutes longer or until they are tender. Remove the pan from the oven and stir in the olives.

Let the vegetable mixture cool to room temperature, then portion out the relish into storage containers, cover, and refrigerate for up to 2 weeks.

RED CABBAGE, APPLE, AND RAISIN SLAW   MAKES ABOUT 6½ CUPS

This slaw is actually a tangy relish that goes beautifully with cold cuts, sausages, pork chops, or cold roasted pork.

8 cups shredded red cabbage
3 tablespoons coarse (kosher) salt
2 firm, crisp tart apples, peeled and
　　shredded
1 cup apple cider vinegar
½ cup red wine vinegar
¾ cup granulated sugar
¼ cup firmly packed light brown
　　sugar
¾ cup peanut oil

10 whole cloves, 10 whole allspice ber-
　　ries, 10 whole white peppercorns,
　　6 dime-size pieces of fresh ginger
　　¼ inch thick, all tied up in a
　　clean square of cheesecloth
⅔ cup golden raisins, plumped in boil-
　　ing water to cover for 10 minutes,
　　drained, and dried thoroughly on
　　paper toweling
salt and freshly ground pepper, to taste

Heap the cabbage in a stainless-steel colander and sprinkle with the coarse salt; toss well and let stand for 3 hours. Press out any excess moisture. Transfer the cabbage to a large nonmetallic bowl. Add the apples.

Combine the vinegars and sugars in a 1-quart saucepan. Cover and cook slowly over a low heat to dissolve the sugar. When the sugar has dissolved, bring the liquid to a boil, and boil for 5 minutes.

Turn off the heat, pour in the oil, and add the spice package and raisins. Let stand at room temperature until the cabbage has been in the colander for the 3-hour time period.

Combine the vinegar and oil dressing with the cabbage and apple mixture and toss well. Let the mixture marinate at room temperature for at least 4 hours. Mix everything around from time to time. Add salt and pepper, to taste.

Remove the cheesecloth bag, and portion the slaw into storage containers, cover, and refrigerate for up to 3 weeks.

Spicy Fruits in Syrup and Fruit Sauces

These are the fruits of autumn, done up piquant and sweet; in combination they are glorious in gift baskets. The Kumquats in White Wine Syrup are an unusual and bright-tasting delight that adds a rich note to duck, turkey, or stuffed fowl. The other preserved fruits serve as gracious notes to light luncheons or light suppers of cold meat or chicken. But they also go well with robust cheeses. Pear Sauce is a great favorite of mine and goes especially well with pound cake, vanilla mousse, or on a puffy German pancake for brunch. All of these look positively glowing in some of those imported canning jars without too much detailing, that have rubber gaskets and hinged lids; they are sleek in the traditional old-fashioned style.

KUMQUATS IN WHITE WINE SYRUP MAKES ABOUT 6 CUPS

The smallest member of the citrus family, kumquats, are unusual in having a sweet rind and tart flesh. If you've always thought of these fruits as decorative rather than edible, this glossy preserved version will introduce you to a delightful surprise. Eaten in their entirety, kumquats lend a special tangy highlight to duck dishes, and I love a bowlful of them on the Thanksgiving table. To make this recipe, I look for oval fruit about the size of a large green olive, because they are especially beautiful when packed in smooth glass jars.

2 pounds kumquats
3 cups dry white wine
3 cups granulated sugar

⅓ cup water
20 whole allspice berries

Lightly pierce the end of each kumquat 2 or 3 times with a thin pointed skewer or larding needle; this prevents the fruit from breaking open in the hot syrup. Once the fruit begins to cook, stay attentive, as kumquats simmered too long will collapse into a puckered state, marring their beauty.

In a straight-sided 10-inch sauté pan, place the kumquats and dry white wine;

bring to a simmer and simmer for 2 minutes. Scoop out the kumquats with a stainless-steel slotted spoon to a side bowl.

Add the sugar, water, and allspice berries. Cook over a low heat until the sugar melts down, then bring the liquid to a boil; boil 4 minutes.

Return the kumquats to the syrup, and simmer gently until they are just cooked and glazed over, about 4 to 5 minutes. While the kumquats are cooking, tip the pan from side to side—gently—to keep the kumquats moving in the syrup; do this about three or four times.

With a slotted spoon, remove the kumquats to a bowl. Boil the syrup for 2 minutes, then pour it over the fruit.

When the kumquats have cooled, transfer them, with all of the syrup, into a sturdy storage container. Cover and refrigerate for up to 6 weeks.

SPICY PEARS WITH GINGER   MAKES ABOUT 8 CUPS

The delicate and subtle pear is remarkably versatile done in this fashion, and the spicy syrup gives the fruit a marvelously seductive taste. These pears have a boldness to them that makes them a delicious complement to meats, cold cuts, and poultry. As gifts, show these off in smooth, rotund glass jars with tight-fitting lids. Decorate with a bit of fresh greenery at Christmas.

3 cups granulated sugar
2 cups apple cider vinegar
3 4-inch cinnamon sticks
8 ¼-inch-thick slices of fresh peeled
*   gingerroot*
10 whole allspice berries

6 whole cloves
¼ cup freshly squeezed lemon juice
1¼ cups water
¼ cup coarsely chopped drained ginger pieces preserved in syrup
8 ripe pears, peeled, halved, and cored

Place the first 7 ingredients in an 8-quart pot. Cover and cook slowly until the sugar dissolves completely. Uncover the pot, add the lemon juice and water, and bring to a boil. Boil the liquid for 4 minutes.

Add the ginger and pears to the pot and cook at a simmer for about 15 minutes, or until tender. Carefully remove the pears to a side bowl. Discard the ginger pieces and boil the liquid for 2 minutes. Pour the syrup over the pears and cool everything to room temperature.

When the pears have reached room temperature, pack them (with syrup) into jars, cover, and refrigerate for up to 6 weeks.

SPICY LADY APPLES

MAKES ABOUT 12 CUPS

Like Spicy Pears with Ginger, these apples have a remarkably lively flavor and delightful fragrance. Lady apples are all of 2 inches at their widest point; they appear in October and remain available throughout early December. The apples are temptingly sweet-tart, with a creamy yellow and patchy rose hue, and are prettiest with their stems attached. Serve this sweet-spicy condiment with pork, roast chicken, or game.

4 cups apple cider vinegar   *10 whole cloves*
4 cups granulated sugar   *6 whole allspice berries*
1 cup water   *6 ¼-inch-thick slices of fresh ginger*
3 4-inch cinnamon sticks   *3 pounds lady apples*

In a 12-quart nonmetallic kettle, place all the ingredients except the apples. Set the pot over a low heat, cover, and cook slowly to dissolve the sugar.

While the sugar is dissolving, prick each apple in 10 random places with the fine point of a skewer or larding needle.

Uncover the pot and bring the liquid to a boil; boil for 6 minutes. Add the apples to the pot and simmer them very slowly until they are just tender, but not collapsed. The apples should retain an edge of firmness if they are to stay whole. Carefully remove the apples to a side bowl with a large nonmetallic sievelike spoon.

Boil down the syrup for 3 to 4 minutes, or until it has condensed slightly. Pour the syrup over the apples and cool to room temperature.

Transfer the apples to clean jars or storage containers, cover, and refrigerate for up to 2 months.

PICKLED PRUNE PLUMS

MAKES 2 POUNDS

Plums turn tender and glossy in this syrup, a true show-off recipe that is as easy to prepare as it is enjoyable to eat. Arrange to give a host or hostess a jar of plums if you know cold buffets and barbecues are a household tradition, or game dinners abound. It is helpful to remember that even-size, firm blue plums behave the best in this recipe. Soft fruit will burst and hopelessly collapse in the hot liquid and only be fit for pureeing at that point.

2 cups water

1 cup apple cider vinegar

1½ cups granulated sugar

2 3-inch cinnamon sticks

1 teaspoon whole allspice berries

1 teaspoon whole cloves

2 pounds Italian blue plums

In a 6-quart casserole, preferably enameled cast iron, place all the ingredients except the plums. Cover the pot, place it over a low heat, and cook the mixture until the sugar dissolves. Uncover the pot, raise the heat to high, and boil the liquid for 4 minutes.

Add the plums to the casserole, adjust the heat so that the syrup simmers slowly, and cook the plums for about 7 minutes. Remove the plums to a bowl with a slotted spoon.

Reduce the syrup to a medium-heavy thickness by boiling for about 4 minutes. Cool the syrup 10 minutes. Pick out the spices and add them to the plums, then strain the cooled syrup over the fruit.

Refrigerate the plums in the syrup, in a covered container, once they have cooled down to room temperature. The plums may be stored in the refrigerator for up to 2 months: if made in October, they will keep until Christmas, *just*.

PICKLED SECKEL PEARS

MAKES 18 PEARS

These stylish little pears look adorable *in* canning jars, and *out*, piled in an antique celadon green bowl. For something special, I dice up some pears and add the cubes to a smoked duck (or turkey) salad, and fold lengths through the more usual chicken salad. If I am a guest at someone's house for Sunday supper, I always take along a jar—the bouncy flavor of the pears is very much appreciated. Note that the peel of seckel pears needs to be taken off carefully so that the fruit will not be misshapen, a job that takes a little patience and a steady hand.

2 cups apple cider vinegar

2 cups granulated sugar

1 cup water

4 4-inch cinnamon sticks

5 thin dime-size slices of fresh ginger,
    smashed with the flat side of a
    cleaver

6 whole cloves

6 whole allspice berries

18 firm but ripe seckel pears

2 tablespoons granular Fresh Fruit
    Preserver

Place the first 7 ingredients in an 8-quart nonmetallic casserole (preferably enameled cast iron). Cover the casserole, set it over a moderately low heat, and cook the mixture until the sugar dissolves completely.

Meanwhile, turn your attention to the pears. Set out a big bowl of water. Peel the pears with a swivel-bladed peeler, leaving the stems intact. Drop the pears into the water as they are peeled. Swirl in the granular fruit preserver.

When the sugar has dissolved completely, uncover the pot, and bring the syrup to a boil. Boil 1 minute. Drain the pears, add them to the syrup, and simmer them until just tender, about 15 minutes. Baste the pears with the syrup from time to time.

Carefully remove the pears from the syrup with 2 slotted spoons to a deep bowl. Boil the syrup for 4 minutes, then strain it over the fruit. Replace the cinnamon sticks, cloves, and allspice berries to the fruit and syrup.

Cool the pears to room temperature, remove the spices, then cover and refrigerate. Refrigerator storage time is 1 month.

PEAR SAUCE

MAKES ABOUT 5 CUPS

A fruit sauce is pure joy to have on hand, so I put by sauces at intervals during each season and use the bounty year-round. Pear Sauce is unusual and delectably rich. Slow cooking melds together the flavors of the spices with the flesh of the pears and intensifies the flavor all the way. This remarkable sauce is delicious with pound cake and ambrosial with a nut-ladden butter cake. Or try it with warm pudding or cold mousse.

*5 pounds ripe and juicy pears, peeled,
  cored, cut into rough chunks, and
  tossed in the juice of 3 large
  lemons
1½ cups water*

*1⅓ cups granulated sugar blended
  with 1 teaspoon ground cinnamon
  and ¼ teaspoon ground allspice
¼ cup apricot liqueur*

Place the pears and water in a large 10-quart nonmetallic kettle. Cover the pot and bring the pears to a simmer. Simmer the pears until they are falling-apart tender, about 30 minutes.

Puree the pears with the liquid in several batches in the bowl of a food processor fitted with a steel blade, or in a blender.

Return the pear puree to the rinsed out pot. Add the sugar and spice blend, cover, and cook over a low heat until the sugar has dissolved. While the sugar is dissolving, in a saucepan bring the apricot liqueur to a boil; set aside.

Uncover the pot, pour in the apricot liqueur, and bring everything to a simmer, stirring all the while. Simmer the sauce until it takes on body and is no longer thin and watery, about 10 to 15 minutes.

Pour the sauce into a sturdy container, cool, cover, and refrigerate for up to 2 months.

Alternately, ladle the sauce into 2 or 3 hot pint jars to ¼ inch of the top; seal with lids and bands. Process the jars in a boiling-water bath (see pp. 8–11) for 15 minutes; cool.

Harvesttime Cookies

Now is the time to invite friends over for a ride into the country and a walk in the woods, then back to the house for mulled wine or cider and something sweet; it's an ideal combination for warming and fortifying guests. You'll also find this combination a welcome standby during the month of December when people are inclined to drop by at odd times. These cookies repeat the scene of the autumn harvest in the list of ingredients—pecans, cranberries, and apples. The selections here are enticing, easy recipes to know for the times when you'd like to bake up something for friends without making an all-day project of it.

PECAN WAFERS

MAKES ABOUT 4 DOZEN

Heaps of whole pecans available at the market in the fall will alert you to the fact that it's time to make these delectable wafers, which seem to taste best when made from freshly cracked pecans. These wafers are sweet, thin, and crisp-chewy.

½ cup unsalted sweet butter
2 cups firmly packed light brown sugar
⅔ cups all-purpose flour (preferably unbleached)
¼ teaspoon salt

2 large eggs, at room temperature
12 ounces (¾ pound) pecans, chopped, plus 1 cup finely chopped pecans
2 teaspoons pure vanilla extract

In a 1-quart saucepan, melt the butter with the brown sugar over a low heat; set aside to cool.

Stir together the flour and salt in a large mixing bowl. Preheat the oven to 350° F.

Beat the eggs into the cooled butter and sugar mixture. Stir in 12 ounces pecans. Make a well in the middle of the flour mixture, pour in the butter-sugar-egg blend, and stir to combine everything. Beat in the vanilla extract.

Line cookie sheets with a length of parchment paper. Drop level tablespoons of batter onto the sheet, about 3 inches apart; each sheet should have only 9 mounds of batter on it. Sprinkle the top of each mound with some chopped pecans and bake the wafers, a sheet at a time, on the middle-level rack of the oven for about 12 minutes, or until set and evenly browned.

Let the wafers cool in the pan for 5 to 6 minutes, then remove them with a wide metal spatula to a cooling rack. When the wafers have cooled, store them in a cookie tin.

OATMEAL NUGGETS WITH CRANBERRIES   MAKES ABOUT 4 DOZEN

These are soft, cakelike cookies that are soothing and restorative, not fussy at all. I pile them up in a basket made out of woven grapevines—the presentation conveys an image of warmth and abundance.

1¾ cups all-purpose flour (preferably
    unbleached)
2 teaspoons baking soda
½ teaspoon salt
1 teaspoon ground cinnamon
½ teaspoon freshly ground nutmeg
1 cup solid shortening
1½ cups firmly packed light brown
    sugar

2 large eggs, at room temperature
½ cup sour cream blended with 2 tea-
    spoons pure vanilla extract, at
    room temperature
2 cups fresh cranberries, picked over
    and coarsely chopped
3¼ cups quick-cooking oatmeal

Sift together the first 5 ingredients onto a sheet of waxed paper; set aside. Preheat over to 375° F.

In the large bowl of an electric mixer, cream the shortening until light on moderately high speed, about 3 minutes. Beat in the brown sugar in two additions, beating for 2 minutes after each portion is added. On moderate speed, beat in the eggs, one at a time, beating for 1 minute after each egg is added. Scrape down the sides of the bowl to keep the mixture even.

On low speed, add half of the flour mixture, and beat it in just until the flour particles have been absorbed. Blend in all of the sour cream–vanilla mixture, then the remaining flour mixture. By hand, stir in the cranberries and oatmeal.

Drop the dough by rounded tablespoons 2 inches apart onto parchment paper–lined cookie sheets (12 mounds of dough to a sheet). Bake the cookies, a sheet at a time, on the middle-level rack of the oven for about 12 minutes, or until they are lightly browned and firm to the touch.

With a sturdy metal spatula remove the cookies to a cooling rack. When the cookies are cooled, store them in an airtight tin.

SHREDDED APPLE COOKIES   MAKES ABOUT 6 DOZEN

Flakes of shredded apple make this cookie tender and moist; grate the peeled apples on the largest holes of a hand-held stainless-steel box grater. Old-fashioned, spicy, and cakelike, these cookies look best filled high in a simple, finely woven basket.

5½ cups all-purpose flour (preferably unbleached)
2 teaspoons baking soda
½ teaspoon salt
2 teaspoons ground cinnamon
½ teaspoon ground allspice
½ teaspoon freshly ground nutmeg
¼ teaspoon ground cloves
1 cup solid shortening

2⅔ cups firmly packed light brown sugar
2 extra-large eggs, at room temperature
½ cup light cream
2 cups (lightly packed measurement) shredded apples, such as Stayman or Jonathan
2 cups coarsely chopped pecans
1 cup golden raisins

Sift together the first 7 ingredients onto a sheet of waxed paper; set aside. Preheat oven to 375° F.

In a large bowl of an electric mixer, cream the shortening until light on moderately high speed, about 3 minutes. Beat in the brown sugar in two additions. Beat in the eggs, one at a time, beating for 1 or 2 minutes after each one is added. Scrape down the sides of the bowl, beat for a minute longer.

On low speed, add half of the sifted mixture and beat just until the particles of flour have been absorbed. Pour in all of the cream and beat it in. Add the remaining sifted mixture and beat it in. By hand, stir in the apples, pecans, and raisins.

Drop the dough by rounded tablespoons onto parchment paper–lined cookie sheets, 12 to a sheet, or about 2½ inches apart. Bake the cookies on the middle-level rack of the oven for about 10 minutes, or until lightly browned and firm to the touch.

Remove the cookies to cooling racks with a wide metal spatula. When the cookies have reached room temperature, store them in a tin.

CRANBERRY-ORANGE DATE COOKIES

These tender-soft cookies feature tart little bits of cranberry in a dough further sharpened by orange juice and rind.

3 cups all-purpose flour (preferably
    unbleached)
¾ teaspoon baking powder
½ teaspoon baking soda
¼ teaspoon salt
1 teaspoon ground cinnamon
½ cup unsalted sweet butter, softened
    at room temperature
1 cup granulated sugar
¾ cup firmly packed light brown
    sugar

1 jumbo egg, at room temperature
2 teaspoons pure vanilla extract
2 tablespoons light cream, at room
    temperature
¼ cup strained, freshly squeezed
    orange juice
1 tablespoon finely grated orange rind
2¾ cups picked over and finely
    chopped fresh cranberries
½ cup finely chopped pitted dates

Sift the first 5 ingredients onto a sheet of waxed paper; set aside. Preheat oven to 375° F.

In the large bowl of an electric mixer, cream the shortening on moderately high speed until light, about 3 minutes. Beat in the granulated sugar; beat for 2 minutes. Then beat in the light brown sugar, scrape down the sides of the bowl, and beat again for a few seconds longer. Beat in the egg, vanilla extract, and cream.

On low speed, beat in half of the sifted dry ingredients. Blend in the orange juice and orange rind, then the remaining sifted mixture, beating just until the flour particles have been absorbed. By hand, stir in the cranberries and dates.

Drop rounded tablespoons of dough onto parchment paper–lined cookie sheets about 2½ inches apart. Bake the cookies on the middle-level rack of the oven one sheet at a time for 10 to 12 minutes, or until lightly browned and firm to the touch.

Let the cookies stand on the sheet for 1 to 2 minutes, then remove them to cooling racks with a wide spatula. When the cookies are thoroughly cooled, store them in airtight tins.

Some Goodies
from the Autumn Breadbasket

These are warm and satisfying quick breads that can be made up instantly as long as a few staples are on hand in the kitchen and some usual baker's ingredients kept at the ready in the pantry (currants, apricots, pecans, walnuts). The fall tradition of fresh cranberries is apparent in the muffins, but the muffins can indeed be baked up at any time of the year as long as you have frozen a few bags of the berries during peak season; or just choose any one of the delectable variations on the Cranberry Muffins recipe.

The wonderful fragrance that pervades the house when you have baked these breads is one reward for your efforts, the other is that friends love to get a batch of these muffins or a loaf of one of the breads for warming up in the morning or for serving at an afternoon coffee, tea, or hot chocolate break.

CURRANT SCONES
MAKES 20 TO 24 SCONES

These scones are flaky, tender, and buttery-rich. Pile them in a calico cloth–lined basket and treat your best friends to a gift of freshly baked teatime or breakfast bread.

3 cups unsifted all-purpose flour (preferably unbleached)
1 tablespoon plus 1½ teaspoons baking powder
3 tablespoons granulated sugar

½ teaspoon salt
8 tablespoons unsalted sweet butter
3 large eggs blended with ¾ cup light cream
⅓ cup dried but moist currants

Into a large mixing bowl, sift together the flour, baking powder, sugar, and salt. Drop in the butter by tablespoonful, and with a round-bladed palette knife cut the butter into the flour until very small bits are formed. The small pea-size dabs of butter should still be quite cool, so don't overwork the dough lest the butter warm up.

Remove ¼ cup egg-cream mixture into a small bowl for glazing the scones later on, set aside. Preheat oven to 450° F.

Make a well in the center of the sifted ingredients and pour in the remaining egg-cream mixture. Add the currants. With a wooden spoon, quickly combine the liquid and dry ingredients into a dough with as few strokes as possible.

Turn out the dough onto a lightly floured board and with a lightly floured wooden rolling pin, gently roll out the dough to a thickness of ¾ inch. Cut out circles of dough with a 2½- to 3-inch biscuit cutter and place the pieces of dough 2 to 3 inches apart on parchment paper–lined baking sheets.

Brush the top of each scone with a thin wash of the remaining egg-cream mixture. Bake the scones, one sheet at a time, on the middle-level rack of the oven for 12 to 15 minutes, or until the tops are golden and the scones are well risen.

Transfer the scones with a wide metal spatula to a cooling rack. When they are room temperature, store them airtight.

Ideally, scones should be made and given as a gift within 2 days of baking. Be sure that the recipient knows to warm the scones before serving (advise of this on the identification tag attached to the gift).

VARIATION: To make Currant-Spice Scones, add 1 teaspoon ground cinnamon, ½ teaspoon ground allspice, ¼ teaspoon ground ginger, and ¼ teaspoon ground nutmeg to be sifted along with the flour, leavening, and salt.

CRANBERRY MUFFINS

MAKES 1½ DOZEN MUFFINS

These round-topped, moist, and tender muffins are so good when warmed up on a blustery fall morning. They are spiced three ways—by cinnamon, allspice, and cloves—and enriched with cream and butter so that what emerges is a very cakelike bread. For a delightful present give a basket of muffins accompanied by a special preserve for a great no-cook breakfast.

1¾ cups all-purpose flour (preferably
unbleached)
½ teaspoon ground cinnamon
¼ teaspoon ground allspice
¼ teaspoon ground cloves
2 teaspoons baking powder
½ teaspoon salt
⅓ cup plus 1 tablespoon granulated
sugar
2 large eggs, at room temperature

½ cup milk, at room temperature
¼ cup light cream, at room tempera-
ture
4 tablespoons melted unsalted sweet
butter, cooled to tepid
2 teaspoons pure vanilla extract
2 teaspoons freshly grated orange rind
1 cup coarsely chopped fresh cranber-
ries

TOPPING:

¼ cup granulated sugar blended with
½ teaspoon ground cinnamon

(continued)

Lightly butter and flour 16 muffin cups measuring 3 inches in diameter; set aside. Preheat oven to 400° F.

Sift the first 7 ingredients into a large mixing bowl. In a smaller mixing bowl, beat the eggs with the milk and light cream; blend in the butter and vanilla extract and stir in the orange rind.

Make a well in the center of the dry ingredients and pour in all of the egg-cream mixture. Add the cranberries. Using a wooden spoon or spatula, combine the liquid and dry ingredients with a few swift strokes, leaving some small lumps.

Spoon the dough into the prepared cups, filling each two-thirds full. Sprinkle the tops of the muffins with a little of the cinnamon-sugar topping.

Bake the muffins on the middle-level rack of the oven for about 20 minutes, or until well risen and a toothpick inserted into the center emerges clean and dry.

Cool the muffins in the cups on a rack for 2 to 3 minutes, then remove them from the cups to a rack to cool completely.

Store the muffins airtight before bundling them up into a gift.

VARIATIONS: *Apricot-Nut Muffins*—Substitute ¾ cup coarsely chopped apricots and ⅓ cup chopped walnuts for the cranberries; mix and bake as directed.

Date-Nut Muffins: Substitute ½ cup coarsely chopped dates and ½ cup coarsely chopped walnuts for the cranberries; mix and bake as directed.

Three-Nut Muffins: Substitute ⅓ cup chopped walnuts, ⅓ cup chopped pecans, and ⅓ cup chopped Brazil nuts for the cranberries; mix and bake as directed.

Raisin Muffins: Substitute ½ cup coarsely chopped dark seedless raisins and ½ cup coarsely chopped golden raisins for the cranberries; mix and bake as directed.

RAISIN-ORANGE LOAF

MAKES ONE 10-INCH LOAF

Quick nut and fruit breads, such as this loaf and the variation that follows, are light and cakelike and wonderful to serve at breakfast, or for a mid-morning or afternoon snack. The texture of this loaf is not too dense—it tastes good with virtually any kind of jam or preserve, especially one that is citrus based.

3 cups sifted all-purpose flour (prefera-
bly unbleached)
½ teaspoon ground cinnamon
¼ teaspoon ground nutmeg
1 tablespoon baking powder
½ teaspoon salt
¾ cup granulated sugar

¾ cup coarsely chopped golden raisins
1 large egg, at room temperature
1½ cups milk, at room temperature
4 tablespoons melted unsalted sweet
butter, cooled to tepid
3 tablespoons finely grated fresh
orange rind

Lightly butter and flour the inside of a 10-inch loaf pan; set aside. Preheat oven to 350° F.

Into a large bowl, sift together the first 6 ingredients; set aside. Place the raisins in a small bowl and toss them with 1½ teaspoons of the sifted mixture.

In another bowl, whisk together the remaining ingredients. Make a well in the center of the sifted ingredients and pour in the egg-milk mixture. Sprinkle with the chopped raisins. Combine all of the ingredients together with a wooden spoon until just blended.

Pour and scrape the batter into the prepared pan and bake the loaf on the middle-level rack of the oven for 50 to 55 minutes, or until a toothpick inserted in the center of the bread emerges clean and dry.

Cool the bread in the pan for 5 minutes, then invert it onto a rack and cool right side up. When room temperature, store the loaf airtight.

VARIATION: To make Raisin-Orange Nut Loaf, combine ¼ cup chopped walnuts and ¼ cup chopped pecans with the raisins. Flour the nuts and raisins with 2 teaspoons sifted flour mixture before combining into the bread batter.

PERSIMMON LOAF   MAKES 1 LOAF

This is an unusually delightful loaf that keeps well.

2½ cups all-purpose flour (preferably
unbleached)
2½ teaspoons baking powder
¼ teaspoon salt
1 teaspoon ground cinnamon
1 cup fresh persimmon puree (see
Note)

1 cup granulated sugar
2 extra-large eggs, lightly beaten, at
room temperature
½ cup vegetable oil
1½ teaspoons pure vanilla extract
½ cup chopped pecans

Lightly butter and flour a 9" x 5" x 3" loaf pan; set aside. Preheat oven to 325° F.

Sift together the flour, baking powder, salt, and cinnamon onto a sheet of waxed paper; set aside.

In the large bowl of an electric mixer, beat together the persimmon puree, sugar, and eggs on moderate speed until well combined, about 4 minutes. Blend in the vegetable oil and vanilla extract; scrape down the sides of the bowl and beat for a few seconds longer.

On low speed, beat in the sifted mixture in two additions, beating just until the flour particles have been absorbed. By hand, stir in the chopped pecans.

99

Turn the batter into the prepared loaf pan. Bake the loaf on the lower-level rack of the oven for about 1 hour, or until a toothpick inserted into the bread emerges clean and dry.

Cool the loaf in the pan on a rack for 10 minutes, then invert it onto another rack, turn it right side up, and cool completely. Store the loaf airtight.

NOTE: To arrive at a cup of persimmon puree, let 2 large persimmons stand at room temperature until thoroughly soft—an index finger pressed into the fruit should not be met with any resistance. Remove the skin with a sharp paring knife, scraping down and off the sweet flesh. Whiz the globs of fruit in a food processor (fitted with a steel blade) or in a blender, or mash it by hand.

Cool Weather Fruit Compotes, Preserves, and Chutneys

Here is a rich variety of fragrant fruit preparations. Most of them can either be stored in the refrigerator or preserved for longer keeping. Either way, they provide down-home pleasure and plain good eating.

The outpouring of cranberry recipes in this section is a celebration of the American cranberry, *Vacinnium macrocarpon*. The berries are highly acidic, which makes them good keepers both in and out of preserved preparations. (They also freeze well and you can stash several bags of them in the freezer where they will keep for up to one year.) Originally, the American Indians boiled up the berries, sweetened them with honey, and ate them with meat.

Going well beyond the Indian's simple sauce, however, here are nine delectable ways to prepare this extra-tart fruit. If I had to choose my favorite, I think it would be the Cranberry and Pecan Conserve. But Cranberry-Apple Preserve is delicious when whisked into the pan juices of cooked pork chops for a quick and novel sauce. Honey-Cranberry Preserve is sensational on thick brioche French toast on Sunday morning. And all cranberries are wonderfully compatible with rich meat, not to mention capon or Cornish hen (I stuff the hens with brown rice, onions, fresh herbs, and a few dabs of Spicy Cranberry Chutney).

In the autumn, especially, preserving provides a warm and lively social backdrop for a congregation of friends, so you could make an afternoon of putting up several batches of something made from cranberries, with friends helping. Not only are these cranberry preparations easy, they hold exceedingly well in the refrigerator for up to two months. Or you can preserve them to produce an array of gleaming jars of ruby-red preserves, conserves, and chutneys for gift-giving year-round.

For instructions on preserving using the boiling-water bath method, see chapter 1, pp. 8–11. This method is suggested in most of the recipes in this section.

CRANBERRY-MAPLE COMPOTE   MAKES ABOUT 6 CUPS

"Fancy grade" maple syrup gives this spicy condiment a rich purity of flavor. Use this quick-to-make blend with chicken, turkey, or pork.

3 cups granulated sugar
4 cups water
2 4-inch cinnamon sticks
9 whole allspice berries, tied up in a
    square of clean cheesecloth
1 plump vanilla bean, split down the
    center to expose the tiny seeds,
    but left whole

¼ cup freshly squeezed lemon juice
½ cup maple syrup
8 cups (2 pounds) fresh cranberries,
    picked over
1 cup dark seedless raisins

In a heavy 8-quart casserole, preferably enameled cast iron, place the first 6 ingredients. Cover the pot and cook the mixture over a low heat to dissolve the sugar. Uncover the pot, bring the liquid to a boil, and boil for 4 minutes.

Add the maple syrup and cranberries; bring to a boil. Reduce the heat so that the mixture simmers, and simmer until the cranberries pop.

Add the raisins and continue to cook until cooked down enough to hold its shape *lightly* when spooned onto a plate, about 15 minutes.

Pour the compote into a sturdy storage container, cool, cover, and refrigerate. The compote stays fresh in the refrigerator for up to 2 months.

Alternately, ladle the boiling-hot compote into 3 or 4 pint jars to ¼ inch of the top; seal with lids and bands. Process jars in a boiling-water bath for 10 minutes; cool.

DRIED APPLE AND CRANBERRY PRESERVE   MAKES ABOUT 7 CUPS

The concentrated taste of dried apple is luscious, soft, and sweet, a perfect contrast to the sharp tang of cranberries. This preserve is delicious with French toast, muffins, and coffee cake.

4 cups (1 pound) dried apple slices
3 cups unsweetened apple juice or
    apple cider
1 cup granulated sugar blended with 1
    teaspoon ground cinnamon, 1 tea-
    spoon ground ginger, and ½ tea-
    spoon ground allspice

½ cup firmly packed light brown
    sugar
4 cups (1 pound) fresh cranberries,
    picked over

Place the apple slices in a heavy 8-quart casserole. Pour on the apple juice or apple cider; bring the liquid to a simmer over a moderate heat. Cover the pot and let the apples simmer in the liquid for 10 minutes. Remove the apples with a slotted spoon to a cutting board, chop them coarsely, and set aside.

Add both sugars to the apple liquid, cover the pot, and cook over a low heat until the sugar dissolves completely. Uncover the pot and boil the syrup for 1 minute.

Put the cranberries and chopped apple into the syrup and bring everything to a boil. Boil the preserve slowly for 10 minutes, or until lightly thickened.

Pour the preserve into a sturdy storage container, cool, seal, cover, and refrigerate for up to 2 months.

Alternately, ladle the boiling-hot preserve into 3 or 4 hot pint jars to ¼ inch of the top; seal with lids and bands. Process the jars in a boiling-water bath for 15 minutes; cool.

HONEY-CRANBERRY PRESERVE

MAKES ABOUT 8 CUPS

Chunks of fresh orange and strained orange juice, along with the brisk tartness of the cranberries provide a tasty balance against the flavor of the honey. The chopped walnuts give the preserve a textural contrast that makes it ideal to serve with nut breads or big, hearty country breads, or as a side dish at the traditional Thanksgiving dinner.

2 cups granulated sugar
1 cup honey
2 cups water
1½ cups strained, freshly squeezed
    orange juice
8 cups (2 pounds) fresh cranberries,
    picked over

⅓ cup diced orange flesh
2 teaspoons ground ginger
½ teaspoon ground allspice
½ teaspoon ground cloves
2 cups coarsely chopped walnuts

In an 8- to 10-quart casserole, preferably of enameled cast iron, or in a large preserving kettle, place the sugar, honey, water, and orange juice. Cover the pot and cook the mixture over a low heat to dissolve the sugar. Uncover the pot, raise the heat to moderately high, and bring the liquid to a boil; boil for 5 minutes.

Add the cranberries, orange flesh, ginger, allspice, and cloves to the pot. Bring the contents of the pot to a boil; boil slowly for 10 to 11 minutes, or until it is beginning to thicken. Add the walnuts and continue cooking for about 4 minutes longer, or until thick enough to hold its shape in a rough mass in the bowl of a spoon.

Pour the hot preserve into a large storage container, cool, cover, and refrigerate. The preserve will keep in the refrigerator for up to 2 months.

Alternately, ladle the boiling-hot preserve into 4 hot pint jars to ¼ inch of the top; seal with lids and bands. Process jars in a boiling-water bath for 15 minutes; cool.

CRANBERRY-APPLE PRESERVE   MAKES ABOUT 6½ CUPS

Equal measures of crisp apple chunks and cranberries and a rich blend of spices combine to form a sultry and satisfying preserve. Use as a spread for toast and English muffins, on warm slices of tea bread, or as a glaze for whole roasted fowl or pork.

4 cups (1 pound) fresh cranberries, picked over

1 pound Golden Delicious apples, peeled, cored, and cut into ½-inch chunks, and tossed in the juice of 1 lemon

2 cups granulated sugar blended with 1 teaspoon ground cinnamon, ¼ teaspoon ground allspice, ¼ teaspoon ground ginger, and ¼ teaspoon ground cloves

2 cups unsweetened apple juice

In an 8-quart kettle or casserole, stir together the cranberries, apples, and sugar-spice blend. Pour in the apple juice.

Cover the pot and cook the mixture over a low heat to melt down the sugar completely. When the granules of sugar have dissolved, uncover the pot and bring the mixture to a boil; boil slowly until thick, for about 15 minutes.

Pour the preserve into a storage container, cover, and refrigerate when cool; the preserve may be stored in the refrigerator for up to 2 months.

Alternately, ladle the boiling-hot preserve into 3 hot pint jars to ¼ inch of the top; seal with lids and bands. Process jars in a boiling-water bath for 15 minutes, then cool.

OVEN-COOKED CRANBERRY-ORANGE CONSERVE MAKES ABOUT 4 CUPS

This conserve is just delicious on warm breads or as a spread for French toast.

4 cups (1 pound) fresh cranberries,
  picked over
1⅓ cups chopped fresh orange flesh
  (about 5 large oranges)
2 cups granulated sugar

2 cups water
1 teaspoon ground cinnamon
½ teaspoon ground allspice
½ cup dark seedless raisins

Gently combine all of the ingredients except the raisins in a 9″ x 14″ baking dish, preferably of porcelain (enameled cast iron may be substituted). If you are using a glass dish, decrease the oven temperature by 25°.

Place the baking dish on the middle-level rack of a *cold* oven. Turn the oven to 325° F. Bake the mixture for about 1 hour, stirring every 15 minutes, when it will begin to thicken. Add the raisins and continue baking for 30 to 40 minutes longer, or until a spoonful holds its shape on a cold plate.

Pour the conserve into a storage container, cover, and refrigerate until cool; the conserve stores in the refrigerator for up to 2 months.

Alternately, ladle the boiling-hot conserve into 2 hot pint jars to ¼ inch of the top and seal with lids and bands. Process the jars in a boiling-water bath for 15 minutes; cool.

NOTE: If you are a lover of spices, add ¼ teaspoon each of ground ginger, cloves, and nutmeg along with the cinnamon and allspice.

CRANBERRY-LEMON CONSERVE WITH ALMONDS MAKES ABOUT 6 CUPS

Almonds that are exceptionally fine and crisp add a crunch against the smoothness of the cooked-down fruit. This conserve is delicious with chicken or duck, as a sort of sweet-savory relish, and is uncommonly good on warm brioche, flaky buttermilk biscuits, currant scones, or warm slices of nut bread.

2¾ cups granulated sugar
2 cups water
⅓ cup chopped lemon flesh (about 1
  very large lemon)
1 teaspoon ground cinnamon
½ teaspoon ground ginger

¼ teaspoon ground cloves
6 cups (about 1½ pounds) fresh cranberries, picked over
¾ cup chopped blanched almonds
  (see Note)

Place the sugar, water, and lemon flesh in a 6-quart casserole or kettle. Cover and cook slowly over a low heat until the sugar has dissolved completely. Uncover the pot, add the spices, and bring the liquid to a boil, stirring. Boil the liquid for 3 minutes.

Add the cranberries, bring to a boil. When the cranberries begin to pop, add the almonds. Boil the cranberry mixture slowly, until it is thick enough to hold its shape in a spoon, about 12 minutes, stirring occasionally.

Pour the conserve into a sturdy storage container, cool, cover, and refrigerate for up to 2 months.

Alternately, ladle the boiling-hot conserve into 3 hot pint jars to ¼ inch of the top; seal with hot lids and bands. Process the jars in a boiling-water bath for 15 minutes; cool.

NOTE: To blanch almonds, bring a large pot of water to a boil (in this case, I fill a 3-quart saucepan two-thirds full of water), drop in the nuts, and turn off the heat. After 4 minutes, drain the almonds in a metal colander or sieve (metal keeps the heat in until all of the almonds are skinned), then, one by one, slip off the skins by pinching them off between your thumb and index finger. To get the nuts extra dry, place them on a shiny cookie sheet, and set them in a low (200° F.) oven to absorb the excess moisture. This will take about 15 minutes. Cool the nuts before chopping them into coarse pieces with a large chef's knife.

CRANBERRY AND PECAN CONSERVE   MAKES ABOUT 8 CUPS

I make this conserve often, mostly in mid-winter, from frozen cranberries (you don't need to defrost them before using). Glowing red in color and glistening with raisins and pecans, Cranberry and Pecan Conserve adds color and rich flavor to poultry, game, and pork, and is a delicious spread for breakfast breads.

3 cups granulated sugar
3 cups water
8 cups (2 pounds) fresh cranberries, picked over
1 cup dark seedless raisins

1½ cups chopped pecans
¼ cup fresh lime juice
2 teaspoons ground cinnamon
1½ teaspoons ground ginger

Place the sugar and water in a 10-quart casserole or kettle, preferably of enameled cast iron. Cover and cook the sugar-water over a low heat to dissolve the sugar completely. Uncover the pot, bring the liquid to a boil, and boil for 3 minutes.

Add the cranberries to the boiling liquid and boil until the cranberries pop. Stir in the remaining ingredients. Bring to a boil again, then reduce the heat so that the mixture boils gently. Continue cooking for about 15 minutes, or until the conserve thickens, stirring frequently.

Pour the conserve into a large storage container, cool, cover, and refrigerate for up to 2 months.

Alternately, pour the boiling-hot conserve into 4 pint jars to ¼ inch of the top and seal with lids and bands. Process pint jars in a boiling-water bath for 15 minutes; cool.

SPICY CRANBERRY CHUTNEY   MAKES ABOUT 8 CUPS

This chutney and the following one each have a distinct identity, but their medium-sharp flavor makes them ideal accompaniments to the same kind of food: country ham, roast chicken, barbecued meat, and as a sandwich spread.

*3 cups granulated sugar blended with
    2 teaspoons ground cinnamon, ¾
    teaspoon ground allspice, ½ tea-
    spoon ground ginger, ¼ teaspoon
    ground nutmeg, ¼ teaspoon
    ground cloves, ¼ teaspoon
    cayenne pepper (or more to
    taste), 1 teaspoon yellow mustard
    seed, and 2 teaspoons coarse
    (kosher) salt*

*4 cups water
¼ cup apple cider vinegar
2 cups finely chopped English walnuts
8 cups (2 pounds) fresh cranberries,
    picked over*

In a 10-quart kettle, place the sugar and spice blend, water, and vinegar. Cover the kettle and cook the mixture over a low heat until the sugar dissolves. Uncover the pot, bring the liquid to a boil, and boil for 3 minutes.

Add the walnuts and cranberries to the pot and continue boiling the mixture until the cranberries pop, stirring frequently.

Continue to cook the chutney, but reduce the heat so that it boils slowly; cook for 15 minutes longer, or until thick.

Pour the chutney into a large storage container, cover, and refrigerate for up to 2 months.

Alternately, ladle the chutney into 4 hot pint jars to ¼ inch of the top; seal with lids and bands. Process the jars in a boiling-water bath for 10 minutes; cool.

CRANBERRY AND PEAR CHUTNEY

MAKES ABOUT 8 CUPS

Three ripe pears get simmered in a vinegar, sugar, and water syrup before the cranberries and spices are added—this mellows the pears and intensifies the flavor of the chutney. This chutney is not too heavily spiced, a perfect companion to turkey, duck, pork, and chicken.

2 cups firmly packed light brown sugar
2 cups water
¼ cup apple cider vinegar
3 ripe pears, peeled, cored, and cut into 2-inch chunks
4 cups (2 pounds) fresh cranberries, picked over

1 teaspoon ground cinnamon
½ teaspoon ground allspice
½ teaspoon ground ginger
½ teaspoon yellow mustard seed

In an 8-quart casserole or kettle, heat the sugar, water, and vinegar over a low heat, covered, until the sugar melts down. Uncover the pot, add the pears, and bring to a simmer. Cover and simmer the pears until they are almost tender, about 5 minutes (if the pears are really ripe).

Uncover the pot, bring the pears and syrup to a boil. Add the remaining ingredients. Bring the contents of the pot to a boil, stirring all the time. Boil slowly until the mixture turns thick, about 15 minutes.

Pour the chutney into a sturdy storage container, cover, and refrigerate for up to 2 months.

Alternately, ladle the boiling-hot chutney into 4 hot pint jars to ¼ inch of the top; seal with lids and bands. Process jars in a boiling-water bath for 10 minutes; cool.

APPLE-CIDERED APPLE BUTTER

MAKES ABOUT 4 CUPS

The trinity of spices found in many apple recipes—cinnamon, allspice, and nutmeg—appear in small quantities here; they do not impose themselves on the royal taste of the apples. Apple butter is a wonderful condiment for breakfast breads, and is an equally good companion to holiday fowl.

3¼ pounds tart apples, stemmed, cored, and cut into rough, unpeeled chunks
6 cups apple cider

2 cups granulated sugar blended with 1 teaspoon ground cinnamon, ½ teaspoon ground allspice, and ½ teaspoon ground nutmeg

(continued)

Place the apple chunks in an 8-quart casserole, preferably made of enameled cast iron. Pour in the apple cider. Bring the cider to a boil, then regulate the heat so that the apples simmer in the cider. Cover the pot and simmer the apples until they are tender, about 20 minutes.

When the apples are very soft, puree the apples and liquid through a food mill with the medium-hole disk in place. Return the pureed apples to the rinsed out pot. Stir in the granulated sugar blend.

Cook the apple-sugar mixture slowly, uncovered, until the sugar dissolves completely, stirring the mixture often. When the sugar has dissolved, turn up the heat, and boil the mixture slowly until of medium thickness; the butter will hold its shape lightly in a spoon. This will take about 30 minutes, stirring the pot from time to time.

Ladle the hot butter into 2 pint jars to ¼ inch of the top; seal with hot lids and bands. Process the jars in a boiling-water bath for 15 minutes; cool.

Alternately, pour the butter into a large storage container, cool, cover, and refrigerate for up to 3 months.

PEAR JAM WITH FOUR SPICES AND WALNUTS   MAKES ABOUT 8 CUPS

The creamy texture of Comice pears, agreeably sweet and fragrant, boils up into a magnificent tender jam. For a special dessert, spread the jam on the bottom of a tart shell that will hold a layer of pastry cream and poached pear slices. Or simply lavish the jam on pear halves that are to be baked. The jam is also marvelous on warm breads.

2 tablespoons granular Fresh Fruit Preserver blended with 2 cups water
8 pounds ripe pears, peeled, cored, and roughly chopped
finely grated rind and juice of 2 large lemons

3 cups granulated sugar blended with 2 teaspoons ground cinnamon, ½ teaspoon ground nutmeg, ½ teaspoon ground ginger, and ½ teaspoon ground cloves
1 cup chopped English walnuts

Place the water and pears in a heavy 10-quart kettle. Bring the contents of the pot to a simmer, covered, then continue simmering until the pears are barely tender, about 10 minutes.

Uncover the pot and add the lemon rind, lemon juice, and granulated sugar-spice blend; stir. Cook the mixture slowly to dissolve the sugar, then once the sugar has dissolved, bring the contents of the pot to a rapid boil. Boil steadily until just beginning to thicken, 20 to 25 minutes.

Add the chopped walnuts and continue boiling for an additional 5 minutes, or until dense enough to hold its shape in a spoon. The mixture will fall from the spoon in sheets, not tiny droplets, when it reaches the proper thickness. This jam must be stirred often as it cooks.

Pour the jam into 4 boiling-hot pint jars to ¼ inch of the top; seal with hot lids and bands. Process the jam in a boiling-water bath for 15 minutes; cool. Jars of jam treated with the boiling-water bath process may be stored for up to 1½ years.

Alternately, pour the jam into a sturdy storage container, cool, cover, and refrigerate for up to 3 months.

LEMON-PEAR BUTTER   · MAKES ABOUT 4 CUPS

Of all the jams and butters I give as gifts, my friends most frequently ask for this one. The pears accept the small amount of spices and lemon (in rind and juice) nicely, and I like to keep the butter free from texture, gossamer and smooth.

4 pounds juicy, ripe pears (preferably Bartlett or Comice), peeled, cored, and cut into rough chunks
2 cups water
¼ cup freshly squeezed lemon juice and grated rind of 2 small lemons

3 cups granulated sugar blended with 1 teaspoon ground cinnamon and ½ teaspoon ground ginger

In an 8- to 10-quart casserole, preferably of enameled cast iron, place the pears, water, and lemon juice. Cover and bring to a simmer. Simmer the pears until they are completely yielding and mushy-tender, about 25 minutes.

Puree the pears with the liquid (in several batches) in the bowl of a food processor fitted with a steel blade, or pass the liquid and pears through a food mill fitted with the smallest hole disk.

Return the puree to the rinsed out pot. Add the sugar and spice blend, and the lemon juice. Cook the mixture over a low heat, uncovered, to dissolve the sugar. Stir frequently. When the sugar has dissolved, bring the contents of the pot to a boil. Boil slowly, stirring often, until the butter has thickened, about 20 minutes.

Ladle the hot butter into 2 hot pint jars to ¼ inch of the top; seal with hot lids and bands. Process the jars in a boiling-water bath for 15 minutes; cool.

Alternately, pour the butter into a sturdy storage container, cool, cover, and refrigerate for up to 3 months.

NOTE: The addition of about ½ cup lightly toasted chopped pecans can be a welcome variation. Add the pecans during the last 5 minutes while the butter is boiling and thickening up.

PEAR-CRANBERRY BUTTER   MAKES ABOUT 5 CUPS

Churning up fleshy pears with a small amount of cranberries produces a festive looking and tasting butter. The pears should be just past the point where slices or chunks could not be handled in a fruit salad or compote—that is, extremely aromatic and bursting with juice. Slatherings of this butter make breakfast and teatime breads memorable.

*4½ pounds ripe pears, peeled, cored,
    and cut into rough chunks*
*½ pound (about 1 cup) cranberries,
    picked over*
*2 tablespoons freshly squeezed lemon
    juice*

3 cups water
*3 cups granulated sugar blended with
    1½ teaspoons ground cinnamon,
    ¾ teaspoon ground allspice, and
    ¼ teaspoon freshly ground nut-
    meg*

Place the pears, cranberries, lemon juice, and water in an 8- to 10-quart casserole or kettle. Cover the pot and bring the water to a simmer over a moderate heat. Simmer the pears and cranberries until they are very tender, about 20 minutes.

Pass the pears and cranberries, with the liquid, through a food mill fitted with the small hole disk.

Rinse out the pot, pour in the fruit puree, and granulated sugar-spice blend. Cook the mixture over a low heat to dissolve the sugar, then bring to a boil. Boil slowly, stirring often, until thick, for about 35 minutes.

Ladle the hot butter into 2 or 3 hot pint jars to ¼ inch of the top; seal with lids and bands. Process the jars in a boiling-water bath for 15 minutes; cool.

Alternately, pour the butter into a sturdy storage container, cool, cover, and refrigerate for up to 3 months.

PUMPKIN BUTTER   MAKES ABOUT 8 CUPS

When the frost is on the pumpkin, or thereabouts, it's time to make up this unusual butter—a 2-day effort but well worth it. This is somewhat of a late October tradition in my house and the production of the butter seems to coincide with getting in the mood for planning out holiday presents. My friends who like to cook a lot of country food love to serve this butter with their main course, especially when game is on the menu, or fried chicken and buttermilk biscuits are featured.

1 5½-pound fresh pumpkin	*2 cups granulated sugar*
1 tablespoon ground cinnamon	*finely grated rind and juice of 5*
2 teaspoons ground allspice	*lemons*
1 teaspoon freshly ground nutmeg	*finely grated rind and juice of 2*
⅛ teaspoon freshly ground white	*oranges*
pepper	*2¼ cups water*
4 cups firmly packed light brown sugar	

Cut the pumpkin into quarters, remove the peel with a sharp knife, and scrape away all of the inner stringy fibers and seeds. Cut each quarter into small chunks and pass the chunks through the finest blade of a meat grinder. The meat grinder is my first choice for reducing the pumpkin into a texture that can best absorb the sugar and spices for marination. If you do not have a meat grinder, a food processor works, too: shred the pumpkin chunks as thin as possible using the shredding disk.

Place the pumpkin in a large mixing bowl, preferably glazed pottery, and stir in the spices. Let stand for 10 minutes, then stir in the citrus rinds and juices. Stir well again. Let the pumpkin mixture stand in a cool place (but not in the refrigerator), uncovered, for 24 hours.

The next day, transfer the pumpkin mixture into a preserving kettle, or large enameled cast-iron pot of 10- to 12-quart capacity. Pour on the water. Add the light brown sugar and granulated sugar. Bring the mixture to a boil slowly over moderately high heat. Cover and boil slowly for 1¼ to 1½ hours, or until the pumpkin is quite soft.

Puree the contents of the kettle, along with a little liquid each time, in a food mill fitted with the fine disk; or spin the mixture, a batch at a time, into a puree using a food processor fitted with a steel blade.

Rinse out the pot and return the puree to it. Boil the puree gently, uncovered, until satiny, about 25 minutes. You need to watch the butter carefully on this final cooking, lest it boil down too much and turn pasty. The butter should be velvety and barely keep its shape in the curve of the spoon when a mound is lifted up from the pot. The butter thickens somewhat on cooling.

Ladle the pumpkin butter into 4 hot pint jars to ¼ inch of the top; seal with hot lids and bands. Process the jars in a boiling-water bath for 15 minutes. Cool.

Alternately, pour the butter into a large storage container, cool, cover, and refrigerate. The butter stores well in the refrigerator for up to 4 months.

ITALIAN BLUE PLUM CONSERVE

MAKES ABOUT 6 CUPS

Turning blue prune plums into conserve is one of the best ways I know to keep the memory of this wonderful fruit for savoring throughout the year. The clingstone plums are treated to a simmering in water with finely chopped orange peel before being boiled to a thickness with sugar, raisins, and pecans. This special recipe comes from Paula Downey (friend of Alice Romejko of the Toasted Texas Pecans and "Z" Relish fame)—a cook with an amazing canning repertoire.

3 pounds Italian prune plums, halved, pitted, and coarsely chopped	*3 cups water*
	4½ cups granulated sugar
1½ medium-size oranges, seeded and finely chopped (including the peel)	*¾ cup dark seedless raisins*
	6 tablespoons chopped pecans

Place the chopped plums, oranges, and water in a 12-quart kettle. Bring to a boil. Partially cover the pot and simmer the fruit until it is tender, about 20 minutes.

Stir in the sugar, raisins, and pecans, and cook slowly until the sugar completely melts down. Bring the mixture to a boil, then boil slowly until thickened, for about 20 minutes.

Ladle the conserve into 3 boiling-hot jars to ¼ inch of the top; seal with hot lids and bands. Process the conserve in a boiling-water bath for 15 minutes. Cool.

Alternately, pour the conserve into a sturdy container, cool, cover, and refrigerate for up to 3 months.

NOTE: For a variation I'll sometimes add a teaspoon of ground cinnamon to a batch of conserve—cinnamon seems to bring out the goodness in plums.

GREEN TOMATO CRISP

MAKES ABOUT 12 CUPS

Although this is a 2½ day project, the recipe is very simple and the results are extraordinary. It will send any sweet pickle lover into ecstasy. The recipe comes from Virginia caterer Liz Taylor (her delightful Pickled Okra recipe appears on p. 43), who once dropped off a lug of green tomatoes along with this recipe and a jar of already made up crisp. Now, I wouldn't let autumn pass without making up at least two batches of the pickle. I seek out firm green tomatoes at farm markets and food cooperatives from mid-September to early October.

7 *pounds solid green tomatoes*
3 *cups pickling lime*
2 *gallons cold water*
6 *cups apple cider vinegar*
5 *pounds granulated sugar*
1 *teaspoon whole cloves*

1 *teaspoon ground mace*
1 *teaspoon ground cinnamon*
1 *teaspoon ground allspice*
1 *teaspoon ground ginger*
1 *teaspoon celery seed*

Slice the green tomatoes ¼ inch thick. In a very large bowl (I use a very wide bowl—16½ inches in diameter—and it works perfectly for this recipe), dissolve the lime in the cold water. Part of the lime will fall to the bottom of the bowl and refuse to dissolve—not a large amount—but that is fine. Dump the tomatoes into the pickling lime solution, making sure that all the slices are immersed. Let the tomatoes stand at room temperature overnight, at least 24 hours.

The next day, drain the slices from the lime solution. Wash out the bowl and fill with fresh cold water. Add the tomato slices. Let the tomato slices stand in the water for 1 hour, then rinse them off and change the water again. Do this three more times, changing the water after each hour is up. After the fourth soaking, drain the slices thoroughly.

Place the remaining ingredients in a nonmetallic 12-quart kettle. Cover the pot and let the sugar melt down completely. When the sugar has dissolved, bring the liquid to a boil.

Remove from the heat and add the sliced tomatoes to the syrup. Let the tomatoes stand in the syrup overnight at room temperature.

The next day, bring the contents of the kettle to a boil over a moderately high heat. Boil the tomatoes in the syrup for 1 hour, or until they turn clear and the syrup has thickened.

Immediately pack the pickles, layering them in 6 hot sterilized pint jars to ½ inch of the top, and pour in enough syrup to cover (to ¼ inch of the top). Seal immediately with hot lids and bands. Cool the jars and store. (Keep the jars in a cool, dark place.)

NOTE: A solution of pickling lime and water is responsible for the firm, brittle-crunchy quality of the pickle (I use Mrs. Wage's Pickling Lime which is available from Dacus, Inc., Tupelo, Mississippi 33901). The lime stiffens the flesh of the tomato, making the slices very hard before they are simmered in a spicy vinegar and sugar syrup.

5

Glorious
Christmas Gifts

THE CHRISTMAS COOKIE TIN

Chocolate Delights

WICKED CHOCOLATE DROPS
CHOCOLATE SQUARES
CHOCOLATE-WALNUT SHORTBREAD
CINNAMON-CHOCOLATE CRISPS
CHOCOLATE-COCONUT MOUNDS
BITTERSWEET CHOCOLATE-CHIP ROUNDS
CHOCOLATE-WALNUT BREAK-UP

Old and New Favorites

VANILLA SHORTBREAD
VANILLA POPPY-SEED SHORTBREAD
BROWN SUGAR–WALNUT SHORTBREAD
BROWN SUGAR–ALMOND SHORTBREAD
LEMON SHORTBREAD
GINGERBREAD PEOPLE
WALNUT CRESCENTS
ALMOND CRESCENTS
COCONUT JUMBLES

SPICE AND FRUIT DROPS

LEMON DELIGHTS

HOLIDAY TEA CAKES

WALNUT POUND CAKE

SOUR CREAM CAKE

SPICE CAKE

PECAN-CURRANT CAKE

CARROT-FLECKED BANANA LOAF

BANANA LOAF WITH APRICOTS

ORANGE BREAD

FRUITCAKES FOR EVERYONE

RICH GINGER CAKE

MY MOTHER'S DARK LUXURY FRUITCAKE

STUFFED APRICOT, FIG, AND PECAN FRUITCAKE

JEWELED CARROT AND FRUIT CAKE

GINGER, APRICOT, AND PECAN FRUITCAKE

PEACH, CURRANT, DATE, AND NUT FRUITCAKE

GRANDMA'S WHITE COCONUT FRUITCAKE

DATE, RAISIN, AND WALNUT CAKE

RAISIN AND ORANGE FRUITCAKE WITH SPICES

A MOSTLY NUT FRUITCAKE

DATE, RAISIN, NUT, AND LEMON FRUITCAKE

FRUITS IN WINE

FIGS WITH RED WINE AND HONEY

GINGER-STUFFED PRUNES SIMMERED IN RED WINE

WHOLE CHESTNUTS IN RUM-SPICE SYRUP

WHOLE CHESTNUTS IN MAPLE LIQUEUR SYRUP

ONE GLORIOUS PUDDING

APRICOT HOLIDAY PUDDING

MINCEMEAT AND NESSELRODE

APPLE MINCEMEAT WITH ALMONDS AND DATES

PEAR MINCEMEAT

FRUIT AND NUT MINCEMEAT

ORANGE MINCEMEAT

NESSELRODE

HARD SAUCES AND SWEET SPREADS

SPICED HARD SAUCE

VANILLA HARD SAUCE WITH APPLE BRANDY

LEMON CREAM

LIME CREAM

SWEETMEATS

CANDIED GRAPEFRUIT PEEL

CANDIED ORANGE PEEL

GRAPEFRUIT SYRUP

PECAN PRALINES

CINNAMONED AND SUGARED PECANS

I get charged up during the month before Christmas and fired with plans for all sorts of kitchen activities. But visions of holiday gift-giving are with me throughout the busy days of fall when I put up batches of conserves, jellies, and butters from late autumn fruits. And baking fever hits me around the end of October when the preserving is just about done. If I'm scrupulous, I have to admit that thoughts of steamed puddings and fruitcakes tug at me during the last sunny days of August.

Prior to this writing, I've never openly admitted thinking about the winter holidays much before the middle of November. I have childhood memories of the comfortable and oftentimes poetic scents of cookies baking and the gentle hum of the electric mixer buzzing along. My mother always made her darkly rich fruitcake (see the recipe for My Mother's Dark Luxury Fruitcake) and everything was right and peaceful.

Since I begin Christmas in the summer when I preserve the fruit and vegetables serially, I'm freed up during the early winter months to do all the baking that is possible with one set of hands. Since I can most food gifts, I now allow cakes and cookies to take over completely.

Mistletoe and pine rope among antique containers, spanking new glass jars, and bottles of rum, cognac, and bourbon—these are the essentials for someone like me, who revels in gathering together everything that is the essence of Christmas. The holidays have then been in my consciousness for a few months already and I know exactly how all the cooking and entertaining will flow.

Preparing for Christmas is also a sensual thing for cooks, because the house takes on the festive scents of baking and cooking. It's nice to begin with the making of fruitcakes and puddings, put up a batch of Nesselrode, and brandy some fruit in anticipation of the forthcoming season, then begin to stir up dozens of cookies as the holiday approaches. Fistfuls of cookies always seem to capture the true character of Christmas, and for me, the baking of them is a cherished sentimental part of my own childhood. The Christmas Cookie Tin offers a collection of cookies which are more or less standard in my home, but you can also look to Old-Fashioned Cookies in chapter 7, Spring Delights, for other ideas, too.

The butter cakes and tea loaves in Wintertime Treats (chapter 6); the pound cakes in Summer Feasting and Harvesting (chapter 3); and the Chocolate-Chestnut Spread with Rum, Twice-Cooked Crispy Walnuts, and Toasted Texas Pecans in chapter 7 would also be excellent choices for Christmas gift-giving.

A special note on preparing fruitcakes and Christmas pudding: If you are of the planning sort, you'll be thinking about fruitcakes well before Christmas. Some cooks I know begin as long as a year in advance, boosting batches of fruit and nuts with a brandy bath, and baking several cakes that will linger on the cool pantry shelf for many months. I have made fruitcakes as late as the beginning of December for the immediate holiday, or a full year in advance (when in the dead of winter I get the urge to candy citrus peel, and use that in fruitcake batter along with the requisite nuts, raisins, and such ingredients).

Most of the recipes in this section benefit greatly from at least a three-week aging period and are even better when held longer and given several moistenings of some liqueur or brandy. For the latter, you must send your psyche into motion before Thanksgiving if you are to enjoy the pleasure of fruitcakes during December. Though fruitcakes are not traditionally thought of as gifts of the harvest, I like to keep their spirit by having them in this Christmas section, even though I advise making them well before winter sets in.

The Christmas Cookie Tin

Inspired by accounts of festive holiday preparations in both real life and story, I enjoy getting a bit excessive in my Christmas cooking, baking, and gift-giving. The seven recipes for chocolate delights are real favorites, and are always first on my list of baked presents. Early in December I begin a relaxed but purposeful gathering of all kinds of chocolate—Dutch-process cocoa, bittersweet bar chocolate, and unsweetened squares of chocolate—to use with abandon in these cookie recipes.

It's been my experience that the chocolate lovers of the world are happiest when they have their favorite flavor in as many different forms as possible. My gift to them (and to myself since I love chocolate too) is a half dozen truly exceptional chocolate cookies—ranging from fudgy to crisp and back to chewy.

As for the Old and New Favorites in this chapter—they are simple and simply delicious. Some are rolled, some are dropped, and some are molded—all are perfect for filling red and green tins. I always make these eight kinds of cookies in double or triple batches to have for my own sweet tooth, and for eager cookie-loving friends who can't wait until Christmas. For holiday baking, you may also want to draw on cookie recipes in other sections of the book. For instance, I suggest some of these from chapter 7: the Traditional (More or Less) Sugar Cookies, Meltingly Rich Sugar Cookies, Sour Cream Sugar Cookies, and Crispy Gingersnaps.

Chocolate Delights

WICKED CHOCOLATE DROPS   MAKES ABOUT 6 DOZEN

These drop cookies are like rich, chunky chocolate candy. They'll melt in your mouth.

5 ounces unsweetened chocolate, cut
    into small pieces
11 ounces bittersweet bar chocolate,
    chopped coarsely, plus 1 pound
    bittersweet bar chocolate, cut into
    1/3-inch pieces with a sharp knife
5 tablespoons unsalted sweet butter, at
    room temperature
1/2 cup all-purpose flour (preferably
    unbleached)

1/2 teaspoon baking soda
1/4 teaspoon salt
4 extra-large eggs, at room temperature
1 1/3 cups granulated sugar
2 teaspoons pure vanilla extract
4 cups English walnuts, coarsely
    chopped into 1/3-inch pieces

Place the unsweetened chocolate, 11 ounces bittersweet chocolate, and table-spoonfuls of butter into the top of a double boiler. Place it over the larger saucepan filled with gently simmering water and let the chocolate and butter melt slowly. Stir from time to time. Remove the chocolate mixture from the heat and let cool to tepid.

In the meantime, sift the flour with the baking soda and salt onto a sheet of waxed paper; set aside. Preheat oven to 350° F.

In the large bowl of an electric mixer, beat the eggs with the sugar and vanilla extract until thick on moderately high speed, about 3 to 5 minutes.

On low speed, blend in the chocolate mixture, scraping down the sides of the bowl to keep the mixture even. Add the sifted dry ingredients and beat slowly until the flour particles have been absorbed. By hand, stir in the 1 pound bittersweet chocolate and the walnuts.

Drop rounded tablespoons of the dough 2½ inches apart onto parchment paper–lined cookie sheets. Bake the cookies, a sheet at a time, on the middle-level rack of the oven for 10 to 13 minutes, or until they are just firm to the touch; the insides will remain quite moist.

Let the cookies remain in the pan for 2 minutes, then remove them with a wide metal spatula to cooling racks. Cool completely and store the cookies airtight.

CHOCOLATE SQUARES
MAKES 16 SQUARES

Fudgy and ornamented inside and out with chopped English walnuts, these are glorious brownielike confections. Individually wrap each square in clear plastic film and store them in an airtight container. (If you make these squares in the summertime, it is a good idea to refrigerate them.)

¼ pound (4 ounces) bittersweet bar chocolate, cut up into rough chunks
1 cup unsalted sweet butter, cut into 2-tablespoon pieces
1½ cups all-purpose flour (preferably unbleached)

¼ teaspoon salt
2 cups granulated sugar
4 extra-large eggs, at room temperature
2 teaspoons pure vanilla extract
1½ cups chopped English walnuts

Lightly butter a 9-inch-square cake pan. Line the bottom of the pan with parchment paper. Butter the paper and dust out the inside of the pan with flour; set aside.

Place the chocolate and butter in the top of a double boiler. Place the top saucepan over the bottom, which has been filled with simmering water. Let the chocolate and butter melt slowly, stirring occasionally. Remove the mixture from the heat and cool to tepid.

Sift together the flour and salt onto a sheet of waxed paper; set aside. Preheat oven to 375° F.

In the large bowl of an electric mixer, beat together the sugar and eggs on high speed for 1 minute. Add the vanilla extract and beat for 30 seconds.

Pour in the cooled chocolate and butter mixture, and beat for 1 minute longer or until it is incorporated, scraping down the sides of the bowl frequently to encourage a quick mix. On low speed, add all of the sifted flour mixture and beat just until the flour particles have been absorbed. By hand, stir in 1 cup walnuts.

Pour the batter into the prepared pan and sprinkle the remaining ½ cup walnuts on top. Bake the squares on the lower-level rack of the oven for 45 to 50 minutes, or until a toothpick inserted into the cake emerges with only a few wet particles clinging to it.

Cool the cake in the pan on a rack for 1 hour, then invert onto another rack, and invert again to cool right side up. Put the cake on a waxed paper–lined tray and refrigerate it for about 5 hours, or until very firm.

With a long sharp knife, cut off the 4 outer edges from the cake. Cut the cake into quarters and cut each quarter into 4 even-size squares. Wrap the squares individually in pieces of plastic wrap, then store them in an airtight container.

CHOCOLATE-WALNUT SHORTBREAD MAKES ABOUT 5 DOZEN

This is a beautiful crisp shortbread made with pure unsweetened cocoa powder. Overlap rounds of shortbread in flower-decorated tins, or pile them in a stenciled box or combine with other chocolate treats on a serving platter. This shortbread looks pretty stamped out with a plain round cutter but cookie cutters in the shape of a star, bell, or doggie bone are fun to use with shortbread dough, and the whimsical shapes delight children.

4 cups all-purpose flour (preferably unbleached)
1 cup Dutch-process cocoa
½ teaspoon baking soda
½ teaspoon salt

2 cups unsalted sweet butter, softened at room temperature
2 cups sifted confectioners' sugar
1 tablespoon pure vanilla extract
¾ cup finely chopped walnuts

Sift together the flour, cocoa, baking soda, and salt onto a sheet of waxed paper; set aside.

In the large bowl of an electric mixer, cream the butter until light on moderately high speed, about 3 to 4 minutes. On low speed, blend in the confectioners' sugar in two additions, scraping down the sides of the bowl often. Blend in the vanilla extract. Still on low speed, beat in the sifted flour mixture in three additions, beating just until the flour particles have been absorbed before adding the next batch. By hand, stir in the chopped walnuts.

Divide the dough in half. Roll out each portion of dough between sheets of waxed paper to a thickness of ½ inch. Refrigerate the waxed paper–wrapped slabs of dough on a tray for about 5 hours, or until very firm. (The dough may be rolled and stored for up to 2 days in the refrigerator. To do so, wrap the firmed-up dough again in sheets of aluminum foil.)

To bake the shortbread, preheat the oven to 325° F. Stamp out rounds of dough with a plain 3-inch round cookie cutter and place the cookies 2 inches apart on parchment paper–lined cookie sheets. Prick the middle of the cookies 3 times with the tines of a fork, to make the traditional shortbread pattern:

• • • •

• • • •

• • • •

Reroll the scraps of dough and stamp out more cookies. Chill the cookies on the sheets for 10 minutes.

Bake the shortbread, a sheet at a time, on the middle-level rack of the oven for about 15 minutes, or until firm to the touch. With a wide metal spatula remove the cookies to a rack. When cooled, store airtight.

CINNAMON-CHOCOLATE CRISPS   MAKES ABOUT 6 DOZEN

These are crunchy chocolate-chocolate-chip cookies with a subtle, almost sexy overtone of cinnamon. Generally speaking, I like chocolate cookies to have the "straight" intense flavor of chocolate, and find the introduction of spices into the dough an intrusion. But this cookie is an exception. The cinnamon makes the cookies a pleasant partner to a spice-scented mug of cocoa or coffee.

2¼ cups all-purpose flour (preferably unbleached)
1 teaspoon baking soda
½ teaspoon salt
½ teaspoon ground cinnamon
1 cup unsalted sweet butter, softened at room temperature
2 cups granulated sugar

2 extra-large eggs, at room temperature
2 teaspoons pure vanilla extract
¼ pound unsweetened chocolate, melted and cooled to tepid
12 ounces (¾ pound) bittersweet bar chocolate, knife cut into ⅓-inch pieces
1 cup coarsely chopped pecans

Sift together the flour, baking soda, salt, and cinnamon onto a sheet of waxed paper; set aside. Preheat oven to 375° F.

In the large bowl of an electric mixer, cream the butter on moderate speed for 3 minutes. Add the sugar and continue creaming for 2 minutes longer, scraping down the sides of the bowl often. Blend in the vanilla extract.

Beat in the eggs, one at a time, beating for about 1 minute after each egg is added. On low speed, beat in the melted chocolate, mixing it in thoroughly, then blend in the sifted flour mixture in two portions, beating just until the flour particles have been absorbed. By hand, stir in the bittersweet chocolate and pecans.

Drop rounded tablespoons of the dough 2½ inches apart onto parchment paper–lined cookie sheets. Bake the cookies, one sheet at a time, on the middle-level rack of the oven for about 10 to 12 minutes, or until firm to the touch.

Remove the cookies to a cooling rack with a wide metal spatula and store the cooled cookies in an airtight container.

CHOCOLATE-COCONUT MOUNDS   MAKES ABOUT 3 DOZEN

Soft and chewy, these are an irresistible combination of two marvelous flavors—chocolate and coconut—especially beloved by all who, like me, are coconut fanciers.

7 ounces bittersweet bar chocolate, cut up into pieces, and 6 ounces bittersweet bar chocolate, cut into ⅓-inch pieces
½ cup unsalted sweet butter, cut into tablespoon chunks
¼ teaspoon salt

¼ cup granulated sugar
3 extra-large eggs, lightly beaten, at room temperature
2 extra-large egg yolks, lightly beaten, at room temperature
2 teaspoons pure vanilla extract
14 ounces sweetened shredded coconut

Place the 7 ounces bittersweet chocolate and butter in the top of a double boiler. Set the top saucepan over the bottom one, which has gently simmering water in it. Let the chocolate and butter melt slowly, stirring occasionally. Remove the mixture from the heat. Wipe the bottom of the saucepan with paper toweling to dry, then pour the chocolate and butter mixture into a large mixing bowl. Preheat the oven to 325° F.

When the chocolate has cooled to tepid, whisk in the salt and sugar. Pour in the beaten whole eggs and whisk again. Blend in the beaten yolks and vanilla extract. Whisk for 1 minute to combine everything together. By hand, stir in the cut-up bar chocolate and coconut.

Drop the mixture by rounded tablespoons 2 inches apart onto parchment paper–lined cookie sheets (12 to a sheet). Bake the mounds on the middle-level rack of the oven for about 20 minutes, or until they are just firm to the touch. The insides will remain moist.

Let the mounds settle on the baking sheet for 2 to 3 minutes, then with a wide metal spatula remove them to cooling racks.

When cooled, store the mounds airtight, but do not stack them too high in the container. It is best to store them in wide, narrow layers.

NOTE: Sometimes, in an extravagant mood, I stir in a cup of chopped walnuts along with the chocolate and coconut.

BITTERSWEET CHOCOLATE-CHIP ROUNDS MAKES ABOUT 4½ DOZEN

Sandy-textured and crisp, these big cookies have bittersweet chocolate chunks dotted throughout. My first choice of chocolate for these is dark Swiss Lindt Excellence. When I first made these cookies (about 10 years ago) I used packaged chocolate morsels but the deep taste of the Lindt chocolate is so good as it melts smoothly and richly on the tongue. Dozens of these cookies look handsome in a big country wicker basket.

2 cups unsalted sweet butter, softened
at room temperature
2 cups granulated sugar
1 tablespoon plus 1 teaspoon pure
vanilla extract
4 cups all-purpose flour (preferably
unbleached)

1 teaspoon salt
2 pounds bittersweet bar chocolate,
knife-cut into ⅓-inch pieces
1 cup coarsely chopped English wal-
nuts

Preheat oven to 350° F. In the large bowl of an electric mixer, cream the butter on moderately high speed for 2 to 3 minutes, or until light. On low speed, beat in the sugar in two additions, beating for 1 to 2 minutes and scraping down the sides of the bowl after each portion of sugar is added. Beat in the vanilla extract.

On low speed, blend in the flour in three additions, beating just until the flour particles are absorbed. With the final portion of flour, add the salt. By hand, stir in the chocolate pieces and walnuts.

Drop rounded tablespoon mounds of dough 2½ inches apart onto parchment paper–lined cookie sheets. Bake the cookies, a sheet at a time, on the middle-level rack of the oven for 10 to 12 minutes, or until the tops feel firm and the cookies are a light golden color all over.

With a wide spatula remove the cookies to a cooling rack. When cooled, store airtight.

CHOCOLATE-WALNUT BREAK-UP   MAKES 3½ TO 4 POUNDS

These are sweet, crunchy, irregular-shaped cookies made with plenty of butter. When cooled, the dough turns very crisp—it is then you "break up" the large piece into smaller odd forms of cookie. These cookies store best in tins, but you may also present them in large Chinese-style take-out containers (secure the pieces in a plastic bag first), or in wide glass jars with painted lids.

4 cups all-purpose flour (preferably un-
    bleached)
½ teaspoon salt
2 cups unsalted sweet butter, softened
    at room temperature
1½ cups granulated sugar
⅓ cup firmly packed light brown
    sugar

3 squares unsweetened chocolate,
    melted and cooled to tepid
¾ pound bittersweet bar chocolate,
    cut into ⅓-inch pieces or the
    same amount of chocolate-chip
    morsels
1¼ cups chopped walnuts

Lightly butter and flour two 15" x 10" x 1¼" jelly-roll pans; set aside. Preheat oven to 375° F.

Sift together the flour and salt onto a sheet of waxed paper; set aside.

In the large bowl of an electric mixer, cream the butter on moderately high speed for 2 to 3 minutes, or until light. On moderate speed, add the granulated sugar and beat it in; add the brown sugar and continue beating for another 1 to 2 minutes, or until it has combined with the butter and granulated sugar. On low speed, add the melted chocolate; beat for 1 minute.

Add the sifted dry ingredients in two additions, beating on low speed just until the flour particles have been absorbed. Then, by hand, stir in the bittersweet chocolate and walnuts.

Divide the dough equally between the 2 pans. (I find it easiest to do this by lining the inside of a scale with plastic wrap, weighing out the full quantity of dough, then dividing it in half portions.) Spread the dough in the pan evenly, using a lightly buttered flexible palette knife. Bake the pans of dough on the upper- and lower-level racks of the oven for 20 to 30 minutes, or until firm and cooked through, but be careful not to overbake (or burn!) the sheets of dough. Reverse the sheets from top to bottom and front to back after about 10 minutes.

Cool the slab of dough in the pan for 5 to 10 minutes, then invert the big rectangular cookies onto cooling racks. Invert again to cool right side up.

When the rectangles have reached room temperature, break them into rough pieces and store airtight.

Old and New Favorites

Part of the pleasure in the actual celebration of the winter holidays comes in the many days preceding, when you begin to swamp pantry and refrigerator with butter, sugar, flour, and spices, and collect rolling pins, special cookie cutters, great big cookie sheets.

Mincemeat, Nesselrode, and fruitcakes having been made, I move into baking a profusion of cookies, substantial cookies, that are not very elaborate. Some rolled, some dropped, some molded, these have become established in my home as the usual sweets to fill red and green tins. I aways have these eight kinds of cookies secured in containers, and make enough (generally a double or triple batch of each) to have for my own sweet tooth, and for anxious cookie-loving friends. You may also draw upon other cookie recipes in this book, and make these your comfortable constants. I like to bake the Traditional (More or Less) Sugar Cookies, Meltingly Rich Sugar Cookies, Sour Cream Sugar Cookies, Crispy Gingersnaps, Molasses-Oatmeal Saucers, Whole-Wheat, Coconut, and Raisin Cookies, and Coconut Rounds.

To mastermind cookie-baking sessions, I gather together tins old and new, cutters, pastry brushes, and my large wooden pastry board. Then I plan for several at-home evenings or afternoons when a dozen or so tins of cookies may be produced. Seal up the tins so that the monsters won't raid them. Better than that, though, is to hide them.

VANILLA SHORTBREAD
MAKES ABOUT 3½ DOZEN

Shortbread is crumbly and buttery, and one of the quickest of all doughs to make. The high butter content makes a tender, firm cookie that can be baked several weeks ahead of the holidays. I love to give shortbread a nutty taste and add finely chopped walnuts or almonds to the doughy mass, or sift top-quality Dutch-process cocoa into the dry ingredients to create a toothsome chocolate version, or flick in some lemon peel for a subtle citrus flavor.

4 cups all-purpose flour (preferably
    unbleached)
½ teaspoon baking powder
½ teaspoon salt

2 cups unsalted sweet butter, softened
    at room temperature
1 cup sifted confectioners' sugar
1 tablespoon pure vanilla extract

Sift together the flour, baking powder, and salt onto a sheet of waxed paper; set aside.

In the large bowl of an electric mixer, cream the butter on moderately high speed for 3 minutes. Add the sugar in two additions, beating on moderately low speed for 2 to 3 minutes after each portion is added. Scrape down the sides of the bowl often to keep the creamed mixture even. Blend in the vanilla extract.

On low speed, add the sifted flour in three additions, beating just until the flour particles have been absorbed.

Divide the dough in half and place each half between 2 sheets of waxed paper. Roll out the dough to a thickness of ½ inch. Place the flat slabs of dough onto a cookie sheet, still enclosed in the waxed paper, and refrigerate them for at least 5 hours, or until very firm. Once firm, the dough may be wrapped in aluminum foil and stored in the refrigerator for up to 3 days.

To bake the shortbread, cut out cookies with a 3-inch cutter of your choice—I like plain circles best, or the simple shape of a bell or rectangle—and place the cookies 2 inches apart on parchment paper–lined cookie sheets. Dip the tines of a fork in flour and carefully pierce the cookies in 3 straight rows, like this

> . . . .
> . . . .
> . . . .

Reroll the scraps and stamp out more cookies. Chill the cookies on the sheets for 10 minutes.

Preheat the oven to 350° F.

Bake the shortbread on the middle-level rack of the oven for about 18 to 20 minutes, or until a pale gold color.

With a wide metal spatula remove the shortbread to a cooling rack. Cool the shortbread, then store airtight.

VARIATION: To make Vanilla Poppy-Seed Shortbread, beat ⅓ cup whole poppy seed into the batter after you have added the confectioners' sugar; 1 tablespoon finely grated orange rind is a pleasant addition to the poppy seed—add it to the butter while it is creaming.

NOTES: Blending the fat and flour together for shortbread may be done in two ways. In the first way, the sugar, flour, and salt is sifted together, then bits of butter are rubbed into the sifted ingredients with your fingertips to form a very crumbly dough. Then the dough is pinched together into a ball, patted into a disk, scored into triangles, and baked. Pie-shaped wedges of dough come out warm from the oven a light biscuit color.

The second method, and this is the one that I use, is one of creaming the butter with the sugar, then adding the flour which has been sifted with a bit of baking powder and salt. I roll out the dough ½ inch thick between sheets of waxed paper and chill the slabs in the refrigerator for half a day (or store them as long as 2 to 3 days, wrapped further in a sheet of aluminum foil). At baking time, I stamp out cookies in the shape of hearts, bells, or circles with sturdy cookie cutters. I prefer this method to the "rubbed-dough" one—the cookie is entirely crisp but still rich and crumbly.

A final baking note: Steep a plump, split vanilla bean in a big jar of confectioners' sugar for 2 weeks and use the sugar in these first 2 shortbread recipes.

BROWN SUGAR–WALNUT SHORTBREAD   MAKES ABOUT 3½ DOZEN

4 cups all-purpose flour (preferably
    unbleached)
½ teaspoon baking powder
½ teaspoon salt
1 teaspoon freshly ground nutmeg
2 cups unsalted sweet butter, softened
    at room temperature

1½ cups firmly packed light brown
    sugar
¾ cup finely chopped walnuts
2½ teaspoons pure vanilla extract

Sift together the flour, baking powder, salt, and nutmeg onto a sheet of waxed paper; set aside.

In the large bowl of an electric mixer, cream the butter on moderately high speed for 3 minutes. Add the brown sugar in two additions, beating on moderate speed for 2 minutes after each amount is added. On low speed, blend in the chopped walnuts and vanilla extract. Slowly beat in the sifted flour mixture in three additions, beating just until the flour particles have been absorbed.

Divide the dough in half and place each half between 2 large sheets of waxed paper. Roll out the dough to a thickness of ½ inch. Place the sheets of dough on a flat cookie sheet and refrigerate them for at least 5 hours, or until firm. Once firm, the dough may be wrapped up in aluminum foil and stored in the refrigerator for 3 days.

To bake the shortbread, cut out cookies with a 3-inch cutter of your choice and place the dough 2 inches apart on parchment paper–lined cookie sheets. Dip the tines of a fork in a little flour and pierce the cookies in 3 straight rows, like this

· · · ·
· · · ·
· · · ·

Reroll the scraps and stamp out more cookies. Chill the cookies on the sheets for 10 minutes before baking.

Preheat oven to 350° F.

Bake the shortbread on the middle-level rack of the oven for 15 to 18 minutes, or until just firm to the touch.

With a metal spatula remove the shortbread to cooling racks. When cooled, store the cookies airtight.

VARIATION: To make Brown Sugar–Almond Shortbread, substitute ¾ cup finely chopped lightly toasted almonds for the walnuts; use 1½ teaspoons pure almond extract and 1 teaspoon pure vanilla extract in place of the whole quantity of vanilla extract.

LEMON SHORTBREAD　　　　　　　　MAKES ABOUT 3½ DOZEN

4 cups all-purpose flour (preferably unbleached)
½ teaspoon baking powder
2 cups unsalted sweet butter, softened at room temperature

1 cup sifted confectioners' sugar
finely grated rind of 4 lemons
2 teaspoons pure lemon extract

Sift together the flour and baking powder onto a sheet of waxed paper; set aside.

In the large bowl of an electric mixer, cream the butter on moderately high speed for 3 minutes. On moderately low speed, add the sugar in two batches, beating for 1 to 2 minutes after each portion is added. Scrape down the sides of the bowl to keep the creamed mixture even. Blend in the lemon rind and lemon extract. Continuing on low speed, slowly beat in the sifted flour mixture in three additions, beating just until the flour particles have been absorbed.

Divide the dough in half and place each half between 2 large sheets of waxed paper. Roll out the dough to a thickness of ½ inch. Place the sheets of dough on a flat cookie sheet and refrigerate them for at least 5 hours, or until firm. Once firm, the dough may be wrapped up in aluminum foil and stored in the refrigerator for 3 days.

To bake the shortbread, cut out cookies with a 3-inch cutter and place them 2 inches apart on parchment paper–lined cookie sheets. Dip the tines of a fork in a little flour and pierce each cookie with the tines in three straight rows, like this

. . . .
. . . .
. . . .

Gather up the scraps of dough, reroll, and cut into more cookies. Chill the cookies on the sheets for 10 minutes.

Preheat the oven to 350° F.

Bake the shortbread on the middle-level rack of the oven for about 15 minutes, or until just firm to the touch on top.

With a wide spatula transfer the shortbread to cooling racks. Store the cooled cookies airtight.

GINGERBREAD PEOPLE
MAKES 4 TO 6 DOZEN (see Note)

Children love to decorate these cakelike gingerbread boys and girls with the traditional raisin eyes, nose, mouth, and buttons. For grownups, they are delicious homey reminders of childhood and Christmases past.

1½ cups dark molasses
1½ cups unsalted sweet butter, cut
* into chunks*
1½ cups firmly packed dark brown
* sugar*
1 tablespoon pure vanilla extract
9 cups all-purpose flour (preferably
* unbleached)*
2 teaspoons baking powder

1 teaspoon baking soda
1½ teaspoons salt
1 tablespoon plus 1 teaspoon ground
* ginger*
1 tablespoon plus 1 teaspoon ground
* cinnamon*
2 extra-large eggs, at room tempera-
* ture, lightly beaten*
dark seedless raisins

Heat the molasses and butter in a 2-quart saucepan until the butter is melted. Pour the mixture into a large bowl, and stir in the sugar and vanilla extract. Cool.

Sift the next 6 ingredients onto a sheet of waxed paper; set aside.

Beat the eggs into the cooled molasses and butter mixture, then turn the mixture into the large bowl of an electric mixer. On low speed, beat in the flour in four additions, beating just until the flour particles have been absorbed. Wrap the dough securely in waxed paper, and chill it for 3 to 4 hours, or until firm enough to roll.

Preheat the oven to 350° F., and on a lightly floured wooden board, roll out the dough, a fourth at a time, to a thickness of ¼ inch. Cut gingerbread men and women, or smaller boys and girls, out of the dough. Arrange the people 3 inches apart on parchment paper–lined cookie sheets. Decorate with the raisins.

Bake the gingerbread people on the middle-level rack of the oven for 12 to 15 minutes, or until just firm to the touch.

Cool the cookies on the sheet for 2 to 3 minutes, then with a wide metal spatula remove them to cooling racks to cool completely. Store the gingerbread people airtight.

NOTE: The yield of this cookie depends on the size of the cutter that you use. A 5-inch gingerbread man/woman cutter will make about 4 dozen cookies; a 3-inch cutter 5½ to 6 dozen.

WALNUT CRESCENTS   MAKES ABOUT 8 DOZEN

These plain, classic cookies are hand-shaped into crescents, or rolled into balls. Everyone seems to have a favorite recipe for them and this one is mine. The wonderful sandy texture is the result of first melting and then completely cooling the butter before adding the dry ingredients. If the butter is not cool, then the baking powder will be activated too soon and that will spoil the lovely texture.

2 cups unsalted sweet butter,
  melted and cooled
2⅓ cups sifted confectioners' sugar
2 teaspoons baking powder

4½ cups all-purpose flour (preferably
  unbleached)
½ cup very finely chopped walnuts

Pour the cooled butter into a large mixing bowl. Stir in ⅓ cup sugar and baking powder. Preheat oven to 350° F.

Sift the flour, a fourth at a time, and stir it into the butter-sugar mixture using a wooden spoon. When all of the flour has been added, blend in the walnuts.

Form teaspoonfuls of dough into balls and shape the balls into even-sized crescents. Place the crescents 2 inches apart onto parchment paper–lined cookie sheets and bake the cookies, one sheet at a time, on the middle-level rack of the oven for 15 minutes, or until a light golden color. With a metal spatula remove the cookies to a rack.

Before serving or giving, dredge the top of the cookies with confectioners' sugar.

VARIATION: To make Almond Crescents, substitute ¾ cup finely chopped blanched and very lightly toasted almonds for the walnuts; add 1 teaspoon pure almond extract along with the confectioners' sugar to the melted butter.

COCONUT JUMBLES   MAKES ABOUT 6 DOZEN

Old-fashioned and buttery-crisp, these cookies are from an old family recipe of mine; my mother made these every December in big batches. This dough needs to chill very well because it is quite sticky, so I prefer to make up the dough a day before baking to ensure good handling.

The jumbles are delicious when topped with sweetened shredded coconut, but if you are baking them with young children, they'll like to brush the tops with some egg white and decorate the cookies with colored sprinkles, coarse sugar, or minuscule cinnamon candies.

5 cups cake flour
3 teaspoons baking powder
1 teaspoon salt
1 cup unsalted sweet butter, softened
    at room temperature
2 cups granulated sugar
1 extra-large egg, at room temperature

4 extra-large eggs, separated, at room
    temperature
2 teaspoons pure vanilla extract
4 tablespoons light cream
about 2 cups sweetened shredded
    coconut

Sift the cake flour with the baking powder and salt onto a sheet of waxed paper; set aside.

In the large bowl of an electric mixer, cream the butter until light on moderately high speed. Add the sugar in two additions, beating for 1 minute after each amount is added. Beat in the whole egg and egg yolks. Blend in the vanilla extract and light cream.

On low speed, add the sifted flour mixture in three additions, mixing just until the flour particles have been absorbed. The dough is sticky at this point.

Divide the dough into 4 portions on 4 sheets of waxed paper; cover each sheet with a second sheet of waxed paper and wrap well. Refrigerate the dough until very firm, preferably overnight.

Preheat oven to 400° F. and on a lightly floured wooden board, roll out each portion of dough to a thickness of ⅛ inch. Stamp out cookies with a 3- or 3½-inch cutter and place the cookies 2 inches apart on parchment paper–lined cookie sheets.

Beat egg whites till frothy, and brush a thin film over the top of each cookie. Sprinkle coconut evenly over the surface. Lightly press down the coconut so that it sticks to the cookie.

Bake each sheet of jumbles on the middle-level rack of the oven for 10 minutes, or until an even golden color. With a spatula remove the cookies to a rack to cool completely. Store airtight.

SPICE AND FRUIT DROPS   MAKES ABOUT 6½ DOZEN

Eggy, rich, and spicy, these drops have more good things in them than most spice-enriched cookies; they are chunky and make excellent cookie-jar cookies. Fill an old glass apothecary jar with the drops, wrap the neck with ribbon and a bouquet of cinnamon sticks and vanilla beans, and present it to someone very special.

5½ cups all-purpose flour (preferably
    unbleached)
2 teaspoons baking powder
¼ teaspoon baking soda
¾ teaspoon salt
1 tablespoon ground cinnamon
1 teaspoon ground ginger
½ teaspoon freshly ground nutmeg
½ teaspoon ground allspice
¼ teaspoon ground cloves
¼ teaspoon ground mace
2 cups unsalted sweet butter, softened
    at room temperature

3 cups firmly packed light brown sugar
5 extra-large eggs, at room temperature
1 tablespoon pure vanilla extract
1 cup plump, dark seedless raisins,
    steeped in boiling water to cover
    for 10 minutes, then drained and
    thoroughly dried on a sheet of
    paper toweling
1 cup dried currants
1 cup coarsely chopped pecans
1 cup coarsely chopped walnuts
1 cup coarsely chopped pitted dates
1 cup finely diced dried apricots

Sift the first 10 ingredients onto a sheet of waxed paper; set aside. Preheat oven to 375° F.

In the large bowl of an electric mixer, cream the butter until light on moderately high speed, about 2 to 3 minutes. Beat in the brown sugar, a cup at a time, beating for about 1 minute after each portion is added. Beat in the eggs, one at a time, beating for 1 minute after each egg is added. Scrape down the sides of the bowl frequently to keep the mixture even. Blend in the vanilla extract.

On low speed, beat the sifted dry ingredients into the creamed batter in four additions, beating just until the flour particles are absorbed. Scrape down the sides of the bowl.

Transfer the batter to a very large bowl. Stir in the remaining ingredients.

Drop the dough by tablespoons 2½ inches apart onto parchment paper–lined cookie sheets. Bake the cookies, a sheet at a time, on the middle-level rack of the oven for 12 minutes, or until firm to the touch.

With a sturdy metal spatula transfer the cookies to cooling racks. When cooled, store airtight.

LEMON DELIGHTS

MAKES ABOUT 5 DOZEN

Fine-grained, crisp, and delightfully lemony.

4½ cups sifted all-purpose flour (preferably unbleached)
1 teaspoon baking soda
1 teaspoon cream of tartar
¾ teaspoon salt
1 cup unsalted sweet butter, softened at room temperature

1 cup vegetable oil
3 cups granulated sugar
1 cup sifted confectioners' sugar
4 extra-large egg yolks, at room temperature
3 tablespoons finely grated lemon rind
1 tablespoon pure lemon extract

Resift the flour with the baking soda, cream of tartar, and salt onto a sheet of waxed paper; set aside.

In the large bowl of an electric mixer, cream the butter until light on moderately high speed, about 2 minutes. On low speed, beat in the vegetable oil in a thin stream; the mixture will appear quite liquid, but that is as it should be. Beat in 1 cup granulated sugar in two portions; add all of the confectioners' sugar and beat it in. Scrape down the sides of the bowl to keep the mixture even. On moderate speed, add the egg yolks, one at a time, beating for a minute or so to combine them into the creamed mixture. Blend in the lemon rind and lemon extract.

On low speed, beat in the sifted flour mixture in three additions, beating just until the flour particles have been absorbed. Refrigerate the dough, covered, until it has firmed up, about 3 hours.

Preheat oven to 375° F. and roll tablespoons of dough into balls, placing the balls 2½ inches apart on parchment paper–lined cookie sheets. With a fork dipped in flour, flatten the dough into a neat round pillow, pressing the tines of the fork in one direction on the dough. After each batch of cookies has been pressed, sprinkle a light haze of granulated sugar on top.

Bake the cookies, a sheet at a time, on the middle-level rack of the oven for 10 minutes, or until firm and a pale golden color.

With a wide metal spatula remove the cookies to a rack. Store the cooled cookies airtight.

Holiday Tea Cakes

WALNUT POUND CAKE

MAKES ONE 10-INCH CAKE

A classically rich pound cake, this nutmeg-scented creation calls for freshly cracked walnuts. But vacuum-packed walnuts are a satisfactory substitute when time is short.

4 cups sifted all-purpose flour (prefera-
    bly unbleached)
1 teaspoon baking powder
½ teaspoon salt
½ teaspoon freshly ground nutmeg
2 cups unsalted sweet butter, softened
    at room temperature

2 cups granulated sugar
8 jumbo eggs, separated, at room tem-
    perature
1 tablespoon pure vanilla extract
pinch of cream of tartar
1 cup very finely chopped walnuts
confectioners' sugar

Lightly butter and flour a plain 1-inch tube pan; set aside. Preheat oven to 300° F.

Resift the flour with the baking powder, salt, and nutmeg onto a sheet of waxed paper; set aside.

In the large bowl of an electric mixer, cream the butter until light on moderately high speed for 3 to 4 minutes. Add the sugar in two additions, creaming for 1 to 2 minutes after each portion of sugar has been added. Beat in the egg yolks, one at a time, beating for a minute after each yolk is added. Scrape down the sides of the bowl often to keep the mixture even.

On low speed, add the sifted flour mixture in three additions, beating just until the flour particles have become absorbed.

In a clean bowl, beat the egg whites until frothy on moderately high speed. Add the cream of tartar and continue beating until firm, not stiff, peaks are formed.

Stir 4 big spoonfuls of the whites into the batter to lighten it, then fold in the remaining whites with the chopped walnuts.

Pour and scrape the batter into the prepared pan, gently leveling the top by shaking the pan from side to side a few times. Bake the cake on the lower-level rack of the oven for 1 hour, or until a toothpick inserted in the cake emerges clean and dry.

Cool the cake in the pan on a rack for 10 minutes, then invert onto another rack; invert again to cool right side up.

When thoroughly cooled, store the cake airtight. Sift confectioners' sugar over the top of the cake before serving.

SOUR CREAM CAKE   MAKES ONE 10-INCH CAKE

Having this cake around gives one a great sense of security—it's sweet, gentle, very moist, and good at all times of the day. The sour cream is what keeps the cake moist and fresh. For gift-giving, decorate it with a thin garland of fresh greens, like tiny sprays of holly, set it in a sturdy box, and wrap in bright tissue (perhaps two contrasting colors) and add a few more greens and a pine cone or two.

3 cups sifted all-purpose flour (prefera-
    bly unbleached)
½ teaspoon baking powder
½ teaspoon salt
1 teaspoon freshly ground nutmeg
1 cup unsalted sweet butter, softened
    at room temperature
3 cups granulated sugar

6 jumbo eggs, separated, at room tem-
    perature
2 teaspoons pure vanilla extract
½ teaspoon pure almond extract
1 cup sour cream, at room temperature
pinch of cream of tartar
confectioners' sugar (optional)

Lightly butter and flour a plain 10-inch tube pan; set aside. Preheat oven to 350° F.

Resift the flour with the baking powder, salt, and nutmeg onto a sheet of waxed paper; set aside.

In the large bowl of an electric mixer, cream the butter until light and fluffy on moderately high speed, about 3 to 4 minutes. Add the sugar in two portions, beating for 2 minutes after each amount is added. Beat in the egg yolks, one at a time, blending for about a minute after each one is added. Beat in the vanilla and almond extracts.

On low speed, add the sifted flour mixture in three additions alternately with the sour cream in two additions, beginning and ending with the sifted mixture. Scrape down the sides of the bowl often to keep the batter even.

In a clean bowl, beat the egg whites on moderately high speed until frothy. Add the cream of tartar and continue beating until firm, not stiff, peaks are formed.

Stir 4 big spoonfuls of the egg whites into the sour cream batter, then fold in the remaining whites with a large rubber spatula until no patches of the white are visible.

Carefully pour the batter into the prepared pan; level the top with a spatula.

Bake the cake on the lower-level rack of the oven for 1 hour and 5 minutes to 1 hour and 15 minutes, or until a toothpick inserted in the cake emerges clean and dry.

Cool the cake in the pan on a rack for 10 minutes; invert the cake onto another rack and invert again to cool right side up.

When cooled, store in an airtight container. Before serving, or giving, sift confectioners' sugar over the top, if you like.

SPICE CAKE   MAKES ONE 10-INCH CAKE

When spices are stirred through a buttery batter, they somehow transform a cake into a country treat. I like to give this substantial, sturdy cake with a basketful of fruit, or a jar of lemon-flavored compote.

3 cups sifted all-purpose flour (preferably unbleached)
1 teaspoon baking powder
½ teaspoon baking soda
½ teaspoon salt
2 teaspoons ground cinnamon
½ teaspoon ground ginger
½ teaspoon freshly ground nutmeg
¼ teaspoon ground allspice

¼ teaspoon ground cloves
1 cup unsalted sweet butter, softened at room temperature
2½ cups granulated sugar
5 jumbo eggs, at room temperature
1 cup buttermilk blended with 2 teaspoons pure vanilla extract
confectioners' sugar (optional)

Lightly butter and flour a fluted 10-inch tube pan; set aside. Preheat oven to 350° F.

Resift the flour with the next 8 ingredients onto a sheet of waxed paper; set aside.

In the large bowl of an electric mixer, cream the butter on moderately high speed for 3 minutes, or until the butter is fluffy. Beat in the granulated sugar in two additions, beating for about 2 minutes after each portion is added. Beat in the eggs, one at a time, beating for about a minute after each egg is added. Scrape down the sides of the bowl to keep the mixture even, and rebeat for a few seconds.

On low speed, add the sifted dry ingredients in three additions alternately with the buttermilk in two additions, beginning and ending with the sifted mixture. Scrape down the sides of the bowl frequently.

Pour and scrape the batter into the prepared pan. Bake the cake on the lower-level rack of the oven for about 1 hour, or until a toothpick inserted into the cake withdraws clean and dry.

Cool the cake in the pan on a rack for 10 minutes, then invert onto another rack to cool completely. Store the cake airtight. Sift confectioners' sugar on top of the cake before serving, or giving, if you like.

PECAN-CURRANT CAKE

MAKES ONE 10-INCH CAKE

Extravagantly good!

2 cups coarsely chopped pecans
2 cups dried, but moist, currants
¾ cup bourbon
3½ cups sifted all-purpose flour (preferably unbleached)
1½ teaspoons baking powder
¼ teaspoon salt
2 teaspoons ground cinnamon

¼ teaspoon freshly ground nutmeg
¼ teaspoon ground allspice
1½ cups unsalted sweet butter, softened at room temperature
2 cups granulated sugar
2 teaspoons pure vanilla extract
7 jumbo eggs, at room temperature
apricot jam (optional)

Combine the pecans, currants, and bourbon in a glazed pottery bowl; cover loosely with a sheet of plastic wrap and let the mixture stand for ½ hour.

Lightly butter and flour a plain 10-inch tube pan; set aside. Preheat oven to 350° F.

Resift the flour with the next 5 ingredients onto a sheet of waxed paper; set aside.

In the large bowl of an electric mixer, cream the butter on moderately high speed until light, about 3 minutes. Add the sugar in two additions, beating for 2 minutes after each portion is added. Beat in the vanilla extract. Beat in the eggs, one at a time, beating for 1 minute on moderate speed after each one is added; scrape down the sides of the bowl often to ensure an even mixture.

On low speed, blend in the dry ingredients mixture in three additions, beating just until the flour particles have been absorbed. By hand, stir in the marinated pecans and currants.

Pour and scrape the batter into the prepared pan. Bake the cake on the lower-level rack of the oven for about 1 hour and 15 minutes, or until a toothpick inserted in the cake emerges clean and dry.

Cool the cake in the pan for 10 minutes, then carefully invert it onto a cooling rack and invert again to cool right side up. When cold, store airtight.

Alternately, when the cake is just warm, douse it with a few teaspoons of bourbon, cool the cake, then store in an airtight tin for at least a week. About 2 hours before serving, or placing the cake in a good-looking tin, glaze the outside with hot sieved apricot jam and arrange a pattern of pecan halves on the top.

CARROT-FLECKED BANANA LOAF   MAKES ONE 9″ x 5″ x 3″ LOAF

The following three recipes produce loaves of distinction that are fun to bake in small 2-cup loaf pans (children love them), as well as in standard loaf pans. They are so good as the highlight of a continental breakfast or tea, whether they are served warm from the oven with country butter or sliced and served a day or so after having been ripened in a cake tin. To give as a gift, wrap up a loaf in clear, heavy plastic wrap, and plunk it, at an odd angle, in a small pine basket. Fill up every space that the bread doesn't with tiny pine cones, bright shiny leaves, and a few sprays of loose pine needles.

2 cups sifted all-purpose flour (*prefera-*
    bly unbleached)
2 teaspoons baking powder
¼ teaspoon baking soda
1 teaspoon ground cinnamon
¼ teaspoon salt
½ cup unsalted sweet butter, softened
    at room temperature
¾ cup granulated sugar

2 large eggs, at room temperature
¾ cup (*lightly packed measurement*)
    shredded carrots (*grate the carrots*
    on the large holes of a hand
    grater)
1 cup (*about 2 medium-small*) pureed
    bananas
¾ cup chopped walnuts

Lightly butter and flour a 9″ x 5″ x 3″ loaf pan; set aside. Preheat oven to 350° F.

Resift the flour with the baking powder, baking soda, cinnamon, and salt; set aside.

In the large bowl of an electric mixer, cream the butter on moderately high speed for 2 minutes. Add the sugar and continue beating for 2 minutes. Beat in the eggs, one at a time, scraping down the sides of the bowl after each egg is added. Beat in the carrots and pureed bananas.

On low speed, add the sifted mixture in two portions, blending just until the flour particles have been absorbed. By hand, stir in the walnuts.

Pour the batter into the prepared pan and bake the loaf on the lower-level rack of the oven for 50 minutes to 1 hour, or until a toothpick inserted into the bread emerges clean and dry.

Cool the bread in the pan on a rack for 10 minutes, then invert it onto another rack, invert again, and cool right side up.

Store the cooled loaf airtight.

BANANA LOAF WITH APRICOTS

MAKES TWO 9″ x 5″ x 3″ LOAVES

This is a dense and fine-grained loaf.

2 cups all-purpose flour (preferably unbleached)
2 cups whole-wheat flour (preferably stone-ground)
2½ teaspoons baking soda
¾ teaspoon salt
1½ teaspoons ground cinnamon
¾ cup diced dried, but moist, apricots

1 cup unsalted sweet butter, softened at room temperature
2 cups granulated sugar
4 extra-large eggs, at room temperature
2 (about 4 medium-size) pureed bananas

Lightly butter and flour two 9″ x 5″ x 3″ loaf pans; set aside. Preheat oven to 350° F.

Sift the flour, baking soda, salt, and cinnamon together onto a sheet of waxed paper; set aside.

Place the apricots in a bowl and stir in 2 teaspoons of the flour mixture; set aside.

In the large bowl of an electric mixer, cream the butter until light on moderately high speed for 2 to 3 minutes. Beat in the sugar in two additions, blending for about 1 to 2 minutes after each portion is added. Beat in the eggs, one at a time, for about 1 minute after each egg is added.

On low speed, blend in the pureed bananas, then the sifted flour mixture in three additions, beating just until the flour particles have been absorbed.

Divide the mixture evenly between the two pans. Bake the loaves on the lower-level rack of the oven for about 1 hour, or until a toothpick inserted into the loaf emerges clean and dry.

Cool the loaves in the pans on a rack for 10 minutes, then invert the loaves on a second cooling rack. Turn the loaves right side up and cool them to room temperature.

Store the cooled loaves airtight.

NOTE: Dates may be substituted for the apricots with tasty results.

ORANGE BREAD   MAKES ONE 9″ x 5″ x 3″ LOAF

A fine small-grained bread that slices into compact, firm pieces.

2 cups all-purpose flour (preferably	*1 extra-large egg, at room temperature*
unbleached)	*⅔ cup orange juice, at room tempera-*
1 cup granulated sugar	*ture*
1 teaspoon baking powder	*4 tablespoons melted and cooled un-*
½ teaspoon baking soda	*salted sweet butter*
½ teaspoon salt	*3 tablespoons finely grated orange rind*
½ cup currants	
½ cup chopped walnuts	

Lightly butter and flour a 9″ x 5″ x 3″ loaf pan; set aside. Preheat oven to 350° F.
In a large mixing bowl, sift together the first 5 ingredients; set aside.

Combine the currants and walnuts in a bowl; stir in 2 teaspoons of the sifted flour mixture and set aside.

In a small mixing bowl, whisk together the remaining ingredients.

Make a well in the middle of the sifted mixture and pour in the orange juice combination. Combine the two together just until the flour particles have been absorbed. Stir in the floured currants and walnuts.

Pour and scrape the batter into the prepared pan and bake the loaf on the lower-level rack of the oven for about 1 hour, or until a toothpick inserted into the bread emerges clean and dry.

Cool the loaf in the pan on a rack for 10 minutes, then invert it onto another rack; turn the loaf right side up to cool completely.

Store the cooled loaf airtight.

Fruitcakes for Everyone

I attend to my fruitcakes with a fanatic devotion, glazing fruit, soaking fruit, blending fruit into buttery batters, sloshing over a few tablespoons of alcohol to age the cake properly; it's a rewarding project, fruitcake-baking, and I'm always coming up with new formulas. Nothing pleases me more than the August-September-October experience of making fruitcakes, perhaps because I love to play with the raw materials.

Thinly sliced, a large fruitcake will serve many persons, and is a perfect gift for those who entertain constantly during the holidays.

I've given fruitcakes, well wrapped in a clean, simple cloth, in antique roasting pans, an enameled Dutch oven (used hearthside in days of old), and in the large perforated basket of an old potato or cruller deep-fat fryer. Always surround the cake with greenery, as the insides of these old containers are no beauties—they look rather bleak.

A *culinary note on lining fruitcake pans:* To prepare the pan for receiving some fruitcake batters (each recipe will specify), it may be necessary to line the pan with heavy brown paper. Here's how I do it:

For a large, plain 10-inch tube pan, also known as an angel food–cake pan, you will need to prepare two separate liners, one for the bottom and another for the sides of the pan. To line the bottom, place the pan on a length of paper. Anchor the pan with one hand and trace around the base with a pencil. Also trace around the inner tube. Cut out the large circle, then fold the circle in half and cut a perfect smaller circle about ⅛ inch over the tracing line (to fit the paper over the tube comfortably). Test the circle to see if it fits comfortably; you may have to make some minor cutting adjustments to the tube opening in the paper.

To line the sides of the tube pan, tear off a length of brown paper that is about 2 inches longer than the circumference of the pan. Measure the height of the pan and trim-cut the paper as deep as the height. Using a firm pastry brush, paint the entire inside of the pan with cool (but still liquid) melted shortening. Put on the bottom paper disk. Fit the long strips on the sides, making several small pleats as necessary, and place one end over the other; seal by dabbing a little bit of liquid shortening along one of the sides and pressing the second side over. If the paper happens to overlap more than 2 inches, trim it off. Brush more melted shortening over the liner paper and on the tube.

RICH GINGER CAKE   MAKES ONE 10-INCH CAKE

Two kinds of ginger—crystallized and preserved in syrup—go into this cake batter. After the cake is baked, a film of ginger glaze is brushed over the finished cake. A ginger lover's dream! Serve thin slices of this cake with a drift of very lightly sweetened and whipped heavy cream.

1 cup crystallized ginger, cut into
    small cubes
1 cup ginger preserved in syrup,
    roughly chopped
1 cup currants
1 cup English walnuts, coarsely
    chopped
1 cup dark rum
3 cups sifted all-purpose flour (prefera-
    bly unbleached)
¾ teaspoon baking powder
¼ teaspoon baking soda
½ teaspoon salt

2 tablespoons freshly ground ginger
    (use dried Jamaican ginger and
    grind it on the smallest holes of a
    hand grater or on a nutmeg
    grater)
2 teaspoons ground cinnamon
1½ teaspoons freshly ground nutmeg
2 cups unsalted sweet butter, softened
    at room temperature
2 cups granulated sugar
6 large or extra-large eggs, separated, at
    room temperature
1 tablespoon pure vanilla extract

GINGER GLAZE:

1 12-ounce jar ginger preserves
3 tablespoons (about 1 large lime)
    freshly squeezed lime juice

2 tablespoons water

Place both kinds of chopped ginger, currants, and walnuts in a large glazed pottery bowl, or a glass bowl. Pour on the dark rum, and mix everything together. Cover the bowl with a piece of plastic wrap and let the mixture marinate at room temperature overnight, or up to 3 days.

On baking day, lightly butter and flour the inside of a 10-inch fluted tube pan; set aside. Preheat oven to 300° F.

Resift the flour with the next 6 ingredients onto a sheet of waxed paper; set aside.

In the large bowl of an electric mixer, cream the butter on moderately high speed for 4 minutes, or until light. Add the sugar in two additions, and continue beating for 2 minutes on moderate speed after each portion of sugar is added. Add the egg yolks, one at a time, beating for 1 minute after each yolk is added. Blend in the vanilla extract. Scrape down the sides of the bowl to keep the mixture even, then beat for a few seconds longer.

On low speed, add the sifted dry ingredients in two additions, beating just until the flour particles have been absorbed. By hand, stir in the marinated nuts-ginger-currants plus any of the rum that may have settled in the bottom of the bowl.

Beat the egg whites until they are foamy, add a pinch of salt, and continue beating until firm, not stiff, peaks are formed. Beat 3 large spoonfuls of the whites into the fruited batter, then fold in the remaining whites until no patches of white show in the batter. This is best accomplished by using a big, wide plastic spatula. It will be necessary to transfer the batter into a very large bowl in order to fold in the egg whites. (I use an enormous, wide stainless-steel bowl.)

Pour and scrape the batter into the prepared pan, and bake the cake on the lower-level rack of the oven for 15 minutes. Reduce the oven temperature to 275° and continue baking the cake for 1 hour and 30 minutes or so, or until a toothpick inserted in the cake emerges without any particles clinging to it.

Cool the cake in the pan on a rack for 10 minutes, then invert it onto a second rack to cool completely.

Store the cake, well wrapped, in an airtight container in the refrigerator for at least 1 week. During that time, baste the top of the cake with a little extra rum, if you like.

To make the glaze, place the ginger preserves, lime juice, and water in a small, heavy saucepan (of about 1-quart capacity). Bring to a boil, stirring, then simmer for 3 minutes.

Strain the preserves through a fine-mesh stainless-steel sieve. Pour the glaze into a clean, dry container, cool to room temperature, then cover and refrigerate. (The glaze may be stored safely in the refrigerator for 8 months.)

When the cake is ready, restore it to room temperature. Heat 1 cup of glaze to boiling, then simmer it for 1 or 2 minutes. Make sure that the outside of the cake is free of any crumbs that may have adhered, then brush an even layer of glaze on the cake with a wide, soft pastry brush.

Decorate the sides of the cake with fresh leaves and extra walnuts, if you like.

MY MOTHER'S DARK LUXURY FRUITCAKE   MAKES ONE 10-INCH CAKE

The fruitcake my mother baked always had to be a deep, dark color, and she settled on this one as her yearly holiday project. It took 24 hours to make. One of my favorite fruitcakes, it stays beautiful and moist for a long time.

1½ cups dates, diced into ½-inch
    pieces
1 cup golden raisins
½ cup dried, but moist, currants
1 cup glazed apricots, diced into ½-
    inch pieces
1 cup glazed peaches, diced into ½-
    inch pieces
1 cup coarsely chopped walnuts
1 cup cream sherry
¼ cup strained, freshly squeezed
    orange juice
¼ cup pineapple juice
2¾ cups cake flour

¾ teaspoon baking powder
1 teaspoon salt
2 teaspoons ground cinnamon
½ teaspoon ground allspice
½ teaspoon ground cloves
½ teaspoon ground mace
½ teaspoon freshly ground nutmeg
½ teaspoon ground ginger
2½ cups unsalted sweet butter, soft-
    ened at room temperature
1¼ cups firmly packed dark brown
    sugar
4 large eggs, at room temperature
½ cup orange marmalade

In a large glazed stoneware bowl, combine the first 9 ingredients. Stir well. Cover the mixture with a sheet of plastic wrap. Let stand overnight in a cool place but not in the refrigerator.

On baking day, lightly butter and flour a plain 10-inch tube pan; set aside. Preheat oven to 250° F.

Sift together the next 9 ingredients on a sheet of waxed paper; set aside.

In the large bowl of an electric mixer, cream the butter until light on moderately high speed, about 2 minutes. Add the sugar in two additions, beating for 1 minute after each amount of sugar is added. Beat in the eggs, one at a time, for 1 minute on moderate speed after each egg is added. Scrape down the sides of the bowl frequently to keep the mixture even. Blend in the marmalade.

On low speed, add the sifted flour mixture in three portions, beating just until the flour particles have been absorbed. By hand, stir in the marinated fruit and nut mixture, including all of the soaking liquid; mix thoroughly.

Turn the batter into the prepared pan. Shake the pan gently to level the top. Bake the cake on the lower-level rack of the oven for 30 minutes. Raise the oven temperature to 275° and continue baking the cake for 2 hours and 15 minutes longer. If the top begins to brown too quickly, lay a sheet of aluminum foil on the top of the cake.

Cool the cake in the pan on a rack for 10 minutes. Invert the cake onto a rack, then invert again to cool right side up.

When completely cool, store airtight in a cool place. Baste occasionally with a little cream sherry, if you like.

STUFFED APRICOT, FIG, AND PECAN FRUITCAKE

MAKES ONE 10-INCH CAKE

A moist and delectable masterpiece.

2 cups small glazed whole apricots
about ⅓ cup dark seedless raisins
3 cups dried, but moist, figs, diced
    into large pieces
3 cups yellow raisins
1 cup diced glazed orange rind
3 cups coarsely chopped pecans
½ cup cognac
2½ cups plus 2 tablespoons all-
    purpose flour (preferably
    unbleached)
1¼ teaspoons baking powder

½ teaspoon salt
1 teaspoon ground cinnamon
1 teaspoon freshly ground nutmeg
¼ teaspoon ground allspice
1 cup unsalted sweet butter, softened
    at room temperature
1 cup granulated sugar
½ cup firmly packed light brown
    sugar
2 teaspoons pure vanilla extract
¼ cup orange juice
6 jumbo eggs, at room temperature

Open up the glazed apricots and distribute the dark raisins evenly in each. Firmly press each apricot shut, then cut in half. Place the apricots in a large bowl. Add the figs, yellow raisins, orange rind, and pecans to the bowl. Pour over the cognac and mix gently; set aside.

Lightly butter and flour a plain 10-inch tube pan; set aside. Preheat oven to 275° F.

Sift together the next 6 ingredients onto a sheet of waxed paper; set aside.

In the large bowl of an electric mixer, cream the butter until light on moderately high speed, about 3 minutes. Add the granulated sugar and beat for 2 minutes; add the light brown sugar and beat for 2 minutes. Scrape down the sides of the bowl and beat for a few seconds longer.

Blend the vanilla extract and orange juice in a small bowl; pour over the fruit, and let stand.

With the mixer on moderately high speed, beat the eggs into the butter-sugar mixture, one at a time for about 1 minute after each egg is added. Scrape down the sides of the bowl after each addition to keep the mixture even.

On low speed, add the sifted flour mixture in two additions, beating until the flour particles have been absorbed. By hand, stir in the fruit-nut mixture.

Turn the batter into the prepared pan and shake the pan gently to level the top.

Bake the cake on the lower-level rack of the oven for 1 hour and 30 minutes. Raise the oven temperature to 300° and continue baking for about 1 hour and 15 minutes, or until a toothpick withdraws without any clinging particles to it. (The fruit is sticky and may adhere to the toothpick—that's all right—but the cake batter should be firm.)

Cool the cake in the pan on a rack for 10 minutes, then invert onto another rack and invert again to cool right side up.

Store the cake airtight. Moisten the cake with a few tablespoons of cognac as it ages, if you like.

NOTE: You can also stuff dates and figs with some contrasting fruit like yellow raisins, or stuff glazed peaches with bits of dried dates. Select fruit for stuffing that is small, otherwise the pieces of fruit will be too large to be suspended in the batter.

JEWELED CARROT AND FRUIT CAKE MAKES ONE 10-INCH CAKE

I bake this carrot cake year-round: the batter is laced with walnuts, currants, apricots, and figs—those are the jewels and it's not as heavy as the traditional fruitcakes. It is an easy Christmas cake to make, and a fine recipe to know, because you can have this one ready in the oven without advance planning (the fruit and nuts do not need to soak), and the finished cake does not depend on a 2-week maturing time to develop its flavor.

3 cups sifted all-purpose flour (preferably unbleached)
2 teaspoons baking soda
¼ teaspoon baking powder
½ teaspoon salt
2 teaspoons ground cinnamon
1 teaspoon freshly ground nutmeg
½ teaspoon ground allspice
¼ teaspoon ground cloves
3 extra-large eggs, at room temperature
2 cups granulated sugar
1½ cups vegetable oil
1 tablespoon pure vanilla extract

2 cups (firmly packed measurement)
   shredded carrots (shred the carrots on the large holes of a hand
   grater)
1 8-ounce tin crushed pineapple
   packed in its own juice
2 tablespoons chopped ginger preserved in syrup
1 cup chopped English walnuts
¼ cup currants
¼ cup finely chopped glazed apricots
½ cup finely chopped dried figs
3 tablespoons cognac

Lightly butter and flour a fluted 10-inch tube pan; set aside. Preheat oven to 350° F.

Resift the flour with the next 7 ingredients onto a sheet of waxed paper; set aside.

In the large bowl of an electric mixer, beat the eggs for 3 minutes on moderately high speed. Add the sugar in two additions, beating for 2 minutes after each amount is added. Add the oil in a steady stream, beating as the oil is poured in. Scrape down the sides of the bowl so that everything combines uniformly. Blend in the vanilla extract.

On low speed, add the sifted mixture in two portions, mixing just until the flour particles have been absorbed. By hand, stir in the shredded carrots and crushed pineapple with all of the packing juices.

In a large bowl, combine the remaining listed ingredients. Pour the carrot batter over the fruit-nut mixture and mix the two together.

Pour and scrape the batter into the prepared pan, shaking the pan gently to level the top. Bake the cake on the lower-level rack of the oven for about 1 hour, or until a toothpick inserted in the cake emerges clean and dry, and the cake pulls away slightly from the sides of the pan.

Cool the cake in the pan on a rack for 10 minutes, then invert it onto a second rack to cool completely.

Store the cake airtight.

GINGER, APRICOT, AND PECAN FRUITCAKE   MAKES ONE 10-INCH CAKE

Preserved ginger, available in small jars in a solution of heavy syrup, is the opulent ingredient in this cake. The ginger is mildly assertive, but you can still taste the smooth richness of the glazed apricots, which are bolstered by a small quantity of apricot liqueur.

2 cups glazed apricots, cut into ½-
   inch cubes
2 cups pecans, coarsely chopped
1 cup coarsely chopped, drained ginger
   preserved in syrup
3 cups all-purpose flour (preferably
   unbleached)
1½ teaspoons baking soda
¼ teaspoon baking powder
½ teaspoon salt

2 teaspoons ground ginger
1 teaspoon ground allspice
¾ teaspoon freshly ground nutmeg
2 cups unsalted sweet butter, softened
   at room temperature
2 cups granulated sugar
6 extra-large or jumbo eggs, separated,
   at room temperature
1 tablespoon pure vanilla extract
¼ cup apricot liqueur

Oil and line with heavy brown paper a plain 10-inch tube pan; set aside. Preheat oven to 250° F.

Combine the apricots, pecans, and ginger pieces in a large bowl; set aside.

Sift together the next 7 ingredients onto a sheet of waxed paper; set aside.

In the large bowl of an electric mixer, cream the butter until light on moderately high speed, about 3 minutes. Add the sugar in two additions, beating for 2 minutes after each portion is added. Add the egg yolks, one at a time, beating for 1 minute on moderately high speed after each yolk is dropped in. Scrape down the sides of the bowl frequently to make sure the mixture beats evenly. Blend in the vanilla extract.

Pour the apricot liqueur over the fruit; stir.

On low speed, add the sifted flour mixture to the creamed butter-sugar-eggs in three additions, beating just until the flour particles have been absorbed. By hand, stir in the fruit-liqueur blend.

Beat the egg whites until foamy in a clean bowl, add a pinch of salt, and continue beating until firm, not stiff, peaks are formed.

Beat a fifth of the egg whites into the fruitcake batter by hand, then fold in the remaining whites.

Carefully pour the mixture into the prepared pan. Gently level the top with a spatula. Bake the cake on the lower-level rack of the oven for 2 hours and 25 minutes, or until a toothpick inserted into the cake withdraws clean of batter (the fruit may turn the toothpick slightly sticky, but that is all right).

Cool the cake in the pan on a rack for 15 minutes. Invert the cake very carefully onto another rack, then invert again to cool right side up. Remove the brown paper.

Store airtight. Moisten the cake with additional tablespoons of apricot liqueur during maturing time, if you like.

PEACH, CURRANT, DATE, AND NUT FRUITCAKE

MAKES ONE 10-INCH CAKE

Plenty of spices and a load of raisins, currants, and glazed peaches make this cake special. And the combination of molasses and melted unsweetened chocolate makes the batter dark and lovely, and very moist.

2 cups golden raisins

2 cups currants

½ cup dark seedless raisins

2½ cups coarsely chopped pitted dates

¾ cup chopped English walnuts

2 cups diced glazed peaches

¼ cup brandy

3 cups plus 2 tablespoons sifted all-purpose flour (preferably un-bleached)

1¼ teaspoons baking powder

1 teaspoon salt

2 teaspoons ground cinnamon

1 teaspoon freshly ground nutmeg

½ teaspoon ground allspice

½ teaspoon ground ginger

½ teaspoon ground cloves

1 cup unsalted sweet butter, softened at room temperature

1 cup firmly packed dark brown sugar

6 jumbo eggs, at room temperature

3 tablespoons dark molasses

1 ounce (1 square) unsweetened choc-olate, melted and cooled

2 teaspoons pure vanilla extract

Oil and line with heavy brown paper the inside of a plain 10-inch tube pan; set aside. Preheat oven to 275° F.

Combine the first 6 ingredients in a large jelly-roll pan; sprinkle with brandy. Set aside.

Resift the flour with the next 7 ingredients onto a sheet of waxed paper; set aside.

In the large bowl of an electric mixer, cream the butter until light on moderately high speed, about 3 minutes. Add the dark brown sugar, and blend together with the butter for 3 minutes on moderately high speed. At moderate speed beat in the eggs, one at a time, for 1 minute after each egg is added. Scrape down the sides of the bowl frequently to keep the mixture light and even. On low speed, blend in the molasses, chocolate, and vanilla extract.

Sift ¼ cup of the sifted flour mixture over the fruit and nuts; mix well.

On low speed, add half of the sifted dry ingredients to the batter and beat just until the flour particles have been absorbed. Scrape down the sides of the bowl and beat for a few seconds. Add the remaining sifted mixture, beat to incorporate the flour; scrape down the sides of the bowl and beat again for a few seconds. By hand, stir in the floured and brandied fruit and nut mixture.

Gently pour the batter into the prepared pan. Level the top with a spatula. Bake the cake on the lower-level rack of the oven for about 2 hours and 45 minutes, or until a toothpick inserted in the cake withdraws without any uncooked batter clinging to it.

Cool the cake in the pan on a rack for 10 to 15 minutes, then invert it onto a second rack and invert again to cool right side up. When cooled, remove the brown paper.

Store the cake airtight. During the maturing time, baste the cake with additional brandy (the same kind used in the cake), if you like.

GRANDMA'S WHITE COCONUT FRUITCAKE   MAKES ONE 10-INCH CAKE

This cake was a specialty of my grandmother Lilly. The trademark of the cake is freshly grated coconut—very elegant; it's relatively light but very fine-grained. It's a cake that is as rich in tradition as it is in good taste.

2 cups golden raisins
2 cups dried, but moist, figs, coarsely
    chopped
2 cups glazed peaches, diced into
    medium-size pieces
1 cup glazed orange peel, diced into
    medium-size pieces
1 cup almonds, blanched and coarsely
    chopped (see Note, Cranberry-
    Lemon Conserve with Almonds,
    p. 104)
½ pound English walnuts, coarsely
    chopped

¼ cup orange liqueur
2½ cups cake flour
2 teaspoons baking powder
1 teaspoon salt
1 cup unsalted sweet butter, softened
    at room temperature
1½ cups granulated sugar
7 extra-large eggs, separated, at room
    temperature
2 teaspoons pure vanilla extract
1 teaspoon pure almond extract
1 cup milk, at room temperature
1 cup freshly grated coconut

Oil and line with heavy brown paper a plain 10-inch tube pan; set aside. Preheat oven to 275° F.

Combine the first 7 ingredients in a large bowl, preferably of glazed pottery; set aside.

Sift together the flour, baking powder, and salt onto a sheet of waxed paper; set aside.

In the large bowl of an electric mixer, cream the butter on moderately high speed for 3 minutes, until light. Beat in the sugar in two additions, blending for 2 minutes after each portion is added. Add the egg yolks, one at a time, for 1 minute on moderately high speed, to mix them in well. Scrape down the sides of the bowl frequently to keep the mixture even. On low speed, blend in the vanilla and almond extracts.

On low speed, add the sifted mixture in three additions, alternately with the milk in two additions, beginning and ending with the sifted mixture. Scrape down the sides of the bowl frequently. By hand, stir in the grated coconut, and the fruit-nut-liqueur blend.

Beat the egg whites in a clean bowl until frothy. Add a pinch of salt and continue beating until firm, not stiff, peaks are formed. Beat 3 big spoonfuls of the whites into the fruitcake batter, then fold in the remaining whites thoroughly but quickly.

Carefully pour and scrape the batter into the prepared pan, leveling the top with a spatula. Bake the cake on the lower-level rack of the oven for 2 hours, or until a toothpick inserted into the cake emerges without any damp cake particles clinging to it.

Cool the cake in the pan on a rack for 10 minutes, then carefully invert the cake onto another rack; invert again to cool right side up. When thoroughly cool, remove the brown paper.

Store airtight. Douse the cake with extra orange liqueur during the time it mellows, if you like.

DATE, RAISIN, AND WALNUT CAKE   MAKES ONE 10-INCH CAKE

The buttery batter is a good showcase for a generous amount of dates, raisins, and walnuts. You'll need a good 24 hours to make this cake, which is packed so full, you'll want to serve it in very thin slices.

2 cups pitted dates, cut into ½-inch pieces	½ teaspoon salt
	2 teaspoons freshly ground nutmeg
1½ cups dark seedless raisins	1½ cups unsalted sweet butter, soft-
2 cups walnuts, coarsely chopped	ened at room temperature
2 cups bourbon	1 cup firmly packed light brown sugar
5 cups sifted all-purpose flour (prefera-	6 jumbo eggs, separated, at room tem-
bly unbleached)	perature
2 teaspoons baking powder	2 teaspoons pure vanilla extract

Combine the dates, raisins, walnuts, and bourbon in a large bowl, preferably of glazed pottery. Mix well. Cover the mixture with a sheet of plastic wrap and let the ingredients marinate overnight or up to 3 days; stir from time to time.

On baking day, oil and line with brown paper a plain 10-inch tube pan; set aside. Preheat oven to 275° F.

Resift the flour with the baking powder, salt, and nutmeg; set aside.

In the large bowl of an electric mixer, cream the butter on moderately high speed until light, about 3 minutes. Add the brown sugar and beat for 4 minutes on moderately high speed. Scrape down the sides of the bowl often with a rubber spatula. Add the egg yolks, beating them in one at a time. Scrape down the sides of the bowl after each yolk is added. Blend in the vanilla extract.

On low speed, add the sifted mixture in two additions, beating slowly just to absorb all the flour particles. By hand, stir in the marinated fruit and nuts (with any of the bourbon that may have settled to the bottom of the bowl).

In a clean bowl, beat the egg whites until frothy. Add a pinch of salt and continue beating the whites until firm, not stiff, peaks are formed. Stir 3 big spoonfuls of the beaten whites into the batter to lighten it, then fold in the remaining whites.

Carefully pour and scrape the batter into the prepared pan, gently leveling the top with a rubber spatula. Bake the cake on the lower-level rack of the oven for 2 hours and 45 minutes to 3 hours, or until a toothpick inserted into the cake emerges without any damp cake particles clinging to it.

Cool the cake in the pan on a rack for 10 minutes, then invert it onto another rack; invert again to cool right side up.

When thoroughly cooled, remove the brown paper and store the cake airtight. Moisten with extra bourbon, if you like, as the cake matures.

NOTE: Paint a not-too-sweet apricot glaze on the top and sides of this cake and decorate the whole cake with big, fat perfect walnut halves and fresh green leaves.

APRICOT GLAZE

Heat 1 cup apricot jam with a tablespoon each of water and lemon juice in a small stainless-steel saucepan over low heat until the jam dissolves. Raise the heat to moderately high and bring the mixture to a boil. Strain the jam through a stainless-steel sieve to remove any lumps, then return it to a clean saucepan; heat the glaze to a simmer before brushing it on the cake.

RAISIN AND ORANGE FRUITCAKE WITH SPICES

MAKES ONE 10-INCH CAKE

In this solidly built fruitcake, apple cider marinates the raisins, currants, walnuts, and orange peel for 24 hours. This is a good change from the usual rum, cognac, or brandy that soaks into fruit mixtures—and so is the English treacle.

2 cups dark seedless raisins
2 cups golden raisins
2 cups finely diced glazed orange peel
2 cups coarsely chopped English
 walnuts
1½ cups good apple cider
3 cups sifted all-purpose flour (preferably unbleached)
1¼ teaspoons baking soda
¾ teaspoon salt
1 teaspoon ground cinnamon
1 teaspoon freshly ground nutmeg
½ teaspoon ground allspice

¼ teaspoon ground cloves
¼ teaspoon ground mace
1 cup unsalted sweet butter, softened
 at room temperature
1¼ cups firmly packed dark brown
 sugar
6 jumbo eggs, at room temperature
½ cup English treacle or dark
 molasses
1½ tablespoons finely grated orange
 rind
2 teaspoons pure vanilla extract

Combine the raisins, orange peel, walnuts, and apple cider in a large bowl, preferably of glazed pottery. Mix well. Cover the bowl with a sheet of plastic wrap and let
stand overnight or up to 48 hours. Stir a few times.

On baking day, oil and line with brown paper a plain 10-inch tube pan; set aside.
Preheat oven to 275° F.

Resift the flour with the next 7 ingredients onto a sheet of waxed paper; set aside.

In the large bowl of an electric mixer, cream the butter until light on moderately
high speed, about 3 minutes. Add the sugar in two additions, creaming on moderately
high speed for 2 minutes after each portion is added. Beat in the eggs, one at a time,
blending well after each addition. Scrape down the sides of the bowl frequently with a
rubber spatula to keep the mixture even. Blend in the treacle or molasses, orange rind,
and vanilla extract.

On low speed, add the sifted flour mixture in two additions, beating just until the
flour particles have been absorbed. Scrape down the sides of the bowl and beat for a
few seconds longer. By hand, stir in the fruit and nut mixture, with any cider that may
linger at the bottom of the bowl.

Pour and scrape the batter into the prepared pan. Bake the cake on the lower-
level rack of the oven for 2 hours and 45 minutes to 2 hours and 55 minutes, or until a
toothpick inserted in the cake emerges without any uncooked cake particles clinging
to it.

Cool the cake in the pan on a rack for 10 minutes. Invert the cake onto another
rack; invert again to cool right side up. When thoroughly cool, carefully remove the
brown paper.

Store the cake airtight; baste the cake with a little apple cider as it matures, if you
like.

A MOSTLY NUT FRUITCAKE

MAKES ONE 10-INCH CAKE

Shredded apple winds its way through the batter which is thick with four different kinds of nuts. A little apple brandy marinating the nuts overnight intensifies the whole batter.

1½ cups coarsely chopped English walnuts
1½ cups coarsely chopped pecans
1 cup coarsely chopped blanched almonds (see Note, Cranberry-Lemon Conserve with Almonds, p. 104)
1 cup coarsely chopped Brazil nuts
1 cup golden raisins
1 cup dark seedless raisins
⅓ cup apple brandy, such as Calvados
3 cups sifted all-purpose flour (preferably unbleached)

1½ teaspoons baking powder
¼ teaspoon baking soda
1 teaspoon freshly ground nutmeg
½ teaspoon salt
1½ cups unsalted sweet butter, softened at room temperature
1½ cups granulated sugar
5 jumbo eggs, at room temperature
2 teaspoons pure vanilla extract
⅓ cup finely shredded tart apple, such as Granny Smith

Combine the first 6 ingredients in a large bowl, preferably made of glazed pottery. Pour on the apple brandy and mix well. Cover the bowl with a sheet of plastic wrap and let stand overnight.

On baking day, oil and line with brown paper a plain 10-inch tube pan; set aside. Preheat oven to 325° F.

Resift the flour with the baking powder, baking soda, nutmeg, and salt onto a sheet of waxed paper; set aside.

In the large bowl of an electric mixer, cream the butter on moderately high speed until light, about 3 minutes. Add the sugar in two additions, beating on moderately high speed for 2 minutes after each portion is added. Add the eggs, one at a time, beating well after each addition. Scrape down the sides of the bowl often to keep the mixture even. Blend in the vanilla extract and apple.

On low speed, add the sifted flour mixture in two portions, beating just until the flour particles have been absorbed. By hand, beat in the fruit and nut mixture.

Pour and scrape the batter into the prepared pan, gently leveling the top with a rubber spatula. Bake the cake on the lower-level rack of the oven for 1 hour and 30 minutes to 1 hour and 40 minutes, or until a toothpick inserted into the cake emerges clean and dry.

157

Cool the cake in the pan on a rack for 10 minutes. Invert the cake onto a second rack; invert again to cool right side up. When thoroughly cooled, remove the brown paper.

Store the cake airtight. As the cake matures, baste with additional apple brandy, if you like.

DATE, RAISIN, NUT, AND LEMON FRUITCAKE   MAKES ONE 10-INCH CAKE

Dark, dense, and delicious! A cupful of black walnuts in the batter of this cake lends distinction to it. And the glazed lemon peel and freshly grated lemon rind beautifully balance the rich dates and nutmeats.

*2 cups pitted dates, cut into ½-inch
    pieces
1 cup golden raisins
1 cup dark seedless raisins
1 cup coarsely chopped pecans
1 cup coarsely chopped black walnuts
1 cup finely diced glazed lemon peel
½ cup cognac
4¾ cups sifted all-purpose flour (pref-
    erably unbleached)
1 teaspoon baking powder
1 teaspoon salt*

*1 teaspoon freshly ground nutmeg
½ teaspoon ground cinnamon
½ teaspoon ground allspice
¼ teaspoon ground cloves
2 cups unsalted sweet butter, softened
    at room temperature
2 cups granulated sugar
3 tablespoons finely grated lemon rind
2 teaspoons pure lemon extract
8 extra-large eggs, separated, at room
    temperature*

Combine the first 6 ingredients in a large glazed pottery bowl. Pour on the cognac; stir.

Lightly oil and line with brown paper a plain 10-inch tube pan; set aside. Preheat oven to 250° F.

Resift the flour with the next 6 ingredients onto a sheet of waxed paper; set aside.

In the large bowl of an electric mixer, cream the butter until light on moderately high speed, about 3 minutes. Add the sugar in two additions, beating for 2 to 3 minutes after each portion is added. Beat in the lemon rind and lemon extract.

With the mixer on moderate speed, beat in the egg yolks, one at a time, blending well after each addition. Scrape down the sides of the bowl often to ensure an even mix.

On low speed, add the sifted dry ingredients in three batches, beating just until the flour particles have been absorbed. By hand, mix in the fruits and nuts.

In a clean mixing bowl, beat the egg whites until frothy. Add a pinch of salt and continue beating until firm, not stiff, peaks are formed. Stir 3 spoonfuls of whites into the batter, then fold in the remaining whites.

Pour the batter into the prepared pan and level the top with a spatula. Bake the cake on the lower-level rack of the oven for 2 hours and 30 minutes to 2 hours and 45 minutes, or until a toothpick inserted in the cake emerges clean and dry.

Cool the cake in the pan on a rack for 10 minutes. Carefully invert the cake onto a rack; invert again onto another rack to cool right side up. When thoroughly cool, remove the brown paper.

Store airtight. During the maturing time, douse the cake with additional cognac, if you like.

Fruits in Wine

FIGS WITH RED WINE AND HONEY   MAKES 2 POUNDS

This wintery compote travels with a pleasant kind of grace to a country house where you may be a summer guest, when wild or cultivated strawberries may be tossed in at the last moment. But for the blustery months of late November and December whip up a simple lush butter cookie to go along with the winey figs and encourage the recipient to enjoy the two together!

4 cups plump, dried whole figs, stemmed	6 whole allspice berries
	6 whole cloves
3 cups dry red wine	2 3-inch cinnamon sticks
½ cup aromatic honey	1 small piece of dried Jamaican ginger

Place the figs and wine in a large nonmetallic bowl and let the figs soak for 2 hours. Drain the figs, reserving the wine; set both aside.

In a nonmetallic 8-quart casserole, preferably of enameled cast iron, pour in the wine and the remaining ingredients. Cover the pot and cook the mixture over a low heat to dissolve the sugar completely. When the sugar has dissolved, raise the heat to moderately high and boil the liquid for 4 minutes, skimming off any grayish foam that may rise to the surface.

Add the figs to the syrup, partially cover the pot, and simmer the figs until they are tender, about 30 minutes. Uncover the pot, strain out the figs and spices to a side bowl. Boil down the syrup until it has condensed slightly, 6 or 7 minutes. Pour the liquid over the figs.

Cool the figs to room temperature, then spoon the figs and liquid to clean glass jars to ½ inch of the top. Cover with lids, and refrigerate for up to 3 months.

GINGER-STUFFED PRUNES SIMMERED IN RED WINE   MAKES 4 POUNDS

These prunes are dressed up on the inside with crystallized ginger. Use them as you would the next 2 recipes and also my Pecan- and Ginger-Stuffed Apricots—that is, carefully cut in half and tucked to the side of a mound of mousse or ice cream or pudding, hot or cold.

5 cups dry red wine
2 cups sugar cubes
4 pounds (about 70) dried, but moist,
  pitted prunes
about 35 pieces of crystallized ginger,
  each piece halved

10 pieces of dried orange peel
10 pieces of dried lemon peel
1 plump and moist vanilla bean, care-
  fully split down the center with a
  sharp paring knife to expose the
  seeds, but left whole

Place the red wine and sugar cubes in a nonmetallic 8-quart casserole, preferably of enameled cast iron. Cover the pot and cook the sugar and red wine over a low heat, until the sugar cubes dissolve completely.

In the meantime, stuff each prune with a piece of crystallized ginger and press shut the prunes with your fingers; set aside.

Uncover the pot, add the orange and lemon peels and vanilla bean. Bring the liquid to a boil over a high heat, boiling for 8 minutes. Add the prunes and simmer them in the syrup for 20 minutes, or until just tender, basting them often.

Remove the prunes to a side bowl with a stainless-steel slotted spoon. Bring the syrup to a boil, boiling for 4 minutes. Pour the syrup over the prunes.

Cool everything to room temperature. Pack the prunes, with syrup and peel (discard the vanilla bean) in clean glass jars to ½ inch of the top. Cover and refrigerate for 6 months to 1 year.

WHOLE CHESTNUTS IN RUM-SPICE SYRUP
MAKES 2 POUNDS (ABOUT 7 CUPS)

Chestnuts put up in syrup may age on the cupboard shelf for up to 1 year. I put them in narrow, fairly deep jars so that I can admire their pattern, and chestnuts stacked in tall jars turn out to be more flavorful (the liquid really covers everything). Use finely diced chestnuts in ice cream and whole chestnuts over; chopped chestnuts are good in mousse and in pastry cream for a tart filling; whole chestnuts in the rum syrup are good paired with meringue desserts.

1½ cups granulated sugar	*6 whole cloves*
2 cups water	*1 cup dark rum*
2 5-inch vanilla beans	*4 cups roasted whole chestnuts (avail-*
2 3-inch cinnamon sticks	*able jarred, imported from*
6 whole allspice berries	*France)*

In a nonmetallic 8-quart casserole, preferably of enameled cast iron, place the first 6 ingredients. Cover the casserole and cook the mixture over a low heat until the sugar dissolves. Uncover the pot, bring the liquid to a boil, boiling for 4 minutes. Pour in the rum; boil for 4 minutes.

Drain the chestnuts of any excess liquid in a colander. Carefully add the chestnuts to the rum syrup and simmer them for 2 minutes.

Cool the chestnuts and spice liquid to room temperature, then pack the chestnuts with the spices in jars and seal tightly. Let the chestnuts stand on a cool pantry shelf for at least 2 weeks before giving or using.

WHOLE CHESTNUTS IN MAPLE LIQUEUR SYRUP

MAKES 2 POUNDS (ABOUT 7 CUPS)

The maple liqueur I use in this recipe comes from Canada and is produced by Rieder Distillery, Ltd.; it is available in 25 fluid ounce bottles.

1½ cups granulated sugar	*3 5-inch vanilla beans*
2 cups water	*2 pounds roasted chestnuts (available*
1 cup maple liqueur	*jarred, imported from France)*

In a nonmetallic 8-quart casserole, preferably of enameled cast iron, place the sugar and water. Cover the casserole, set it over a low heat, and cook slowly until the sugar has dissolved.

Uncover the pot, add the maple liqueur and vanilla beans and bring the mixture to a boil. Boil for 4 minutes, then simmer the mixture for 4 minutes.

Add the chestnuts to the simmering mixture and continue to cook slowly for 2 minutes.

Cool the chestnuts to room temperature, then pack in clean jars with the vanilla beans and syrup. Store the chestnuts on a cool shelf in the cabinet or pantry. Let the chestnuts stand for 2 weeks before using or giving.

One Glorious Pudding

One of the nicest tributes to Christmas puddings occurs in Dickens's *A Christmas Carol* when Bob Cratchit applauds Mrs. Cratchit's handiwork. Although steamed puddings come in a wide variety of flavors and many combinations of ingredients, they are always a rich dessert—dense, moist, and satisfying. The traditional holiday puddings of Britain, which we have adopted in this country, consist of dried fruits, fruit peels, bread crumbs, suet, eggs, flour, and sugar.

Steamed puddings are great gifts to make for several reasons. First, they are properly sumptuous to end a festive meal. And they can be made well in advance of the holidays because they keep for months in the refrigerator—the suet, sugar, and alcohol all act as preservatives. Also, they are especially welcome, because they are fairly complicated to make, and people tend not to make them for themselves—unless they are British or diehard traditionalists.

The classic mold used for steaming puddings is a heatproof pudding basin, but I use a decorative metal pudding mold that has a tight-fitting lid with a ring attached so that it is easy to remove from the simmering kettle. When the pudding has finished steaming (about 2 hours), it is unmolded and stored. On serving day, the aged pudding is replaced in the mold and resteamed to warm it up.

It's customary to place a sprig of holly atop the pudding, pour warmed brandy over it and around the base (it should be set on a heatproof dish), and set it alight. What a beautiful sight!

APRICOT HOLIDAY PUDDING   SERVES 15

This lovely steamed pudding is the best and oldest in my collection. It has a simple purity of flavor that I prefer to the customary plum pudding.

2 cups dried apricots, cut into ⅓-inch
  pieces
1 cup milk
¾ cup light cream
1¾ cups sifted all-purpose flour (preferably unbleached)
2 teaspoons baking powder
½ teaspoon baking soda
½ teaspoon salt
2 teaspoons ground cinnamon
1 teaspoon freshly ground nutmeg
½ teaspoon ground ginger

½ pound finely shredded suet (shred
  the suet while it is cold on the
  fine shredding holes of a hand-
  held stainless-steel grater)
½ cup unsalted sweet butter, softened
  at room temperature
1 cup granulated sugar
3 jumbo eggs, lightly beaten, at room
  temperature
finely grated rind of 3 lemons
1⅓ cups (lightly packed measurement) moist white bread crumbs

In a 1½-quart saucepan simmer the apricot bits in the milk and light cream, covered, for 25 minutes, or until the apricots are very tender. Drain apricots, reserving the cream mixture; set aside uncovered.

Heavily butter the inside of an 8-cup metal pudding mold and butter the inside of the lid, too; set aside. Have a large kettle half full with simmering water; make sure that you have placed a round metal cooling rack or trivet on the bottom.

Resift the flour with the next 6 ingredients onto a sheet of waxed paper; set aside.

In the large bowl of an electric mixer, cream the suet with the butter on moderate speed for 3 minutes. Blend in the sugar and beat for 3 minutes. Add the beaten eggs in two portions, beating well after each amount is added. Scrape down the sides of the bowl to keep the mixture even.

On low speed, beat in the lemon rind. Blend in the flour, in two additions, alternately with the milk-cream that has been drained from the apricots, beginning and ending with the sifted mixture. Continuing on low speed, beat in the bread crumbs. By hand, stir in the apricots.

Turn and scrape the batter into the prepared pudding mold, leveling the top with a spatula.

Place the pudding in the kettle on the rack, in the center, and pour in enough boiling water to rise two-thirds up the side of the mold. Cover the kettle and simmer the pudding for 2 hours.

While the pudding is simmering, check the level of water from time to time, and take care to keep the level about halfway up the sides of the mold.

Remove the mold to a cooling rack, let stand for 10 minutes, then uncover the pudding. Cool the pudding, then invert onto the flat base of a storage container that has been lined with plastic wrap. (I use a large cake box that has a tight-fitting lid.) Wrap the cooled pudding in plastic wrap, cover airtight, then refrigerate.

While the pudding is aging, you may sprinkle it with brandy once in a while—delicious.

To serve, carefully return the pudding to a heavily buttered mold, cover tightly with the lid, and steam for 1 hour to heat it through completely. Invert the pudding on a heatproof platter, decorate with holly, douse with warmed brandy, then set off with a match.

NOTE: When I make many puddings for gifts, I often vary the flavor by using diced dates, diced peaches, or chopped glazed orange and lemon peel in place of the apricots. The dates and glazed fruits need only be simmered in the milk and cream for 5 minutes.

Mincemeat and Nesselrode

For me, mincemeat and Nesselrode—two very different but equally delightful blends of fruits and nuts—have become synonymous with holiday feasts, and I cannot imagine a Christmas without them. I never let a fall pass without blending up both mixtures: to let the mincemeat steep properly you have to allow at least a month. It's best, then, to begin making these well in advance of the holidays.

It could be looked upon as a breach of tradition, but I strongly favor the lighter taste of mincemeat made without meat. Both Fruit and Nut Mincemeat and Orange Mincemeat are examples of my allegiance to the nonmeat combinations—they are loaded with fruit, spices, and spirits and are very good indeed. These take their cue from those English mixtures where fruit, nuts, and spices dominate.

Nesselrode, on the other hand, has no traditional connection with Christmas but is such a luxurious blend of glazed fruits, chestnuts, and cognac that it has become my own personal tradition. Mincemeat virtually stands for mince pies and tarts, but Nesselrode may find its way into custard puddings, fruitcakes, and ice cream with equal grace and style.

APPLE MINCEMEAT WITH ALMONDS AND DATES

MAKES ABOUT 13 CUPS

This is a fresh, no-cook, "vegetarian" mincemeat that is particularly light. It is best used in filling a 2-inch deep, 9-inch tart shell made with a rich, firm pastry dough. Top it off with a circle of dough.

A quart quantity of mincemeat makes the perfect size gift, and glass preserving jars with rubber gaskets and wire-hinged lids show off this mincemeat best. Before the jars are closed, you could dip circles of brown paper cut to fit the top of the jar in a little apple brandy and place them directly on top of the mincemeat. Then seal the jars. This adds an extra grace note of flavor.

4 pounds tart cooking apples, peeled, cored, coarsely chopped, and tossed in ¼ cup freshly squeezed lemon juice
1½ cups dark seedless raisins
1½ cups currants
½ cup golden raisins
2½ cups halved seedless green grapes
¾ cup chopped whole dates
½ cup slivered blanched almonds (see Note, Cranberry-Lemon Conserve with Almonds, p. 104)

2 tablespoons finely grated lemon rind
2 cups firmly packed light brown sugar
1¾ cups granulated sugar
2½ teaspoons ground cinnamon
1½ teaspoons freshly ground nutmeg
1 teaspoon ground allspice
½ teaspoon ground cloves
10 tablespoons (½ cup plus 2 tablespoons) melted and cooled unsalted sweet butter
¾ cup apple brandy, such as Calvados

In a very large round bowl, preferably of glazed stoneware, stir together the first 10 ingredients. Let stand for ½ hour, stirring frequently.

Blend in the spices. Pour on the butter and brandy and spoon through the liquid. Let the mincemeat stand at room temperature, loosely covered with a sheet of plastic wrap, until the sugar has completely dissolved (this will take about half a day). Stir often.

Parcel out the mincemeat into jars. Cover the jars and refrigerate the mincemeat for at least 5 days before using or giving as gifts. The mincemeat will keep in the refrigerator for up to 1 month.

PEAR MINCEMEAT   MAKES ABOUT 17 CUPS

The luxurious richness of this mincemeat makes it ideal as a filling for small turnovers or little double crust tarts. These sweet pastry gems are delicious warm with mulled wine and cider and they would look charming nestled among other baked things as a gift for the holidays.

5 pounds ripe but firm pears, peeled,
   cored, and coarsely chopped
4 cups (2 pounds) golden raisins
4 cups (2 pounds) currants
2 cups (1 pound) pitted dates, diced
2 cups (1 pound) glazed lemon peel,
   diced
2 cups (1 pound) English walnuts,
   coarsely chopped

2 pounds suet, sent through the finest
   blade of a meat grinder
5 cups firmly packed light brown sugar
1 cup lemon marmalade
2 teaspoons ground cinnamon
2 teaspoons ground allspice
1 teaspoon freshly ground nutmeg
½ teaspoon ground cloves
3 cups brandy

In a large glazed pottery or glass bowl, combine the first 7 ingredients. Crumble on the brown sugar and stir it into the fruit.

Blend in the lemon marmalade and spices. Pour on the brandy and stir everything together very well.

Let the mincemeat stand at room temperature, lightly covered with a sheet of plastic wrap, for about half a day, so that the sugar melts down completely. Stir up the mincemeat now and again.

When the sugar has dissolved, pack the mincemeat into jars, cover, and refrigerate. Store the mincemeat in the refrigerator for up to 1 month; the mincemeat should "age" for a week in the refrigerator before using or giving.

FRUIT AND NUT MINCEMEAT
MAKES ABOUT 4½ QUARTS

Spoon this mincemeat and the Orange Mincemeat in the following recipe into clear, heavy preserving jars that close with a good seal. A cap of fabric stretched over the lid and secured with a silky cord turns each jar into a charming gift.

4 cups dried, but moist, currants
2 cups golden raisins
2 cups dark seeded raisins
2 cups walnuts, chopped
2 cups almonds, blanched (see Note,
   Cranberry-Lemon Conserve with
   Almonds, p. 104)
2 pounds tart apples, peeled, cored,
   roughly chopped, and tossed in
   the juice of 1 lemon (about 4
   cups sliced and lightly packed)

1¾ cups glazed orange peel, coarsely
   chopped
2 pounds dark brown sugar
1 tablespoon ground cinnamon
2 teaspoons ground allspice
2 teaspoons freshly ground nutmeg
2 teaspoons ground ginger
2 cups brandy or rum
finely grated rind of 3 lemons
1 pound finely grated beef suet

In a large bowl, preferably of glazed pottery, combine the first 7 ingredients. Sprinkle on the brown sugar and spices, and stir everything together. Pour in the rum or brandy, sprinkle on the lemon rind and suet, and mix it all together using your hands (they are the best set of tools you'll find for this final blending).

Cover the bowl loosely with a sheet of plastic wrap and let stand at room temperature for 24 hours.

Pack the mincemeat in jars to ⅛ inch of the top, then cover with the lids. Refrigerate the mincemeat for up to 6 months.

ORANGE MINCEMEAT　　　　　　　MAKES ABOUT 3 QUARTS

12 oranges, washed well	*¼ cup firmly packed light brown*
3 cups golden raisins	*　sugar*
2 cups currants	*1 cup orange liqueur, such as Coin-*
1 cup diced glazed orange peel	*　treau or Grand Marnier*
1 cup diced glazed lemon peel	*1 tablespoon ground cinnamon*
1½ cups coarsely chopped walnuts	*1 teaspoon freshly ground nutmeg*
2 cups shredded beef suet	*½ teaspoon ground cloves*
2¾ cups granulated sugar	

With a swivel-bladed peeler, remove the outer peel (with none of the white pith) from 6 oranges. Entirely peel all 12 oranges with a very sharp fruit knife. Chop the orange flesh coarsely. Finely chop the peel from the 6 oranges, using either a large chopping knife or a food processor fitted with a steel blade.

Place the orange flesh and chopped peel in a large bowl, preferably of glazed pottery. Stir in the next 8 ingredients and mix well. Let stand 20 minutes.

Pour on the orange liqueur, and sprinkle the fruit with the spices. Mix well again.

Cover the bowl with a sheet of plastic wrap and let stand at room temperature overnight, or up to 36 hours.

Parcel out the mincemeat into jars, filling them up to ⅛ inch of the top. Cover and refrigerate for up to 6 months.

NESSELRODE　　　　　　　　MAKES ABOUT 6 CUPS

Traditional Nesselrode combines Maraschino cherries with citron, ginger, and chestnuts and enough rum to bathe the ingredients. I have substituted glazed peaches and apricots for the cherries, and use a little of both orange and lemon peel. You'll find this recipe easy to make and delicious blended into ice cream, bread pudding, mousse, and fruitcake. It makes a delightful gift for cook friends who love to prepare desserts.

1 cup diced glazed peaches
1 cup diced glazed apricots
1 cup crystallized ginger
1 cup diced glazed orange peel

½ cup diced glazed lemon peel
1½ cups diced chestnuts in syrup
½ cup dark rum
¼ cup cognac

Combine all but the last 2 ingredients in a large nonmetallic bowl, preferably of glazed pottery. Pour in the rum and cognac, and mix well.

Let the Nesselrode stand for 2 hours at room temperature, lightly covered with a sheet of plastic wrap. Stir several times during the 2 hours.

Spoon the Nesselrode into clean glass jars to ¼ inch of the top. If you like, moisten brown paper circles (cut to fit the insides of the jars) with a little extra rum or brandy, place them directly on top of the Nesselrode, and cover the jars with lids.

Refrigerate the jars until you are ready to give them away, but do not use the mixture for at least 2 days after making up a batch.

Hard Sauces and Sweet Spreads

Pudding and fruitcake just isn't pudding and fruitcake without a bit of hard sauce nearby. A little covered pot of the stuff should be tucked into the cake box as part of the presentation for either dessert.

I pack the sauce into earthenware containers that have hinged lids and press a round of brown paper that has been lightly soaked in brandy right on top of the sauce before fastening the lid. This further perfumes the sauce as it mellows in the refrigerator.

SPICED HARD SAUCE

MAKES 1⅓ CUPS

12 tablespoons (½ cup plus 4 tablespoons) unsalted sweet butter, softened at room temperature
2 cups sifted confectioners' sugar, resifted with ¼ teaspoon cinnamon, ¼ teaspoon ground allspice, ¼ teaspoon freshly ground nutmeg

2 tablespoons brandy or dark rum
2 teaspoons pure vanilla extract

In the large bowl of an electric mixer, cream the butter until light on moderately high speed. On low speed, beat in the sifted sugar-and-spices in three portions, beating for about a minute after each amount of sugar has been added. Beat in the brandy or rum and vanilla in small dribbles.

Pack the hard sauce into containers and level the tops. Cover and refrigerate for up to 2 weeks.

VANILLA HARD SAUCE WITH APPLE BRANDY   MAKES ABOUT 1⅓ CUPS

12 tablespoons (½ cup plus 3 tablespoons) unsalted sweet butter,
softened at room temperature
2 cups sifted confectioners' sugar

2 tablespoons apple brandy, such as
Calvados
2 teaspoons pure vanilla extract

In the large bowl of an electric mixer, cream the butter until light on moderately high speed, about 3 minutes. On low speed, beat in the sugar in three portions, blending thoroughly before adding each next batch of sugar. Slowly beat in the apple brandy and vanilla extract. Beat for 1 minute on high speed.

Pack the hard sauce into containers, cover, and refrigerate for up to 2 weeks.

LEMON CREAM   MAKES ABOUT 3½ CUPS

Lemon and lime creams are smooth and rich, to be enjoyed as spreads for warm breakfast or teatime breads, in between cake layers, or underneath fresh fruit in a tart. These are big-batch cream recipes, which I make in a very large professional double boiler. But you may wish to halve the recipe.

2 cups granulated sugar
¼ teaspoon salt
1 cup freshly squeezed lemon juice
(about 6 large lemons)
2 tablespoons finely grated lemon rind

6 large eggs, at room temperature
6 large egg yolks, at room temperature
1 cup unsalted sweet butter, cut up
into chunks

In the top saucepan of a double boiler, whisk together the sugar, salt, lemon juice, and rind. Beat in the eggs, one at a time; beat in the egg yolks, one at a time.

Place the saucepan over the bottom saucepan, which has been filled with gently simmering water. Cook and whisk over very low heat for 5 minutes.

Begin adding the butter in chunks, letting each bit melt down into the mixture before adding the next, whisking all the while. After all of the butter has been added, continue to cook the mixture until it has thickened up, keeping the heat low and constant, lest the eggs scramble the cream.

When thickened, after 15 to 20 minutes, pour the cream into clean, pretty jars to ¼ inch of the top. Close the jars and store the cream in the refrigerator for up to 1 month.

VARIATION: To make Lime Cream, substitute 1 cup lime juice for the lemon juice. I find grated lime rind too bitter to include in the cream, so I omit the rind from the recipe. Makes about 3 cups.

Sweetmeats

These are old-fashioned sweets, the kind people think of when they remember holidays past. And they are best produced in large amounts and consumed in moderate quantities.

People love to get small packets of these—plain glass canisters are nicest. You might want to use three graduated ones and use the largest for the pralines. Or you can use jars for the peel and nuts and put the pralines in a cookie tin or Shaker box. Decorate the containers with calico covers and ribbons and set them in a splendid garden basket for relatives and friends.

CANDIED GRAPEFRUIT PEEL   MAKES ABOUT 6 DOZEN PIECES

Candied grapefruit peel is such a great luxury to have at hand: I love thin pieces of it after dinner as a wonderful kind of sweetmeat. First I squeeze the grapefruit and make Grapefruit Syrup (see the recipe below) to be used in fruit salads and thirst-quenching drinks. Then I peel back all of the remaining flesh and remove the harsh-tasting pith from the grapefruit sections. After the grapefruit strips are boiling water–bathed and simmered in syrup, I roll them in finely crushed sugar crystals. I use the English white crystals made by Tate and Lyle and crush a mound of it with a rolling pin. Crystals are preferable to plain granulated sugar.

6 very large thick-skinned grapefruit   *about ⅓ pound white sugar crystals,*
3 cups superfine sugar   *crushed*

Quarter the grapefruit and remove the peel (if you are making Grapefruit Syrup, juice the grapefruit first). With a sharp serrated fruit knife, carefully cut away the thick white pith from the underside of the grapefruit peel. Cut the sections of grapefruit into even-size narrow strips, about ⅓ inch thick and 2½ inches long.

Place the peel in a large nonmetallic pot of 10- or 12-quart capacity. Cover the peel with plenty of cold water. Bring to a boil, boil for 3 minutes, and drain. Repeat the process four more times, covering the peel with water, boiling, draining. Dump the peel into a colander.

Rinse out the pot. Pour in the superfine sugar, cover the pot, and place it on a low heat until the sugar melts down completely. Uncover the pot and add the peel. Cook the peel slowly until tender and transparent, and glazed all over, stirring the peel from time to time. The glazing process takes from 50 minutes to 1 hour and 20 minutes for the peel to become tender and yielding.

With tongs, remove the peel from the syrup to lightly oiled cooling racks. Let stand for about 1 hour to cool down completely, then roll the peel in crushed sugar crystals. Store the peel in a tin on the shelf of a cool pantry.

VARIATION: To make Candied Orange Peel, substitute 12 oranges, sectioned and peeled, for the grapefruit.

GRAPEFRUIT SYRUP   MAKES 3½ CUPS

This is a superbly refreshing syrup; it's splendid sloshed over wedges of winter fruit such as grapefruit, oranges, or grapes. Fruit syrups such as this one also make a fine base for homemade sorbet (pour it in a little puddle), or a light citrus ice milk.

6 cups grapefruit puree (6 very large   *2 cups granulated sugar*
  grapefruit, sectioned, seeded, and   *¼ cup black currant liqueur (crème de*
  pureed in a blender, or flesh   *cassis)*
  finely squeezed)

Combine the grapefruit puree and granulated sugar in a 4-quart nonmetallic saucepan. Cover the pot and cook slowly over a low heat; cook until the sugar has dissolved completely, about 15 minutes. Uncover the pot, pour in the liqueur, and bring the liquid to the boil. Lower the heat and simmer for 10 minutes.

Pour the syrup through a fine-meshed stainless-steel sieve placed over a large bowl. Press down on the solids to extract every last drop of syrup.

Cool the syrup to room temperature, then decant it into pretty 1-cup bottles, cap, and refrigerate for up to 1 year.

PECAN PRALINES

MAKES ABOUT 2 DOZEN

Between turns at the electric mixer and cookie-baking my way through the first part of December, I make these pralines, a dashing candy. Crack open the pecans just before assembling the remaining ingredients. And you will need a trusty candy thermometer with clear, large, and readable numbers for the recipe to work smoothly. I like to let the pralines "ripen" for 2 days before eating or giving so that the sweetness and nuttiness have a chance to grow in flavor.

2 cups firmly packed light brown sugar
2 cups granulated sugar
1 cup light cream
¼ cup unsalted sweet butter, softened
at room temperature

pinch of salt
3 cups fresh pecan halves, cut into
rough ½-inch pieces

Line 2 cookie sheets with parchment paper; set aside.

Place the sugars and light cream in a heavy 6-quart casserole, preferably of enameled cast iron. Cover and place over a low heat to dissolve the sugar. When the sugar has dissolved completely, uncover the pot, hook on the candy thermometer so it drops into the liquid, and raise the heat to moderately high. Bring the liquid to a boil, and boil to 228° F. exactly.

Immediately add the butter by tablespoonfuls, then the salt and pecans; stir briefly, and continue cooking to 236°.

When the mixture reaches 236°, remove the saucepan from the heat, and cool the mixture to 200°. Stir 1 minute with a sturdy wooden spoon until thick and glossy.

From an oiled tablespoon immediately drop heaping mounds of the candy mixture 4 inches apart onto the cookie sheets.

Cool the praline patties to room temperature, then peel them off the paper. Store the pralines in a tin.

CINNAMONED AND SUGARED PECANS

MAKES 3 CUPS

Pecans tossed in cinnamon and coated in a light syrup are very welcome as a partner to the Candied Grapefruit Peel.

1¾ cups granulated sugar
½ cup light corn syrup
½ cup plus 2 tablespoons water
3 cups fresh pecan halves

2 teaspoons ground cinnamon
¼ teaspoon salt
2 teaspoons pure vanilla extract

Place the sugar, corn syrup, and water in a heavy 6-quart saucepan. Cover the pot and place it over a low heat to dissolve the sugar, about 15 minutes

While the sugar is melting down, toss the pecan halves with the cinnamon and salt in a large bowl; set aside.

Uncover the pot, raise the heat to moderately high, attach a candy thermometer so it drops into the liquid, and boil the liquid until it reaches 237° F. Immediately remove the hot syrup from the heat and quickly stir in the vanilla extract and nuts.

Without haste, pour the sugar-syruped nuts onto a lightly oiled surface (see Note). With 2 oiled forks, separate out the nuts so that they no longer cling together. When the nuts have cooled down to room temperature, break off any large clumps of nuts with your fingers.

Store the nuts in an airtight tin.

NOTE: Ideally, you should have a smooth cold slab of marble to pour the hot nuts on after they are glazed in the syrup; a well-oiled jelly-roll pan with a release surface such as Teflon works as well.

6

Wintertime Treats

BUTTER CAKES AND TEA LOAVES

LEMON–POPPY-SEED BUTTER CAKE
SOUR CREAM BUTTER CAKE
CREAM CHEESE AND DATE BUTTER CAKE
DATE AND LEMON BUTTER CAKE
COCONUT BUTTER CAKE
CHOCOLATE BUTTER CAKE
PECAN-CARROT BUTTER CAKE
PECAN BUTTER CAKE
CARROT-COCONUT LOAF
BANANA-COCONUT BREAD
DATE LOAF
SWEET POTATO BREAD
RHUBARB BREAD
PARMESAN CHEESE SHORTBREAD

DRIED WINTER FRUIT MEDLEYS

PICKLED FIGS
APRICOTS IN APRICOT LIQUEUR

FIGS WITH GINGER AND VANILLA
PRUNE-STUFFED PEACHES
PECAN- AND GINGER-STUFFED APRICOTS
DRIED PEACH, APRICOT, AND PEAR COMPOTE

GRANOLA

CINNAMON-COCONUT GRANOLA
GRANOLA WITH DRIED FRUIT
GRANOLA SAUCERS

A RUSTIC PÂTÉ

Retreating to the stove is the best defense against the winter cold, and many people that I know do more baking in January and February than they do during the holiday season. So while some may take to the ski slopes, I like to set up shop near the oven, at home, cozy and warm. It is then that I like to bake butter cakes and tea loaves for giving. Old-fashioned, wholesome and full of flavor, these cakes and loaves are good, honest sweets that friends always love to receive. Because these bakery gems have a country taste and look to them, their presentation should be relaxed and earthy looking. To package them I make use of warm winter spices, especially beribboned piles of cinnamon sticks, and I often set them in substantial rush or reed baskets.

During winter (and the holidays that open the season) shops usually offer the best selection of dried fruit, which is easy to stock in the pantry for making last-minute sweet and savory fruit medleys. Figs, prunes, and apricots, all plump and moist, are given a spicy bath in a sugar syrup and look inviting when packed in the syrup in clear glass jars. On a cold, gray February or March day these add a bright note and make cheering gifts.

I like to use heavy earthenware casseroles or yellowware bowls for holding winter gifts of cookies or big batches of granola. A painted pine candle box or wood-rimmed horsehair sieve is also a charming way to hold small individual loaves of tea bread, and not-too-deep lacquered trays with shiny black finishes make cakes look glamorous. Preserved fruit is made for old-time canning jars, which can be decorated with the festive baubles and edible garnishes described in chapter 2, pp. 17–20. Often I decorate winter food presents with appealing fruits of the season—rosy-cheeked apples, slender or tubby pears, lemons, limes, oranges or tangerines, and very small persimmons. Tea loaves get settled in a lattice woven basket on a bed of juniper, cedar, or Spanish moss and whatever fruit that strikes my fancy—perhaps lady apples or glossy lemons—surround the loaf. And when I fill a canister with a jar of any of the dried fruit medleys, I circle the top of the jar with a wreath of small fruits (kumquats with their leaves are handsome) and that automatically holds the jar in place.

As for the tea loaves, the combinations of ingredients are free and easy, and their shelf life spans at least three to four days. Wrap the breads in clear cellophane and tie them up with a length of brightly colored ribbon. Lipped trays, both old and new, lined with patchwork fabric or a bottom padding of cedar, juniper, or Spanish moss are good supports for presenting home-baked loaves.

These loaves may be baked in the standard loaf pan, but try miniature loaf pans for a dramatic effect when you heap several different breads together.

Butter Cakes and Tea Loaves

Brighten anyone's day by giving them one of the butter cakes and you'll see smiles of gratitude even in the gloomiest weather. The flavor of each loaf has a distinct personality and an uncontrived appeal. And while they are especially well suited for wintertime giving, there is no law that says you can't delight a host or hostess with one of these in spring, summer, or autumn too.

Several friends of mine, among whom are a couple of caterers, regularly make and present the Chocolate Butter Cake as a gift when they are invited for lunch, dinner, or tea. Once, within a two-week period, I was served four slices of Chocolate Butter Cake on four different occasions—a period I think of as the Invasion of the Chocolate Butter Cakes.

To pack these cakes, I like to stash them in a box and wrap them in shiny, brightly colored wrappings.

LEMON–POPPY-SEED BUTTER CAKE   MAKES ONE 10-INCH CAKE

Light and lemony, plain but luscious, here is a butter cake of great potential. Match slices of this cake with a refreshing homemade lemon ice cream, poached pear slices, or chunks of fresh peaches marinated in a little brandy with slivers of lemon rind.

2¾ cups sifted all-purpose flour (pref-
    erably unbleached)
2¼ teaspoons baking powder
1 teaspoon baking soda
½ teaspoon salt
1 cup unsalted sweet butter, softened
    at room temperature
1¾ cups granulated sugar

4 jumbo eggs, separated, at room tem-
    perature
finely grated rind of 3 lemons
2 teaspoons pure vanilla extract
1 cup buttermilk, at room temperature
⅓ cup poppy seed
confectioners' sugar

Lightly butter and flour a fluted 10-inch tube pan; set aside. Preheat oven to 350° F.

Resift the flour with the baking powder, baking soda, and salt onto a sheet of waxed paper; set aside.

In the large bowl of an electric mixer, cream the butter until light on moderately high speed, about 3 minutes. Add the sugar in two additions, beating for 2 minutes after each addition. Add the egg yolks, one at a time, beating on high speed for about 1 minute after each yolk is added. Scrape down the sides of the bowl with a rubber spatula to ensure an even mixture. Beat in the lemon rind and vanilla extract.

On low speed, beat in the flour mixture in three additions and buttermilk in two additions, beginning and ending with the dry ingredients. Stir in the poppy seed.

In a separate, clean bowl, beat the egg whites until they are foamy. Add a pinch of salt and continue to beat them until firm, not stiff, peaks are formed. Vigorously stir 3 big spoonfuls of the egg whites into the poppy-seed cake batter, then fold in the remaining whites to lighten up the batter. Fold in the whites quickly, but carefully.

Pour and scrape the batter into the prepared pan, and shake the pan briskly a few times to level the top. Bake the cake on the lower-level rack of the oven for 55 minutes, or until a toothpick emerges clean and dry.

Cool the cake in the pan for 10 minutes, then turn it out of the pan—carefully—onto a metal cooling rack to cool completely.

Store the cake airtight. At serving time, dust the cake with confectioners' sugar lightly sifted over the top.

SOUR CREAM BUTTER CAKE   MAKES ONE 9-INCH CAKE

With its splendid moist texture and its swirl of cinnamon and walnuts, this is a fine homemade alternative to gooey-sweet morning pastries. It will dignify even the most informal of breakfast trays—or tea trays for that matter.

2½ cups unsifted all-purpose flour
(preferably unbleached)
2½ teaspoons baking powder
½ teaspoon baking soda
½ teaspoon salt
1 cup sour cream, at room temperature
2 teaspoons pure vanilla extract

1 cup unsalted sweet butter, softened
at room temperature
1¾ cups granulated sugar
3 extra-large eggs, at room temperature
½ cup finely chopped walnuts
1½ teaspoons ground cinnamon
confectioners' sugar

Lightly butter and flour a plain 9-inch tube pan; set aside. Preheat oven to 325° F.

Sift together the flour, baking powder, baking soda, and salt onto a sheet of waxed paper; set aside.

In a small bowl, combine the sour cream and vanilla.

Beat the butter in the large bowl of an electric mixer until it is light and fluffy; do this on moderately high speed for about 3 minutes. Add 1½ cups of the sugar in two additions, beating for 2 minutes after each amount of sugar is added. Beat in the eggs, one at a time, blending well after each addition. When all of the eggs have been added, beat the mixture on high speed for 1 minute. Scrape down the sides of the bowl to ensure an even mix.

On low speed, blend in half of the flour mixture, then all of the sour cream–vanilla mixture, and finish with the remaining flour mixture.

Combine the remaining ¼ cup sugar, walnuts, and cinnamon in a small bowl.

Pour half of the cake batter into the prepared pan. Scatter half of the walnut mixture over it. Pour in the remaining batter, shake the pan slightly to level the top, then sprinkle on the rest of the walnut mixture.

Bake the cake on the lower-level rack of the oven for about 55 minutes, or until a toothpick inserted into the cake emerges clean and dry.

Cool the cake in the pan on a wire rack for 10 minutes, invert onto another rack, then invert again to cool right side up.

Store the cake airtight. Sift confectioners' sugar over the top before serving.

CREAM CHEESE AND DATE BUTTER CAKE   MAKES ONE 9-INCH CAKE

In the kingdom of butter cakes, the next two cakes are doubly rich—the first gets a full half pound of cream cheese and butter; the second is enriched with butter and buttermilk. Use dates that are completely plump and chubby looking. For both recipes, the sweet, grand Medjool date is worth seeking out, although the Deglet Noor variety also works. Dates keep well under refrigeration, but they should be wrapped tightly because they easily draw in the smells of other food.

2½ cups sifted cake flour
2 teaspoons baking powder
½ teaspoon salt
1 cup finely chopped dates
1 cup unsalted sweet butter, softened
    at room temperature
8 ounces cream cheese, at room tem-
    perature

1½ cups granulated sugar
4 jumbo eggs, at room temperature
2 teaspoons pure vanilla extract
½ cup chopped walnuts
confectioners' sugar

Lightly butter and flour a fluted 9-inch tube pan; set aside. Preheat oven to 325° F.

Sift together the flour, baking powder, and salt onto a sheet of waxed paper; set aside.

Place the dates in a bowl and toss them with 1 tablespoon of the sifted flour mixture.

Beat the butter in the large bowl of an electric mixer on moderately high speed for 1 minute. Add the cream cheese and continue beating until both are light and very fluffy, about 3 minutes. Add the sugar in three additions, beating on moderately high speed for 1 minute after each addition. Continue beating the mixture on medium speed for a full 4 minutes. Underbeating at this point will cause the cake to be heavy textured.

Add the eggs, one at a time, beating for about 1 minute after each egg is added. Scrape down the sides of the bowl often. Blend in the vanilla extract. On low speed, beat in the sifted mixture in two additions, just until the flour particles have been absorbed; the mixture will be as smooth as buttercream. By hand, stir in the floured dates and walnuts.

Turn and scrape the batter into the prepared pan. Shake the pan gently to level the top. Bake the cake on the lower-level rack of the oven for about 1 hour and 15 minutes, or until a toothpick inserted in the cake emerges clean and dry.

Cool the cake in the pan on a wire rack for 10 minutes, then invert it onto a second rack to cool completely.

Store the cake airtight. Sift confectioners' sugar over the top before serving.

DATE AND LEMON BUTTER CAKE MAKES ONE 10-INCH CAKE

Dotted with bits of chopped date and grated lemon peel, this spicy cake has a texture somewhere between compact and airy. Because it keeps well, it makes an ideal gift.

4 cups sifted all-purpose flour (preferably unbleached)
1 teaspoon baking soda
1 teaspoon baking powder
½ teaspoon salt
1 teaspoon ground cinnamon
1 teaspoon freshly ground nutmeg
1 cup finely chopped dates

1 cup unsalted sweet butter, softened
at room temperature
2 cups granulated sugar
4 jumbo eggs, at room temperature
2 teaspoons pure vanilla extract
1½ cups pure, rich buttermilk, at
room temperature
finely grated rind of 3 lemons
confectioners' sugar

Lightly butter and flour a plain 10-inch tube pan; set aside. Preheat oven to 325° F.

Sift together the first 6 ingredients onto a sheet of waxed paper; set aside.

Place the dates in a bowl and toss them with 1 tablespoon of the sifted mixture.

Beat the butter in the large bowl of an electric mixer on moderately high speed for 1 minute. Add the sugar in two additions, beating for 1 minute after each portion is added. Scrape down the sides of the bowl. Beat in the eggs, one at a time, for 1 minute on moderate speed after each egg is added. Blend in the vanilla extract.

On low speed, beat in the sifted mixture in three additions alternately with the buttermilk in two additions, beginning and ending with the sifted mixture. Scrape down the sides of the bowl often. By hand, stir in the lemon rind and dates.

Turn and scrape the batter into the prepared pan. Bake the cake on the lower-level rack of the oven for 1 hour and 20 minutes to 1 hour and 30 minutes, or until a toothpick inserted in the cake emerges clean and dry.

Cool the cake in the pan on a wire rack for 10 minutes, then invert it out onto a second rack. Invert the cake again and cool it right side up. When thoroughly cooled, store airtight.

Sift confectioners' sugar on top of the cake just before serving or giving.

COCONUT BUTTER CAKE

MAKES ONE 10-INCH CAKE

This cake recipe is a cherished one that I have taken out of my paternal grandmother's black notebook of handwritten recipes. Usually, Grandma Lilly would turn the batter for this cake into a large metal baking pan in the shape of a lamb, decorate the cake, and serve it forth on my birthday.

Grandma used fresh coconut and so do I. But I bake the cake in a big fluted tube pan; the lamb mold remains only a particularly beautiful memory.

3 cups sifted cake flour
2½ teaspoons baking powder
½ teaspoon salt
1 cup unsalted sweet butter, softened
    at room temperature
1 1-pound box confectioners' sugar,
    sifted

4 jumbo eggs, separated, at room tem-
    perature
1 cup fresh coconut milk (see Note)
2 teaspoons pure vanilla extract
1¼ cups freshly grated coconut

Lightly butter and flour a fluted 10-inch tube pan; set aside. Preheat oven to 350° F.

Resift the cake flour, baking powder, and salt onto a sheet of waxed paper; set aside.

Beat the butter in a large bowl of an electric mixer on moderately high speed for 3 minutes, or until light and fluffy. Add the sugar in three additions, beating slowly at first to incorporate it into the butter, then on high speed for 1 minute after each addition. Scrape down the sides of the bowl often to ensure an even mix. Add the egg yolks, one at a time, beating for about 1 minute after each one is added.

On low speed, beat in the sifted mixture in three additions and the coconut milk in two, beginning and ending with the sifted mixture. Blend in the vanilla extract. By hand, stir in the grated coconut.

Beat the egg whites in a clean bowl until they are foamy. Add a pinch of salt and continue beating until firm, not stiff, peaks are formed. Quickly stir several spoonfuls of the beaten whites into the coconut batter to lighten it up, then fold in the remaining whites, carefully but thoroughly.

Pour and scrape the batter gently into the prepared pan. Bake the cake on the lower-level rack of the oven for about 55 minutes, or until a toothpick inserted into the cake emerges clean and dry.

Let the cake cool in the pan on a wire rack for 10 minutes. Invert the cake onto another cooling rack to cool completely.

Store airtight. Sift confectioners' sugar over the top of the cake just before serving.

NOTE: To make fresh coconut milk, Grandma always took aside about 1½ cups of the freshly grated nut, put it in a bowl, and poured over about 1⅓ cups boiling water. After 45 minutes, she squeezed the coconut meat with her hands to extract every last drop of liquid, then measured out 1 cup coconut milk for this recipe.

CHOCOLATE BUTTER CAKE

MAKES ONE 10-INCH CAKE

Unsweetened cocoa powder gives this cake an excellent depth of flavor. It is of utmost importance, as any chocolate purist will tell you, to use Dutch-process cocoa: this means that the cocoa has been processed with alkalai to neutralize the acids, rendering it quite dark, full flavored, and rich.

3 cups sifted all-purpose flour (prefera-
bly unbleached)
1 cup unsifted Dutch-process cocoa
(stir the cocoa with a fork to aer-
ate it, then lightly spoon it into a
measuring cup)
3 teaspoons baking powder
½ teaspoon salt
1 cup unsalted sweet butter, softened
at room temperature

3 cups granulated sugar
3 jumbo eggs, at room temperature
1½ cups milk and ¼ cup light cream,
blended together, at room tem-
perature
1 tablespoon pure vanilla extract
confectioners' sugar (optional)

Lightly butter and flour a plain 10-inch tube pan (not fluted); set aside. Preheat over to 325° F.

Resift the flour with the cocoa, baking powder, and salt onto a sheet of waxed paper, set aside.

Beat the butter until it is light and fluffy in the large bowl of an electric mixer using moderately high speed, about 2 minutes. Add the sugar in three additions, beating for 1 minute after each portion is added. Beat on high speed for 1 minute. Beat in the eggs, one at a time, beating for 1 minute after each one is added. Scrape down the sides of the bowl to make sure that the mixture is light and even. Beat for 30 seconds.

On low speed, beat in the sifted mixture in three additions and the milk-cream combination in two additions, beginning and ending with the sifted ingredients. Slowly, beat in the vanilla extract.

Turn and scrape the batter into the prepared pan. Bake the cake on the lower-level rack of the oven for about 1 hour and 25 minutes, or until a toothpick inserted in the cake emerges clean and dry.

Cool the cake in the pan on a wire rack for 10 minutes. Turn out of the pan onto a wire rack and invert onto another rack to cool right side up.

Store the cake airtight. If you like, confectioners' sugar may be sifted over the top of the cake before serving.

PECAN-CARROT BUTTER CAKE

MAKES ONE 10-INCH CAKE

The pecan (*Carya illinoensis*) was popular as far back as colonial times, when George Washington and Thomas Jefferson planted seeds for trees at Mount Vernon and Monticello. Since then, many varieties have been cultivated in Texas, Georgia, Oklahoma, Louisiana, and Alabama.

Freshly shelled pecans have smooth ribbed tops. When chewed, the meat is oily and not at all dry. I always chop pecans (and every other kind of nut) by hand, using a very long chef's knife. Dump the pecans in a quantity of no more than 2 cups onto a large chopping board. Place the knife in the middle of the pecan heap and hold down the top of the knife with 3 fingers. Grasp the handle firmly and swing the knife from side to side, cutting the nuts as you go. Keep chopping, sweeping the nuts into a rough pile, chopping over and again, until you have cut the pieces into the desired size. Pecans do not arrive out of the blender or food processor in good condition; I find that the electric action releases the essential oils of the nutmeat while haphazardly chopping them.

2¾ cups sifted all-purpose flour (preferably unbleached)
2 teaspoons baking powder
1 teaspoon baking soda
2 teaspoons ground cinnamon
½ teaspoon ground ginger
½ teaspoon freshly ground nutmeg
¼ teaspoon ground cloves
½ teaspoon salt
1 cup unsalted sweet butter, softened at room temperature
1¾ cups granulated sugar

¼ cup firmly packed light brown sugar
5 jumbo eggs, separated, at room temperature
1 cup milk, at room temperature
2 teaspoons pure vanilla extract
1¾ cups shredded carrots (grate them on the large holes of a hand-held box grater)
¾ cup finely chopped fresh pecans
½ cup sweetened shredded coconut
confectioners' sugar (optional)

Lightly butter and flour a 10-inch tube pan; set aside. Preheat oven to 350° F. Resift the flour with the next 7 ingredients onto a sheet of waxed paper; set aside.

In the large bowl of an electric mixer, cream the butter on moderately high speed until light and fluffy, about 3 minutes. Add the granulated sugar in two additions, beating well after each addition. Add the light brown sugar; beat for 2 minutes. Add 2 egg yolks and beat for 2 minutes on high speed. Add 2 more yolks and beat for 2 minutes on high speed. Add the remaining yolk and beat for 1 minute.

On low speed, blend in the sifted mixture in three additions with the milk in two additions, beginning and ending with the sifted mixture. Blend in the vanilla extract. By hand, stir in the carrots, pecans, and coconut.

Beat the egg whites in a clean bowl until they turn foamy. Add a pinch of salt and continue beating until firm, not stiff, peaks form. Beat one-fifth of the whites into the carrot batter, then fold in the remaining whites, quickly and thoroughly.

Carefully pour and scrape the batter into the prepared pan. Bake the cake on the lower-level rack of the oven about an hour, or until a toothpick inserted in the cake emerges clean and dry.

Cool the cake in the pan on a wire rack for 10 minutes. Turn out the cake onto another wire rack to cool completely.

Store airtight. Dust the top of the cake with sifted confectioners' sugar, if you like, right before serving.

PECAN BUTTER CAKE

MAKES ONE 10-INCH CAKE

3 cups sifted cake flour
2½ teaspoons baking powder
¾ teaspoon salt
½ teaspoon freshly ground nutmeg
½ teaspoon ground mace
1 cup unsalted sweet butter, softened
    at room temperature
2 cups granulated sugar

4 jumbo eggs, separated, at room temperature
1 tablespoon pure vanilla extract
1 cup milk
1 cup finely chopped fresh pecans
confectioners' sugar

Lightly butter and flour a fluted 10-inch tube pan; set aside. Preheat oven to 350° F.

Resift the cake flour with the baking powder, salt, nutmeg, and mace onto a sheet of waxed paper; set aside.

In the large bowl of an electric mixer, beat the butter until light and fluffy on moderately high speed, about 3 minutes. Add the sugar in two additions, beating on high speed for 2 minutes after each addition. Add the egg yolks, one at a time, blending them well on moderately high speed. Scrape down the sides of the bowl with a rubber spatula often to make sure that the beaten mixture is blended evenly.

On low speed, beat in the vanilla extract. Slowly beat in the flour mixture in three additions alternately with the milk in two additions, beginning and ending with the flour mixture. By hand, stir in the chopped pecans.

Beat the egg whites in a clean bowl until foamy. Add a big pinch of salt and continue beating the whites until firm, not stiff, peaks are formed. By hand, beat several large spoonfuls into the batter, then fold in the rest of the whites carefully and thoroughly.

Quickly pour and scrape the batter into the prepared pan. Bake the cake on the lower-level rack of the oven for about an hour, or until a toothpick inserted in the cake emerges clean and dry.

Cool the cake in the pan on a wire rack for 10 minutes, then invert onto another rack to cool completely.

Store airtight. Sift confectioners' sugar on top of the cake just before serving.

CARROT-COCONUT LOAF   MAKES ONE 9″ x 5″ x 3″ LOAF

Just about every good produce department in major supermarkets carries carrots by the bunch, with their fluffy green tops slouching to one side of the bin. Absolutely and positively use these bunch carrots for grating in this recipe—they are very sweet. Carrots entombed in cellophane bags are tough and have a withered, dry taste.

2 cups all-purpose flour (preferably
    unbleached)
2 teaspoons baking soda
½ teaspoon salt
1 teaspoon ground cinnamon
½ teaspoon ground allspice
¼ teaspoon ground ginger
1 cup granulated sugar
3 extra-large eggs, at room temperature

1 cup vegetable oil
2½ teaspoons pure vanilla extract
2 cups (lightly packed measurement)
    grated carrots (grate the carrots
    on the large holes of a hand-held
    grater)
1 cup (lightly packed measurement)
    sweetened shredded coconut

Lightly butter and flour a 9″ x 5″ x 3″ loaf pan; set aside. Preheat oven to 350° F.

Sift together the first 7 ingredients onto a sheet of waxed paper; set aside.

In the large bowl of an electric mixer, beat the eggs on high speed for 3 minutes. Add the oil, ½ cup at a time, beating for 1 minute on moderate speed after each portion is added. Beat in the vanilla extract. Beat the mixture on moderately high speed for 2 minutes, until lightly thickened.

On low speed, beat in the sifted mixture in two additions, scraping down the sides of the bowl after each part is added. By hand, stir in the carrots and coconut.

Turn and scrape the batter into the prepared pan. Bake the loaf on the lower-level rack of the oven for 50 minutes to 1 hour, or until a toothpick inserted into the loaf emerges clean and dry.

Cool the loaf in the pan on a wire rack for 10 minutes; invert the loaf onto a second rack, move it right side up, then cool completely.

Store the loaf airtight.

BANANA-COCONUT BREAD   MAKES TWO 9″ x 5″ x 3″ LOAVES

This firm-textured tea bread has a wonderful flavor and (handy) capacity to keep very well. In my baking kitchen, farm-fresh buttermilk appears frequently, as I happen to like the rich delicate quality it imparts—especially in this loaf. Most of the coconut in this recipe appears in the batter, but a smaller quantity gets scattered over the top as a final lacy cloak. On baking, it turns a light golden color and crisps up slightly, a delicious addition and subtle refinement.

4 cups sifted all-purpose flour (preferably unbleached)
2¼ teaspoons baking powder
1 teaspoon baking soda
¾ teaspoon salt
13 tablespoons (1 cup less 3 tablespoons) unsalted sweet butter,
  softened at room temperature

1⅓ cups granulated sugar
4 extra-large eggs, at room temperature
1 tablespoon pure vanilla extract
6 tablespoons buttermilk, at room temperature
2 cups pureed bananas (about 4
  medium-size)
2 cups sweetened shredded coconut

Lightly butter and flour two 9″ x 5″ x 3″ loaf pans; set aside. Preheat oven to 350° F.

Resift the flour with the baking powder, baking soda, and salt onto a sheet of waxed paper; set aside.

In the large bowl of an electric mixer, beat the butter for 2 minutes on moderately high speed. Add the sugar in two additions, beating for 2 to 3 minutes after each portion is added. Add the eggs, one at a time, beating each for 1 minute on moderately high speed before adding the next.

On low speed, blend in the vanilla extract, buttermilk, and bananas. Scrape down the sides of the bowl with a rubber spatula to keep the mixture even. Still on low speed, add the sifted mixture in two additions, beating just until the flour particles have been absorbed. By hand, stir in 1¾ cups coconut.

Pour the batter into the prepared pans, dividing it evenly between them, then sprinkle the remaining coconut over the top of each loaf. Bake the bread on the lower-level rack of the oven for 50 to 55 minutes, or until a toothpick inserted in the loaf emerges clean and dry.

Cool the loaves in the pans on wire racks for 10 minutes, then pop them out of the pans and let them cool right side up.

Store airtight.

DATE LOAF   MAKES ONE 9″ x 5″ x 3″ LOAF

This loaf has a real mother lode of dates and nuts. I get very emotional about this kind of loaf and firmly believe it to be one of the most genteel things to have around the house (yours or someone else's). Weekend hostesses will just love to slice it up and set it out with some scoops of fine country butter or a smooth mound of fresh cream cheese as part of a no-cook breakfast or tea.

1½ cups warmed milk
1¼ cups chopped moist dates
2½ cups all-purpose flour (preferably
  unbleached)
1⅓ cups granulated sugar
2¼ teaspoons baking soda

½ teaspoon salt
¾ cups chopped walnuts
2 extra-large eggs, at room temperature
1½ teaspoons pure vanilla extract
3 tablespoons unsalted sweet butter,
  melted and cooled to tepid

Lightly butter and flour a 9″ x 5″ x 3″ loaf pan; set aside.

Pour the warmed milk into a bowl, add the chopped dates, and stir them around in the milk. Let the mixture stand until it reaches room temperature.

Sift together the flour, sugar, baking soda, and salt into a big bowl; set aside. Preheat oven to 350° F.

Put the walnuts in a small bowl and stir in 1 teaspoon of the sifted flour mixture.

In the bowl of an electric mixer, beat the eggs, vanilla extract, and butter on high speed for 2 minutes.

Make a big well in the middle of the sifted mixture and pour in both the egg mixture and the milk-date mixture. Swiftly stir everything together until combined, but do not overbeat.

Pour and scrape the batter into the prepared pan and bake the loaf on the lower-level rack of the oven for about an hour or so, or until a toothpick inserted in the loaf withdraws clean and dry.

Cool the loaf in the pan on a wire rack for 10 minutes, then invert it out and cool right side up.

Store airtight. It is best to allow this loaf to mellow at room temperature for 24 hours before eating or giving.

SWEET POTATO BREAD MAKES TWO 9″ x 5″ x 3″ LOAVES

This is an ideal bread to make when the baking–gift-giving mood strikes—the aroma of the spices lingers in the kitchen long after baking time is up, and it is hard to allow these loaves to mellow.

4 cups all-purpose flour (preferably unbleached)
2 teaspoons baking soda
½ teaspoon baking powder
1 teaspoon salt
1½ teaspoons ground cinnamon
½ teaspoon ground ginger
½ teaspoon ground allspice
¼ teaspoon freshly ground nutmeg

¼ teaspoon ground cloves
1 cup finely chopped walnuts
½ cup dried, but moist, currants
⅔ cup solid shortening
1½ cups granulated sugar
4 large eggs, at room temperature
1 cup light molasses
2 teaspoons pure vanilla extract
2 cups pureed cooked sweet potatoes

Lightly butter and flour two 9″ x 5″ x 3″ loaf pans; set aside. Preheat oven to 350° F.

Sift together the first 9 ingredients onto a sheet of waxed paper; set aside.

Place the walnuts and currants in a bowl. Stir in 1 tablespoon of the sifted mixture; set aside.

In the large bowl of an electric mixer, cream the shortening until light, about 3 minutes on moderately high speed. Add the sugar in two additions, beating for 2 minutes after each portion is added. On moderate speed, add the eggs, one at a time, beating for 1 minute after each is added.

On low speed, blend in the molasses and vanilla. Scrape down the sides of the bowl often to keep the mixture even. Still on low speed, add half of the sifted mixture and beat just until the flour particles have been absorbed. Add all of the pureed sweet potatoes, beat slowly until incorporated, then add the remaining sifted mixture. By hand, stir in the walnuts and currants.

Divide the batter evenly between the two prepared loaf pans. Bake the loaves on the middle-level rack of the oven for about 1 hour, or until a toothpick inserted in the cake emerges clean and dry.

Cool the cakes in the pan on wire racks for 10 minutes, turn them out, and let them cool right side up.

Store the loaves airtight. Let the loaves mature for 1 day before eating or giving.

RHUBARB BREAD MAKES TWO 8″ x 4″ x 3″ LOAVES

Pockets of rhubarb in a plain buttermilk tea bread.

*2¾ cups plus 3 tablespoons sifted
all-purpose flour (preferably
unbleached)*
1 teaspoon baking soda
½ teaspoon salt
1 teaspoon ground cinnamon
¼ teaspoon ground allspice
¼ teaspoon freshly ground nutmeg
⅔ cup vegetable oil

1 cup firmly packed light brown sugar
½ cup firmly packed dark brown sugar
1 jumbo egg, at room temperature
*1 cup buttermilk blended with 1 tea-
spoon pure vanilla extract, at
room temperature*
1 cup thinly sliced fresh rhubarb
3 tablespoons finely chopped walnuts

Lightly butter and flour two 8″ x 4″ x 3″ loaf pans; set aside. Preheat oven to 350° F.

Resift the flour with the next 5 ingredients onto a sheet of waxed paper; set aside.

In the large bowl of an electric mixer, beat the oil with both sugars for 4 minutes on moderate speed. Beat in the egg.

On low speed, add the sifted dry ingredients in three additions alternately with the buttermilk in two additions, beginning and ending with the dry ingredients. Scrape down the sides of the bowl often to keep the batter even. By hand, stir in the rhubarb and walnuts.

Pour and scrape the batter into the prepared pans, gently leveling the top. Bake the loaves on the lower-level rack of the oven for about 40 minutes, or until a tooth-pick inserted into the bread withdraws clean and dry.

Cool the loaves in the pan on a rack for 10 minutes. Invert the loaves onto another rack, then turn them right side up and cool them to room temperature.

Store the loaves airtight.

PARMESAN CHEESE SHORTBREAD MAKES ABOUT 1½ DOZEN

Biscuits such as these are one of the finer luxuries to have on hand. Savory shortbread tastes right with cold food, and the dough can be made up to 2 days in advance, so if you want to serve it warm from the oven, there's no need to get frantic right before serving time. To get these biscuits as a gift is heaven; I pack up a lot of them in bold plaid canisters.

2 cups all-purpose flour (preferably
    unbleached)
¼ teaspoon salt
⅛ teaspoon cayenne pepper
¼ teaspoon baking powder

1 cup unsalted sweet butter, softened
    at room temperature
1 cup (lightly packed measurement)
    freshly grated imported Parmesan
    cheese

Sift together the flour, salt, pepper, and baking powder onto a sheet of waxed paper; set aside.

In the large bowl of an electric mixer, cream the butter on moderately high speed for 2 minutes. On low speed, add the flour mixture in two additions, beating slowly just until the flour particles are absorbed.

By hand, work in the cheese, blending it in with a wooden paddle or spoon.

Place the dough between two large sheets of waxed paper; roll out the dough to an even thickness of a scant ½ inch. Put the rolled-out dough, which is enclosed in waxed paper, on a cookie sheet and refrigerate for 5 hours, or until very firm. Once firm, the dough may be wrapped again in aluminum foil and stored in this fashion in the refrigerator for up to 2 days.

To bake the shortbread, line a cookie sheet with parchment paper. Cut out 3-inch rounds of dough with a plain circle cutter and place them 2 inches apart on the parchment paper. Dip the tines of a fork in flour and pierce the rounds with the tips of the tines in 3 rows:

· · · ·
· · · ·
· · · ·

Chill the rounds for 15 minutes.

Bake the biscuits, a sheet at a time, on the middle-level rack of a preheated 375° F. oven for 12 to 15 minutes, or until a light golden color and firm to the touch.

With a wide metal spatula remove the shortbread to a cooling rack.

When cooled, store airtight.

Dried Winter Fruit Medleys

Dried fruits are lovely winter companions to spices, liqueurs, aromatic brown sugar, and citrus peel flavorings. These medleys, once put up and jarred, are beautiful gifts for bringing to an open house during the very cold months of January and February. Some can be put to use as spoonfuls of whimsy for serving with slices of my butter cake or pound cake (notably the Apricots in Apricot Liqueur, Figs with Ginger and Vanilla, Pecan- and Ginger-Stuffed Apricots, and Dried Peach, Apricot, and Pear Compote), and the Pickled Figs are awfully good with smoked chicken, smoked turkey, pork, or lamb.

PICKLED FIGS

MAKES 2 POUNDS

In autumn, when late-season fresh figs are available, I love to boil up the syrup outlined below and submerge whole figs in it. But using that method, the fruit only keeps in the refrigerator for 2 weeks. The handy alternative is to carefully simmer whole dried figs in the same syrup and the resulting "compote" is a real treat, as sweetly pungent as the version using fresh figs, but richer. Select very small dried figs; they should be cooked to tenderness but also retain a slight firmness. Pickled figs are positively delicious with pork or lamb (hot or cold), and turkey.

2½ cups water
1½ cups apple cider vinegar
1 cup firmly packed light brown sugar
2 3-inch cinnamon sticks

8 whole cloves
8 whole black peppercorns
2 pounds dried figs

Place all the ingredients but the figs in a 6-quart casserole. Cover the pot and cook the liquid over a low heat to completely melt down the sugar. Uncover the casserole, raise the heat to high, and boil the syrup for 1 minute.

Add the figs to the pot, cover, and simmer slowly until the figs are tender, but not mushy, about 20 minutes. Remove the figs to a bowl with a slotted spoon.

Boil down the syrup until it is condensed and syrupy, about 5 to 6 minutes. Strain the syrup over the fruit, then add the cooked spices.

Cool the spiced figs to room temperature, then cover and refrigerate. The figs keep under refrigeration for at least 4 months.

APRICOTS IN APRICOT LIQUEUR

MAKES 4 POUNDS

These fancy apricots look gorgeous when packed in decorative jars. Buy the softest, lushest apricots you can find, as the liqueur will only enhance the flavor of the dried fruit, not tenderize it. Drained and chopped, these apricots are a handy addition to some yeast breads and coffee cakes, and are delicious in mincemeat, puddings, and fruitcake. For gift-giving, place the apricots and liqueur in a clean jar, angle a whole vanilla bean in full view, and close the jar. Decorate with a fabric top, if you like, and include a helpful tag that describes some uses for the apricots.

4 pounds compact, whole dried apri-
    cots, preferably Turkish

4 supple vanilla beans
apricot liqueur

Lightly pack the apricots in four pint jars, filling each jar about two-thirds full. After one-third of the jar is filled, slide in a vanilla bean. Pour on enough liqueur to cover the fruit, about ¾ cup for each jar.

Put the lids on the jars and let the apricots stand for 1 day at room temperature, then refrigerate.

The apricots may remain in the refrigerator for at least 8 months. They get better and better as the weeks go by.

FIGS WITH GINGER AND VANILLA   MAKES 2 POUNDS

Use these figs as you would the Pickled Figs. I usually make this recipe when I receive dried figs as gifts and they mount up on a shelf in the pantry. If the figs you use are not perfectly moist, soak them in hot English Breakfast tea to cover for 2 hours, then drain them very well (too-dry prunes respond to this gentle plumping, too).

2 cups water
1 cup granulated sugar
⅛ teaspoon salt
¾ cup apple cider vinegar
2 3-inch cinnamon sticks
4 ½-inch-thick pieces of fresh ginger,
    lightly smashed with the broad
    side of a knife or a cleaver

½ teaspoon whole allspice berries
1 small vanilla bean, split down the
    center with a sharp knife (the pod
    should still remain whole)
2 pounds dried, but moist, figs

Place all the ingredients except the figs in a 6-quart casserole, preferably of enameled cast iron. Place the casserole over a low heat and cook the mixture until the sugar has dissolved completely. When the sugar has melted down, uncover the pot and bring the syrup to a boil; boil for 2 minutes.

Add the figs to the pot, cover the pot partially, leaving about 2 inches open at the top. Simmer the figs for about 20 minutes, or until just tender. Remove the figs and spices to a bowl with a slotted spoon.

Boil down the syrup until it has condensed lightly, about 4 minutes, then strain the syrup over the figs.

Let the figs cool to room temperature, then cover and refrigerate. The figs keep very well under refrigeration for about 4 months.

PRUNE-STUFFED PEACHES   MAKES 4 DOZEN

The stuffed fruits in this and the next recipe are essentially sweetmeats, very rich and elegant, looking lovely in a cognac syrup flavored with cinnamon and vanilla. These small treasures are best served one to a person as a garnish to a perfectly poached pear sitting atop a thin fruit puree or custard sauce; placed strategically, carefully halved, on the side of fluffs of mousse or ovals of ice cream; or anywhere a final, sweet playful fillip is needed for a dessert. They are great fun to make, and children have a good time stuffing the fruit (their small fingers can maneuver in the fruit easily).

4 dozen small dried, but moist, whole
    peaches
2 dozen small pitted prunes
2 cups granulated sugar
3 cups water

¼ cup cognac
2 4-inch cinnamon sticks
2 small vanilla beans, split down the
    center to expose the tiny seeds,
    but not halved

Put out the peaches and prunes on a working surface. Cut the prunes in half the long way. Stuff each peach with a prune half, securing it well within the cavity of the peach. Set the stuffed peaches aside.

In a 6- to 8-quart casserole, preferably of enameled cast iron, place the remaining listed ingredients. Cover the pot and set it over a low heat. Cook the mixture until the sugar has dissolved completely. Uncover the pot, raise the heat to high, and boil the liquid for 2 minutes.

Add the fruit to the pot, adjust the heat so that the liquid simmers slowly, and cook the fruit until it has plumped up, about 7 minutes (the timing depends upon the moistness of the fruit; some dried fruit may take as long as 15 to 20 minutes to plump). Remove the fruit from the syrup with a slotted spoon to a bowl—easy does it.

Boil the syrup for about 5 minutes to condense it. Cool the syrup, pick out the spices, and add them to the fruit, then strain the syrup over the fruit.

When the fruit has reached room temperature, store it in a tightly covered container in the refrigerator. It can be stored up to 3 months.

NOTE: Fruit prepared in this fashion can take a lot of spices, so feel free to add a fingerful of whole allspice berries or cloves as you like; the spices end up floating in the syrup, mingling around the fruit here and there.

PECAN- AND GINGER-STUFFED APRICOTS   MAKES 3 DOZEN

3 dozen small whole dried apricots
3 dozen pecan halves
about 1 10-ounce jar ginger preserved
   in syrup
1½ cups granulated sugar

2½ cups water
¾ cup apricot liqueur
6 thin slivers of lemon peel
3 4-inch pieces of cinnamon stick

Place the apricots and pecans on a working surface. Remove 18 pieces of ginger from the syrup, and cut each piece in half with a sharp paring knife.

To stuff each apricot, place a ginger piece on the flat side of a pecan and insert both in the cavity of the apricot. Make sure that the stuffing is well inside the fruit.

In a large casserole of 8-quart capacity, preferably enameled cast iron, place the remaining listed ingredients. Cover the pot and cook the mixture over a low heat to dissolve the sugar. When the sugar has dissolved, uncover the pot and raise the heat to high; boil the liquid for 4 minutes.

Add the fruit to the casserole. Lower the heat so that the liquid simmers, and simmer the fruit until plump and just tender, about 9 to 18 minutes.

Remove the fruit with a slotted spoon to a container. Let the syrup cool for 15 minutes, then pick out the spices and add to the container.

Bring the syrup to a boil; boil for 1 minute. Cool the syrup to room temperature. Strain it over the fruit.

When the fruit has cooled completely, cover the container and refrigerate. The fruit may be stored in the refrigerator for up to 3 months.

NOTE: Tangerine or orange peel may be substituted for the lemon peel, and walnut halves may be exchanged for the pecans. For added spiciness, see Note in preceding recipe.

DRIED PEACH, APRICOT, AND PEAR COMPOTE

MAKES ABOUT 3½ POUNDS

The January *angst* for a good cook is the stark realization that summer's ambrosial fruits and vegetables are nowhere in sight. To tide me over until strawberry season, I like to have this cold-weather compote, which looks just lovely when it is put up in stylized jars, with the spices included. If you know that the compote will not be consumed in a few days after cooking it, do not pack the spices in, but add a fresh cinnamon stick and a few cloves to the jar on gift-giving day instead.

1 *pound dried apricots*	2 *4-inch cinnamon sticks*
1 *pound dried peaches*	½ *cup* liquid *brown sugar*
¾ *pound dried pear slices*	3 *whole allspice berries*
¾ *pound prunes, with pits in*	3 *whole cloves*
2 *cups sweet white wine*	*juice of 1 lemon, strained*
1 *cup water*	

Place the apricots, peaches, pears, and prunes in a bowl. Pour on the white wine and water, and add the cinnamon sticks, and let stand for a half hour.

In the meantime, place the remaining listed ingredients in a 3-cup saucepan. Bring to a boil; set aside.

Transfer the fruit mixture to a large 6-quart casserole, preferably of enameled cast iron. Bring the liquid to a simmer, then simmer the fruit until it is barely tender, not completely soft, about 10 minutes. Remove the fruit to a side bowl with a slotted spoon.

Pour the brown sugar mixture into the casserole. Bring all of the liquid to a boil and boil it down until it is reduced by about a third, and is syrupy. Strain the syrup over the cooked fruit.

Transfer the compote to a storage container. Pick out the cooked spices and add them to the fruit if you are using it within 3 or 4 days, otherwise float a cinnamon stick or a few allspice berries in the compote for effect shortly before presenting as a gift.

Store the cooled compote in the refrigerator, covered, for up to 1 month.

Granola

It is fun to mix up a batch of this rich-tasting breakfast cereal when you get to add walnuts, apricots, coconut, peaches, sesame seeds, and pears to spiff up drab oatmeal.

I find that oatmeal cookies—the big chunky ones—are very good indeed if granola is exchanged for the quantity of plain oatmeal. One time I had a fair amount of Cinnamon-Coconut Granola stored in one of my antique apothecary jars. What I wanted to make was a few dozen oatmeal cookies, but I was without the "quick-cooking" oatmeal. Nevertheless, I mixed up a batter with well-crumbled granola instead, following one of my oldest oatmeal cookie recipes, and baked large saucerlike cookies.

They were richly spiced and eminently portable, which makes them a splendid office snack or picnic addition, and a sturdy gift (granola cookies seem indestructible).

CINNAMON-COCONUT GRANOLA
MAKES ABOUT 14 CUPS

8 cups "quick-cooking" oatmeal
2 cups shredded coconut
2 cups chopped pecans
¼ cup unprocessed bran
¼ cup sesame seeds
¼ teaspoon salt

1 tablespoon ground cinnamon
¼ teaspoon freshly ground nutmeg
1 cup honey
½ cup safflower oil
2 teaspoons pure vanilla extract
1 cup dark seedless raisins

In a large bowl, stir together the first 8 ingredients. Preheat oven to 325° F.

Pour the honey and safflower oil into a 3-cup saucepan and bring to a simmer. Remove from the heat and stir in the vanilla extract. Pour this over the oatmeal mixture, blending everything together with a large fork.

Turn out the granola mixture into a lightly oiled jelly-roll pan and bake it on the middle-level rack of the oven for about 35 minutes, or until it is toasty.

Let the granola cool on the sheet for a half hour, then slide it into a bowl. Stir in the raisins.

Store the granola in airtight jars.

GRANOLA WITH DRIED FRUIT
MAKES ABOUT 14 CUPS

6 cups "quick-cooking" oatmeal
1 cup unprocessed bran
1½ cups chopped walnuts
½ cup sesame seeds
⅓ cup plus 2 tablespoons dark, rich
   honey blended with ¼ cup plus 2
   tablespoons safflower oil and 2
   teaspoons pure vanilla extract

1 cup dark seedless raisins
1½ cups chopped dried apricots
1 cup chopped dried peaches
1 cup chopped dried pears

Preheat the oven to 325° F. Place the oatmeal, bran, walnuts, and sesame seeds into a bowl. Pour over the honey-oil-vanilla mixture and combine it with the oatmeal with a fork to coat the flakes and nuts well.

Scatter the mixture on a well-oiled jelly-roll pan and bake on the middle-level rack of the oven for about 35 minutes, or until it colors lightly.

Cool the nut and oatmeal combination for 30 minutes, then stir in all of the fruit.

Store the granola in airtight tins.

NOTE: For exceptionally good granola cookies, use a couple of cups of your own homemade granola in this recipe.

GRANOLA SAUCERS

Make sure that 2½ cups of home-produced granola is free of all big lumps; break up very big clumps with your fingertips. Sift together 2 cups (unsifted) unbleached all-purpose flour with 1¼ teaspoons baking powder, ¼ teaspoon baking soda, ¼ teaspoon salt, 1½ teaspoons ground cinnamon, ½ teaspoon ground allspice, ¼ teaspoon ground ginger, ¼ teaspoon freshly ground nutmeg.

In the large bowl of an electric mixer, cream 6 tablespoons unsalted sweet butter, softened at room temperature and 6 tablespoons soft solid shortening. Beat in ½ cup granulated sugar and ¼ cup firmly packed light brown sugar until light and fluffy. Beat in 2 extra-large eggs, at room temperature, one at a time, and 2 teaspoons pure vanilla extract. By hand, stir in the 2½ cups granola. Drop the cookies by double tablespoons onto parchment-lined cookie sheets, 9 to a sheet, or about 3 inches apart. Bake the cookies, a sheet at a time, on the middle-level rack of a preheated 375° F. oven for 12 to 13 minutes, or until they are just firm to the touch. Transfer the cookies to a cooling rack with a wide spatula. Bake the remaining cookies in this fashion.

When the saucers have cooled thoroughly, pack them in airtight tins where they will keep for about 3 weeks.

An extra ½ cup quantity of raisins, coconut, or chopped dates (or other diced dried fruit) may be stirred into the batter with the granola.

A Rustic Pâté

This is a fine gift for friends who truly appreciate a good pâté and will use it straight away for lunch on the porch or deck. The ingredient list reflects my personal preference to combine two kinds of meat with poultry, add freshly chopped herbs for a bit of zip, and tuck cognac-soaked strips of country ham within all. Pork fat happens to be a requisite (and maligned) addition to pâté, and you should not think of jettisoning it.

The fat that keeps the pâté from turning heavy can be ground along with the veal and pork if your butcher is agreeable. A well-stocked meat department also will be able to sell you, inexpensively, fresh thin sheets of fatback—smooth fat from the back of the pig—for lining the bottom and sides of the baking pan. I use a 5-cup rectangular enameled cast-iron terrine that measures 4 inches wide by 10 inches long (creating 10 good-size slices).

Meat loaves intrigue me, possibly because I can haul out jars of different condiments to use as satellite things to spice up the loaf. Eggplant Relish with Paprika and Oregano, Pickled Pearl Onions with Vermouth, Red Onion and Currant Marmalade, and Pickled Okra, all are dandy sweet and tart adjuncts to the pâté below:

THE PÂTÉ

MAKES ONE PÂTÉ ABOUT 3½ POUNDS

¼ pound skinless and boneless chicken breast, cut into ¼-inch-thick strips

1 2-ounce-thick slice country ham, cut into ¼-inch-wide strips

¼ cup cognac

2¼ teaspoons coarse (kosher) salt

freshly ground white pepper, to taste

⅛ teaspoon ground allspice

1 medium sweet white onion, finely chopped

3 tablespoons unsalted sweet butter

freshly ground black pepper, to taste

2 teaspoons finely chopped fresh rosemary

2 teaspoons finely chopped fresh thyme

¼ teaspoon ground bay leaf plus 1 small imported bay leaf

1 pound lean pork, coarsely ground

½ pound lean veal, coarsely ground

¾ pound pork fat, ground

2 large eggs, lightly beaten, at room temperature

10 to 12 sheets of fatback (pork fat)

Marinate the boneless chicken breast pieces and country ham strips in the cognac for 1 hour. Season with ¼ teaspoon salt, white pepper, and allspice and refrigerate for 1 hour. Drain the cognac from the chicken and ham into a small cup and set aside.

In a small skillet, soften the chopped onion in the butter over a moderately low heat. Season with 2 teaspoons salt and black pepper. Fold through the rosemary, thyme, and ground bay leaf. Set aside.

In a large mixing bowl, beat together the pork, veal, and ground pork fat (if it has not already been combined in grinding by your butcher). Beat in the eggs, then the cognac that has been reserved from the chicken and ham marination. Stir in the onion and spices.

Line the inside of a 5- to 6-cup rectangular terrine with sheets of fatback, making sure that the fat covers the bottom without too much of an overlap. Any fat that extends past the sides to the top of the terrine may be folded over after the pâté mixture is spooned in. Preheat oven to 350° F.

Spread one-third of the ground meat and onion mixture on the bottom of the lined terrine. Smooth over. Lay on one-half of the chicken and ham strips. Spread on the second third of the ground meat mixture, and lay on the remaining chicken and ham strips. Top with an even layer of the remaining ground meat mixture. Press the bay leaf flat on top of the pâté, in the center. Cover the top with pieces of pork fat.

Wrap the top of the terrine with a double layer of aluminum foil and put on the terrine's lid. Place in a large roasting pan and pour in enough hot water to rise at least a third of the way up the sides of the terrine. Bake the pâté on the middle-level rack of the oven for 1 hour and 30 minutes. The pâté is done when it shrinks slightly from the sides of the pan and oozes a clear yellow liquid, not tinted with red.

Remove the terrine from its water bath and place on any large pan that has a lip, such as a jelly-roll pan. Remove the lid and weigh it down by placing a brick or another terrine filled with weights on top of the pâté. Cool the terrine, weighted, for at least 3 hours. Chill the pâté overnight, with the weights on.

The next day, clean the sides of the pan, place on a fresh covering of plastic wrap and aluminum foil, and store in the refrigerator until needed, or up to 2 weeks.

Remove the pâté from the mold; wrap up into a neat block for presentation.

VARIATIONS: Try ¼ cup chopped pistachio nuts, green and bright, scattered over each of the chicken and ham layers.

Instead of the ham, use 2 ounces thin slices of boiled tongue or a 2-ounce chunk of tongue, cubed.

Instead of the ground veal, try ¾ pound ground skinless and boneless dark meat of chicken; then use ¼ pound bottom round of veal cut into strips in place of the chicken breast.

7

~~

Spring Delights

FANCY FLAVORINGS

Potions
BRANDY VANILLA EXTRACT
BRANDIED LEMON FLAVORING
BRANDIED ORANGE FLAVORING

Aromatics
FLAVORED HONEY
HERB SUGARS
DRIED ORANGE OR LEMON PEELS

SWEET AND SPICY PRESERVES AND PICKLES

RED ONION AND CURRANT MARMALADE
RHUBARB AND RAISIN CONSERVE
RHUBARB CHUTNEY
PICKLED PEARL ONIONS WITH VERMOUTH
CARROT-LEMON PRESERVES
SWEET AND HOT MUSTARD
GARLIC-IMBUED OLIVES

GREEN OLIVES WITH CELERY AND ONION
HOT PEPPERED OLIVES

NUTS: DRAMATIC AND SPIRITED

TWICE-COOKED CRISPY WALNUTS
TOASTED TEXAS PECANS

OLD-FASHIONED COOKIES

Sugar Cookies
TRADITIONAL (MORE OR LESS) SUGAR COOKIES
MELTINGLY RICH SUGAR COOKIES
SOUR CREAM SUGAR COOKIES

Gingersnaps
CRISPY GINGERSNAPS
MOLASSES GINGERSNAPS

Oatmeal Cookies
OATMEAL AND DATE COOKIES
MOLASSES-OATMEAL SAUCERS
OATMEAL WAFERS
MOLASSES AND SPICE COOKIES
WHOLE-WHEAT, COCONUT, AND RAISIN COOKIES
PEANUT BUTTER COOKIES
COCONUT ROUNDS
ORANGE–POPPY-SEED COOKIES

A LUXURIOUS SWEET SPREAD

CHOCOLATE-CHESTNUT SPREAD WITH RUM

The pastel scene of spring is repeated in light and luxurious gifts that just lift you out of winter's doldrums. Begin with making a simple batch of sweet flavorings that will keep you and the happy recipients in good supply for any kind of confection you'll want to whip up. Lemon, vanilla, and orange flavorings are lovely looking in slender-necked bottles; honeys and sugars, scented with herbs and spices, are good for filling clear glass screw-top jars. Set the jarred extract or aromatic in some old-fashioned antique tin can and put plenty of Spanish moss around to hold the jar in place; tie the neck of the jar with colored raffia or ribbon to match the contents of the gift. Turn-of-the-century stoneware crocks are also fun to fill with any of the refreshing flavorings or sweet and spicy preserves.

A whole basketful of potions and aromatics is just like composing a big mixed bouquet of spring flowers; each has a different color, visual texture, and, of course, culinary use. Since spring is somewhat an early taste of summer, you might reach into Summer Feasting and Harvesting, chapter 3, and look at the dips and savory snacks for additional ideas to enliven and tantalize, and combine those in one container, too.

Tea bins with slanted lids that lift up, tin measures (these are graduated cups with exterior quantity markings and handles), flour sifters shaped like a huge scoop, or a colander of wire mesh outlined in tin or wood are enchanting packages for any of the springtime preserves or old-fashioned cookies. Glass beakers and lightweight enameled white bowls and pots are also perfect containers for spring cookie extravaganzas—the cookies have elegance in the see-through glass cylinders and a down-home appeal in the enameled pots and pans.

I turn to cookie-making in the spring because cookies are easy and light and go well with citrus mousses and early summer fruit compotes (especially strawberries, shiny and sweet, available during late May). And speaking of strawberries, one of the best add-ons to a bowl of strawberries is the Chocolate-Chestnut Spread with Rum on some thin, sturdy butter cookies.

Spring is the time to create soft little compositions—such as one perfect batch of cream-colored sugar cookies heaped in a pink lacquered bowl, or jars of Carrot-Lemon Preserves, made with slender reed-thin young carrots decorated with fresh galax leaves and capped with a circle of orange dotted Swiss fabric bound in ribbon. Food gifts should keep the delicate and informal qualities of the season even if the food is bright and bold.

My favorite gift, so appropriate for spring, is an Easter basket filled with any of the old-fashioned cookies in this chapter (which I routinely make for the baskets); the baskets are decorated with confetti colors of ribbon and tied to the sides are fresh spring flowers—a garland of narcissus or snowdrops, or later, tulips and daffodils.

Fancy Flavorings

Extracts and flavorings are terrific pantry staples to have on hand for your own personal use or for gift-giving. My favorite time of the year to start up big batches is during the spring, so that they have a chance to mature and mellow for summertime fruit desserts and fall and winter baking. These flavorings are so simple to make—requiring less than an hour in the kitchen—yet they become beautiful, refreshing gifts.

Potions

BRANDY VANILLA EXTRACT
MAKES 4 CUPS

Your baking buddies, makers of custards and wobbly Bavarians, and assorted others who love to poach fruit, make compotes, and otherwise revel in desserts, will absolutely love this extract (and the next citrus flavoring as well).

12 plump, pliable vanilla beans, about
    6 inches long

4 cups good brandy

Split each vanilla bean lengthwise down the center to expose the tiny seeds, using a very sharp paring knife.

In a jar deep enough to hold the vanilla beans without bending them, lower in the beans. Pour in all of the brandy. Cover tightly and let the flavors exchange and enlarge for about 2 weeks, storing the extract on a cool, dark shelf. Shake up the bottle once a day, or as often as you can remember to (no harm if a day or so elapses); this encourages all the goodness from the beans to permeate the brandy.

Parcel out 1 cup of brandied extract to each of 4 slender bottles, add 3 beans to each, and cap tightly. I'm fond of using clear glass bottles that are lightly patterned and are closed by a beautiful procelain top and rubber gasket.

BRANDIED LEMON FLAVORING   MAKES 4 CUPS

The old-fashioned system of steeping peel in brandy is to remove ribbony strips of peel from lemons (or oranges) and plunk them in a quart of brandy, so giving the brandy the energy of bold citrus.

4 medium-size lemons	*½ cup granulated sugar*
4 cups brandy	*½ cup water*

Using a serrated fruit knife and a slightly exaggerated sawing motion, remove the peel from the lemon in a few long coils. The white pith, a thickness just under the peel, would lend a bitter taste to the brandy, so take off the peel without digging into the pith. If some pith comes off with the peel, cut it away.

Drop the peel into a 6-cup screw-top jar. Pour on the brandy. Let this stand for 4 days for a proper infusion.

In the meantime, put the sugar and water in a 3-cup saucepan, the heavier the better (I use enameled cast iron for all sugar syrups). Cover and cook over a low heat, until the sugar melts completely—every last grain must be dissolved. Uncover, raise the heat to high, and bring the liquid to a boil; boil for 1 minute. Remove the syrup from the heat to cool. Pour the cooled syrup into a container, cover, and refrigerate (this will keep for at least 6 months).

After 4 days, strain out the peel from the brandy with a stainless-steel slotted spoon. Stir in the sugar syrup.

Pour the flavoring into clean small bottles with tapered necks. Close tightly. Store in a cool cupboard.

VARIATIONS: To make Brandied Orange Flavoring, use the peel of 3 medium-size bright-skinned oranges in place of the lemon peel.

Once in a while, I'm inclined to use tangerine peel, and what results is a highly agreeable, if not downright poetic, tangerine brandy flavoring, a splash of which is lovely in a winter fruit salad or spun into a homemade tangerine sorbet.

Aromatics

FLAVORED HONEY

MAKES 1 CUP

A few thin sticks of cinnamon, a sprinkling of cloves, several allspice berries, each may transform and cause to shine a cup of plain clover honey. Use very handsome jars to package flavored honey, the kind made of moderately thick glass just a shade over a cup in capacity, and topped off with a white porcelain screw-top lid. Some of these are available with hand-painted tops.

1 cup clover honey
2 cinnamon sticks, or
1 small imported bay leaf, or
2 pieces dried Jamaican ginger, or

¼ teaspoon perfect whole allspice
  berries, or
¼ teaspoon perfect whole cloves

To add cinnamon sticks, bay leaves, or ginger pieces, pour the full cup of honey into a jar, then put the spices in. Close the jar.

To add allspice berries or cloves, pour in half of the honey, drop in half of the spices, then pour on the remaining honey. Top the honey with the last of the spices and close.

Store the honey on a cool, dry shelf, away from any light, for 2 weeks before giving away or using.

HERB SUGARS

MAKES 2 CUPS

In her extremely versatile and cheery little book *Herbs for Every Garden* (E. P. Dutton, 1966, 1973) the author Gertrude B. Foster suggests a use for some herbs that I find a wonderful adjunct to some phases of cookery. She imbues granulated sugar (or confectioners' sugar) with leaves of rose geranium, peppermint, spearmint, lemon verbena, or rose petals. As the leaves dry out, the sugar draws in the marvelously rich flavor of the herb. When you dig into the sugar by the teaspoon, tablespoon, or even cupful, simply flick aside the herbs and use the sugar. Granulated sugar done this way is so good in sugar and water syrup for glossing over fresh fruit; superfine herb sugar (especially a blend made of peppermint and spearmint, or of lemon verbena) gives a bright, refreshing taste to summer beverages; and cookies and cakes that have confectioners' sugar in their mixtures snap to attention when you first steep herbs in before using in baking.

First, Gertrude Foster's instructions, then mine:

"All of the sweet herbs that go into fruit cups, cold drinks, cake icings and baked cookies lend themselves to putting up in granulated sugar to flavor it. The principle is the same as that used for vanilla beans which flavor a whole pint of sugar with one or two pods. Simply put a few fresh leaves of rose geranium, or peppermint or lemon verbena in a screw-top jelly jar, and fill to the brim with granulated or confectioner's sugar, depending on how you want to use it later. The leaves may stay in the jar, becoming dried as their flavor is absorbed by the sugar. They may be sifted out when you want to use a tablespoonful or half-cupful of the sweeting in desserts. Rose petals may be substituted for herb leaves if you have the fragrant old roses. I use confectioner's sugar, flavored with rose geranium leaves or apothecary's rose petals, to make the thin white icing I pour on raised coffee cake. You might like mint-flavored granulated sugar to sprinkle on cut up fruit, particularly orange, grapefruit, and bananas. If you want to make colorful gifts from herb sugars, get some paste vegetable colorings and work into the granulated sugar after sifting out the herb leaves. Pack in little glass jars and label with suggestions for use."

MY HERB SUGAR:

2 cups granulated sugar, or confection-
ers' sugar, or superfine sugar,
pressed free of all lumps

1 ounce rose geranium, or peppermint,
or spearmint, or lemon verbena,
or fragrant rose petals

In a 2-cup jar, place a third of the sugar and cover with about ⅓ ounce of clean, very dry herbs. Add the second third of sugar and herbs. Finish the layering with the remainder of the sugar and the remainder of the herbs. Cover the jar.

Keep the sugar on a cool shelf away from light for about 2 weeks before giving as a gift or using. The sugar keeps beautifully for 1 year.

DRIED ORANGE OR LEMON PEELS

For orange and lemon peels to send forth their full flavor in syrups, slowly simmered fricassees and ragouts, in milk steeped for custards, and so on, the peel must be stripped of firm, fresh fruit that is neither shriveled nor badly pockmarked. Then, and only then, with good peels at hand, do you get out your sewing basket and string the peels for drying out. The leathery dried pieces may be lightly packed in a special jar and stored. I like to remind those who get the peels (usually with some kind of fruit bread or cake) that these, though seemingly common, contribute a glossy zest to marinated and simmered vegetable mixtures and all kinds of marinades for meat, fish, and fowl.

lemon or orange peels   a small trussing needle or strong nee-
sturdy white sewing thread   dle used for needlepointing

The citrus peel must be free of any lingering white pith; scrape off the pith with a small sharp knife, if necessary. Cut the peel into 2-inch lengths.

Thread your needle. String the peel, piercing it in the center, and leave about 2 inches between each piece. Suspend the line of peel to hang it (in a closet on a rod; between cabinets), or place it on a wire mesh cooling rack. Dry the peel for about 3 days, or until it hardens up a bit and is no longer moist.

Gently pull the peel from the string and store airtight in jars. The peel keeps for at least 6 months.

Sweet and Spicy Preserves and Pickles

These vibrant, sweet, and savory "put-ups" turn the spring kitchen glowing. When deep pink stalks of rhubarb are plentiful, stir up slices of the fruit with vinegar, spices, and sugar for two zesty-tasting blends—these go well with spring lamb and carry well into summer when a jar or two should be tucked into the picnic basket and served along with anything barbecued, or cold roasted chicken or roasted pork.

The mustard is a smooth, thickish spread that can be used as is or whisked into mayonnaise and vinaigrette dressings; if you use eggs purchased at a health-food store to make the mustard (these are from hens that are not fed arsenicals or antibiotics and the yolks are quite yellow), you will arrive at mustard the shade of the first jonquil of spring. The Sweet and Hot Mustard stores well for many months and the spring is an ideal time to make it so that you'll have plenty of it on hand for summer vegetable and poultry salads.

Many of the recipes in this section can be canned by the boiling-water bath method. See chapter 1, pp. 8–11 for instructions.

RED ONION AND CURRANT MARMALADE   MAKES ABOUT 6 CUPS

Of all the relishes and similar things to savor this light yet perky marmalade is perhaps the easiest to prepare. And it's one of the most satisfying onion condiments to have on hand. I love it with slices of pâté, cool slices of roasted pork, and anything skewered and grilled.

8 tablespoons safflower oil
3½ pounds sweet red onions, thinly
*   sliced*
1 cup granulated sugar
⅓ cup red currant vinegar (available
*   at specialty food stores)*

1 cup sweet red vermouth
¼ cup black currant liqueur (crème de
*   cassis)*
½ cup dried, but moist, currants

In a 6-quart casserole, preferably of enameled cast iron, place the oil, onions, and granulated sugar. Put the pot over a moderate heat, and cook, stirring, just until the oil begins to sizzle. Reduce the heat to low, cover the pot, and cook the onions slowly until they have softened completely, about 20 minutes.

Uncover the pot, stir in the vinegar, vermouth, and liqueur. Bring the contents of the casserole to a boil, then boil the mixture slowly until lightly thickened, about 35 minutes. Add the currants, and continue boiling for 5 to 9 minutes longer, or until the marmalade holds its shape lightly in a spoon.

Ladle the marmalade into a clean, dry storage container and cool to room temperature. Cover and refrigerate. The marmalade may be stored in the refrigerator for up to 4 months.

RHUBARB AND RAISIN CONSERVE   MAKES ABOUT 6½ CUPS

Fanciers of tart (and much-neglected) rhubarb will adore turning chunks of it into conserve and chutney. The sweet-sour taste and plum-red color nicely offset game and rich poultry. My favorite way for using the chutney is to serve a bowl of it with hot pastry turnovers filled with ground meat or vegetables, or both.

3 cups granulated sugar
1/4 cup firmly packed light brown
   sugar
1/4 cup apple cider vinegar
2 tablespoons minced fresh ginger
1 teaspoon ground cinnamon

1 teaspoon ground allspice
1/4 teaspoon ground cloves
4 pounds firm, fresh rhubarb, cut into
   1 1/2-inch chunks
1 cup dark seedless raisins

    In an 8-quart nonmetallic casserole or kettle, place all but the last 2 ingredients. Cover the pot and cook the mixture over a low heat to dissolve the sugar. Uncover the pot, raise the heat to moderately high, and boil the liquid for 4 minutes.

    Add the rhubarb to the kettle and bring everything to a boil, stirring. Boil for 2 minutes. Reduce the heat so that the mixture simmers steadily, and cook for about 35 minutes, or until it barely holds its shape in a spoon. Add the raisins and continue to simmer for 5 to 10 minutes longer, until a little spooned onto a plate stays in shape but still remains soft, not pastelike.

    Pour the boiling-hot conserve into hot jars to 1/4 inch of the top; seal with hot lids and bands. Process pints in a boiling-water bath for 15 minutes; cool.

    Alternately, ladle the hot conserve into a sturdy container, cool to room temperature, cover, and refrigerate. The conserve keeps well in the refrigerator for at least 6 months.

    NOTE: I don't find raw rhubarb exceptionally hardy, despite its rather strong looks, so I plan to use the moist, firm stalks as soon as they arrive in my kitchen. If you must store rhubarb, place the lengths in a plastic bag, seal, refrigerate, and use within the next 36 hours.

RHUBARB CHUTNEY   MAKES ABOUT 4 CUPS

Spiced four ways, this chutney has a brisk, fruity flavor.

4 cups granulated sugar
1 cup water
1/2 cup apple cider vinegar
1 teaspoon ground cinnamon
1 teaspoon ground ginger
1/2 teaspoon ground allspice
1/2 teaspoon yellow mustard seed
1/2 cup chopped fresh lemon pulp
   (about 2 large lemons)

1/2 cup chopped fresh orange pulp
   (about 3 large oranges)
3 pounds rhubarb, cut into 1 1/2-inch
   cubes
1 cup currants
1 cup coarsely chopped English
   walnuts

In a 6- to 8-quart casserole, preferably of enameled cast iron, place the first 9 ingredients. Cover the pot and cook the mixture over a low heat to dissolve the sugar. When the sugar has dissolved, uncover the casserole, raise the heat to moderately high, and bring the contents to a boil; boil for 2 minutes.

Add the rhubarb to the casserole, bring the mixture to a boil, stirring. Reduce the heat so that everything simmers at a lively bubble, and simmer for 30 minutes, stirring from time to time.

After 30 minutes, add the currants and nuts. Continue to simmer the fruit and nut combination, about 10 minutes longer, until finally thick enough to form a light mass in a spoon.

Ladle the boiling-hot chutney into 2 hot pint jars to ¼ inch of the top; seal with hot lids and bands. Process the chutney in a boiling-water bath for 10 minutes; cool.

Alternately, spoon the chutney into a solid storage container, cool completely, cover, and store in the refrigerator. The chutney will keep for 4 months under refrigeration.

PICKLED PEARL ONIONS WITH VERMOUTH   MAKES ABOUT 12 CUPS

If you want to get terribly exotic, use red pearl onions in the recipe that follows; either way, choosing yellow or red, the very best onions approach the size of a large thumbnail and so turn this into a project for a determined cook, or for a cook and one extra set of enlisted hands. But the results are definitely worth all the work of blanching and peeling the onions. These are delicious with hamburgers, grilled steak or chicken, meatloaf, or pâté.

1 cup light olive oil
1 cup vegetable oil
1 cup white vermouth
¾ cup white wine vinegar
½ cup granulated sugar
1 tablespoon coarse (kosher) salt
5 garlic cloves, peeled and halved
1 teaspoon whole black peppercorns, lightly cracked in a mortar and pestle
¾ teaspoon fennel seed, lightly crushed in a mortar and pestle

2 tablespoons minced fresh thyme
¾ cup thick tomato puree (preferably homemade from ripe summer tomatoes)
¾ cup dried, but moist, currants
7 pounds perfect white or red pearl onions, blanched in boiling water for 2 minutes and peeled, leaving the root intact (trim any strands from the roots with a sharp paring knife)

In a 10- to 12-quart nonmetallic kettle, pour in the olive oil and vegetable oil. Add the vermouth, vinegar, sugar, and salt. Cover the kettle and cook over a low heat until the sugar has dissolved. Uncover the pot, add the garlic, peppercorns, fennel, thyme, and tomato puree. Bring everything to a boil; boil for 5 minutes.

Add the currants and onions to the pot and simmer slowly, with the lid on askew, for about 13 minutes, or until the onions are no longer rock-hard, but cooked through and still slightly crunchy.

Remove the solids from the pot (onions, currants, garlic cloves) with a slotted spoon to a bowl. Boil down the liquid until very lightly thickened, about 4 minutes. Cool the liquid; pour over the onions.

Refrigerate the onions in a covered container; the onions will keep for up to 3 months.

CARROT-LEMON PRESERVES   MAKES ABOUT 8 CUPS

Once a gardener friend dropped off 10 pounds of newly dug baby carrots right on my doorstep. They were divine. After I turned 4 pounds into an enormous pot of cream of carrot soup (with leeks, thyme, and pinches of cinnamon and nutmeg), I made preserves with the rest. Carrot preserves, you say? Yes! The contents of the preserving kettle looks like a mess of baby food at first, but soon the mixture thickens into something you would use as a spread for tea breads and muffins (especially Whole-Wheat Muffins with Currants and Bran Muffins), toast and coffee cake.

6 pounds fresh bunch carrots, peeled	1 teaspoon freshly ground nutmeg
5 cups granulated sugar	1 teaspoon ground cinnamon
finely grated rind of 4 lemons	½ teaspoon ground allspice
juice of 3 lemons, strained	1 cup chopped walnuts

Cut the carrots into 2-inch lengths. I own a steamer which is large enough to hold 6 pounds of carrots; those of you whose kitchen is equipped with a small basket-type steamer that fits in a saucepan will have to steam the carrots in about three shifts. Steam the carrots for 7 minutes or until tender.

Dump the soft, hot carrots into an 8 to 10-quart preserving kettle and mash them coarsely with a potato masher or sturdy wooden spoon. Stir in the sugar, lemon rind and juice, and spices. Cook the contents of the pot slowly over a low heat to melt down the sugar. When the sugar has dissolved, bring the mixture to a boil.

Boil the mixture for 20 minutes, at which point it should take on body. Add the walnuts and continue boiling, stirring frequently, about 10 minutes longer, until the mixture is thick enough to stand in a little mound on a cold plate.

Pour the boiling-hot preserves into hot half-pint or pint jars to ⅛ inch of the top and seal immediately with hot lids and bands.

SWEET AND HOT MUSTARD
MAKES ABOUT 1¾ CUPS

This tantalizing mustard is made from powdered mustard, a mixture of ground yellow and brown seeds of the plant. When the powder is blended with sugar and liquid (in this case, two kinds of vinegar), the explosion of "hotness" develops, and when left to "mature" overnight—a necessity—loses its raw taste. Dollops of the prepared mustard could find their way into dressings for cold poultry, seafood, or salads made from such strong-flavored greens as arugula or mâche. Generous slatherings of it do nicely over flank steaks or chicken parts bound for the grill or on pork loins to be roasted.

1 2-ounce tin dry mustard (preferably Colman's)
1 cup granulated sugar
½ cup rich wine vinegar

½ cup champagne vinegar
¼ teaspoon salt
2 extra-large or jumbo eggs, well beaten, at room temperature

In a nonmetallic bowl, preferably of china or glazed pottery, blend together the mustard and granulated sugar.

Whisking all the while, slowly pour in the vinegars. Blend in the salt. Let the mixture stand overnight, uncovered. (A whiff of this clears up your sinuses.)

The next day, transfer the mustard solution to the upper saucepan of a double boiler. Beat in the eggs. Have the bottom of the double boiler ready with very slowly simmering water (a few lazy bubbles hitting and breaking the surface now and again). Put on the top saucepan and cook the mustard for about 15 minutes, stirring, until it is thick enough to coat the spoon.

Pour the hot mustard into 2 hot half-pint jars to ¼ inch of the top; cover with lids and bands; process jars in a boiling-water bath for 10 minutes; cool.

Alternately, pour the mustard into one or two jars, cool to room temperature, then cover and refrigerate. The mustard keeps for at least 6 months under refrigeration. Portion out to a small beautiful jar when you need to.

NOTE: This recipe doubles successfully, but you will need a large (commercial) double boiler to cook it in; or, use 2 graduated saucepans, one inside the other.

GARLIC-IMBUED OLIVES
MAKES ABOUT 6 CUPS

Olives, spruced up with, oh, say, bay leaves, hot peppers, oregano, garlic, a little olive oil, and bottled, is the kind of undemanding type of cooking I like to do when a quick gift is needed. Or, when I pass by an ethnic market or delicatessen and cannot resist buying a few pounds of the green or black olives, I usually treat them this way, if I'm not using them for some kind of spread.

For packing up the olives, any clean glass jar works, but I am enchanted by the pale green glass preserving jars from Italy with rubber gaskets and hinged lids. The jars are rounded and shapely and the olives look gorgeous in them; avoid, however, darker glass jars in shades of amber or, heaven forbid, a reddish-orange color.

3 pounds large green olives, pickled in
brine, well drained (see Note)
15 small garlic cloves, peeled but left
whole

3 imported bay leaves, each broken in
half
light, fruity olive oil

Lightly crack each olive with a cleaver to split it slightly, then drop it into a large bowl.

Dump the garlic cloves and bay leaf halves into the bowl. Pour on enough olive oil to make everything glisten, about ¾ cup.

Cover the bowl and refrigerate the olive mixture for 1 day, drawing a spoon through it once or twice.

If you are jarring the olives for immediate gift-giving, leave in the garlic cloves (they may stay in about 4 days); if not, remove and discard the garlic. Spoon the olives into jars, including some of the oily liquid, cover tightly, and refrigerate. Olives can be stored about 3 or 4 weeks. (After that, they lose their pungent taste and get soft.)

NOTE: The "Sevillana" olive, translated as "the olive of the Queen," looks large, plump, and green, and for me, has the best flavor for marinating. Smaller Spanish olives ("manzanilla") would be my second choice in the selection of a green olive. I just like the ample look of big, voluptuous olives. The oil-cured black olives are best bought out of bulk containers at specialty food shops; taste one before leaving the store with pounds of them—they should be soft, not hard as a pellet, and lightly smoky-tasting on the tongue.

GREEN OLIVES WITH CELERY AND ONION   MAKES ABOUT 6 CUPS

3 pounds green olives, pickled in brine,
well drained (see Note, Garlic-
Imbued Olives)
6 ribs of celery, preferably taken from
celery hearts, thinly sliced
2 small red onions, finely diced

2 teaspoons dried oregano
½ teaspoon whole black peppercorns,
lightly crushed in a mortar and
pestle
about 1 cup light, fruity olive oil

Lightly crack each olive to split it slightly, but don't mangle it, using a medium-weight cleaver to accomplish the job.

Place the olives in a bowl with the celery, onion, oregano, and peppercorns. Pour on about 1 cup olive oil, or enough to make the olives, celery, and onions shine.

Spoon the olive mixture equally in jars, along with any oil that may have settled to the bottom of the bowl, and cover the jars. Refrigerate the olives for up to 3 weeks.

HOT PEPPERED OLIVES   MAKES ABOUT 6 CUPS

3 pounds oil-cured black olives (see
Note, Garlic-Imbued Olives)
4 large garlic cloves, peeled and lightly
crushed with the blade of a knife
4 jalapeño peppers, halved down the
center (use rubber gloves to pro-
tect your hands while cutting
them), and deseeded

2 teaspoons dried oregano
¼ teaspoon whole black peppercorns,
cracked in a mortar and pestle
about ¾ cup light, fruity olive oil

Using a cleaver, lightly crack each olive to open it slightly.

Combine the next 5 ingredients in a large bowl; let stand for 1 hour. Stir in the oil.

If you are packing the olives to give away at once, leave the hot peppers in with the olives, distributing the pepper halves in equal amounts. If you are keeping the olives for a few days, remove the peppers after 24 hours, then, if you like, *insert 1 whole, fresh pepper* to each jar at packing up time, for color. Refrigerate the olives for up to 3 weeks.

Nuts: Dramatic and Spirited

I am most grateful to caterer Mimi Davidson for allowing me to share the recipe for Twice-Cooked Crispy Walnuts and for agreeing to let me include my own twists and turns to the method. All of the nuts are delicious, but the most asked-for recipe is the walnut one.

For gifts, bind jars of nuts with gingham fabric, especially the spring pastel colors, and attach a bunch of cinnamon sticks or savory packets to the side of the jars for a light and gossamer look.

TWICE-COOKED CRISPY WALNUTS

MAKES 8 CUPS

I received this incredible walnut recipe (of probable mixed ancestry) from my pastry-chef friend Mimi Davidson, who caters an outstanding chocolate dessert for a Washington, D.C., restaurant—a chocolate Bavarian molded in a thin, fudgy chocolate case—in addition to baking teatime specialties, like gorgeous tarts and plain cakes. Everyone I know raves about these nuts. They are light, crunchy, barely salted, and not too sweet. You can eat them anytime, but they're awfully good with drinks, scattered on top of chicken salad, and over poached fruit.

12 cups water
8 cups perfect walnut halves
1 cup granulated sugar

1 quart, 6 ounces fresh vegetable oil
about 1/4 teaspoon salt (preferably
freshly milled kosher salt)

It is very important to follow the directions *to the letter*; timing the walnuts as they are boiled should be done with a *reliable* minute-timer.

Bring the water to a boil in a 10-quart pot. When the water boils vigorously, add the nuts; stir for 10 seconds. Let the water return to a boil (the pot is still uncovered) and boil for *exactly* 1 minute. Pour the water and nuts in a large colander. Shake the colander for 1 minute or so to drain the nuts well.

Transfer the drained, still steamy nuts into a large bowl. Pour the sugar over them and stir. The heat of the nuts will dissolve the sugar.

In the meantime, pour the vegetable oil into a *heavy* 10-inch-wide straight-sided pan (I use a sauté pan with 3-inch sides—it works perfectly). Heat the oil to 350° F.

Stir the nuts again; check to see that the sugar has completely melted down in a glossy coating all over the nuts. There may be a small puddle of sugar-water at the bottom of the bowl, but that is to be expected.

While the oil is heating, line the insides of 2 large jelly-roll pans with clean, heavy paper bags. Keep one pan near the stove, the other on a convenient work surface.

With a scoop or measuring cup, add about 1½ cups of nuts to the hot oil. Fry the nuts for 3 to 4 minutes, or until golden. The nuts should not turn too dark or they will taste burnt; if they are pale and undercooked, they will have no flavor and not be crispy at all. The color should be that of medium amber. Quickly after they are cooked remove the nuts with a slotted spoon to the brown paper. Continue to fry the nuts in 1½ cup batches.

Make sure that you scatter the nuts on the brown paper in 1 layer. As the brown paper becomes covered with nuts (about halfway through), transfer the cooked nuts to the second pan to degrease thoroughly. When all of the nuts have been fried and transferred to the second pan, let them cool completely. Sprinkle the nuts evenly with the salt.

Store the nuts in a cookie tin. Do *not* store in plastic containers or in plastic bags, as the plastic turns the nuts soggy.

TOASTED TEXAS PECANS MAKES 4 CUPS

This goodie comes from the files of my long-time friend Alice Romejko, Texas born and bred. (You'll find another Alice R. recipe, "Z" Relish, in chapter 3.) Alice and her husband love to entertain, and their family Christmas celebration is a personal favorite of mine—it is a terrific blend of traditional holiday food lovingly prepared. For this recipe, I buy pecan halves with perfect anatomies because gifts of these nuts look the nicest when the nuts are not broken or chipped.

4 cups pecan halves
2 tablespoons melted unsalted sweet
butter
½ teaspoon salt
¼ teaspoon cayenne pepper

4 tablespoons Worcestershire sauce
½ teaspoon ground cinnamon
drops of hot pepper sauce, such as
Tabasco, to taste

Preheat oven to 275° F.

Place the pecans in a large bowl. Stir in the melted butter and salt. Add the remaining ingredients and mix well.

Turn the spiced pecans onto a cookie sheet and even them out into 1 layer. Bake the nuts on the middle-level rack of the oven for 30 minutes, or until all of the seasonings have been absorbed. From time to time, stir up the nuts with a spoon.

Cool the nuts in the pan until they have reached room temperature, then store in a covered tin.

NOTE: According to your taste, the amount of Worcestershire sauce may be increased by a tablespoon, and the hot pepper sauce may be shaken on for extra fire.

Old-Fashioned Cookies

A filled cookie jar, to have and to give, is the heart of festivity. Cookies are a light-hearted thing, easy to make and pack, and refreshingly varied in scope. They come in a variety of moods—dense and thick and rich; short, buttery, and sinful; perfectly formed and architectural; and playfully childlike. Likewise, the containers you reach for can be chosen to imitate each feeling.

I like to find packaging to suit the personality of the baked gems. I have seen extraordinary terra-cotta containers made to resemble burlap bags, with all the appropriate sags and folds, and this would make an outstanding vessel for wrapped cookies. Pewter pails, a stoneware basin, a large metal brioche mold, or a fabric-lined ceramic flowerpot all have pleasing lines and will show off the cookies in a wonderful, ornamental way.

Sugar Cookies

TRADITIONAL (MORE OR LESS) SUGAR COOKIES MAKES ABOUT 4 DOZEN

When it comes to sugar cookies, it's their plainness that charms me, and their opulent flavor never bores. Risky to the waistline, however, is to have them within handy reaching distance on the kitchen countertop in a big old glass jar. I love to use butter that is churned from raw cream (another health-food store item) in the following recipes. It gives a deep, rich flavor to the cookies.

3 cups all-purpose flour (preferably
unbleached)
½ teaspoon baking powder
½ teaspoon salt
1 cup unsalted sweet butter, softened
at room temperature
1½–2 cups granulated sugar

4 large or extra-large egg yolks, at
room temperature
2 teaspoons pure vanilla extract
2 tablespoons light cream, at room
temperature
multicolored sprinkles (optional)

Sift together the flour, baking powder, and salt onto a sheet of waxed paper; set aside.

In the large bowl of an electric mixer, cream the butter on moderate speed for 3 minutes. Add 1½ cups sugar in two additions, beating for a minute after each portion is added. Add the egg yolks, one at a time, beating for a minute after each is added. Beat in the vanilla extract and light cream. Add the sifted mixture on low speed in two additions, beating just until the flour particles are absorbed; scrape down the sides of the bowl after each amount of flour is added.

Chill the dough, wrapped in waxed paper, for about 4 hours, or overnight, so that it has firmed up and is easy to roll.

Preheat oven to 375° F. Divide the chilled dough into three portions. Roll out a segment of dough on a lightly floured wooden board to a thickness of about ¼ inch. Cut out cookies—I use a 3-inch round scalloped cutter—and place them on a parchment paper–lined cookie sheet 1½ to 2 inches apart. Shower the tops of the cookies with sugar or sprinkles.

Bake the cookies, a sheet at a time, on the middle-level rack of the oven for 8 to 10 minutes.

With a wide spatula remove the cookies to wire racks to cool completely. Layer them carefully in a tin, cover, and store airtight for up to 1 week.

MELTINGLY RICH SUGAR COOKIES   MAKES ABOUT 6 DOZEN

As the name declares, the cookies melt in your mouth; they are slightly sandy textured and crisp, and my holiday cookie basket would not be without them.

5 cups sifted all-purpose flour (prefera-	1 cup vegetable oil
bly unbleached)	1 cup sifted confectioners' sugar
½ teaspoon baking soda	2 cups granulated sugar
½ teaspoon cream of tartar	4 extra-large egg yolks, at room tem-
½ teaspoon salt	perature
1 cup unsalted sweet butter, softened	1 tablespoon plus 1 teaspoon pure
at room temperature	vanilla extract

Sift together the flour, baking soda, cream of tartar, and salt onto a sheet of waxed paper; set aside.

In the large bowl of an electric mixer, beat the butter on moderately high speed for 3 minutes. With the mixer going, beat in the oil, pouring it in a thin, steady stream; scrape down the sides of the bowl to encourage an even blend. The mixture will be somewhat liquid—that is to be expected.

On low speed, add the confectioners' sugar; beat for 1 minute. Add 1 cup granulated sugar, beat for another minute. Add the egg yolks, one at a time, blending for about 30 seconds on high speed after each yolk is dropped in. Beat in the vanilla extract.

On low speed, quickly but thoroughly incorporate the sifted ingredients, adding the mixture in three additions.

Cover the bowl with plastic wrap or aluminum foil and let the dough chill in the refrigerator until it has firmed up, about 5 hours. If you like, transfer the dough to a storage container, cover, and keep the dough in the refrigerator for up to 5 days before baking.

Preheat oven to 375° F. Take up level tablespoons of dough, roll them into balls, and then roll them in granulated sugar. Place the balls 2½ inches apart on parchment paper–lined cookie sheets. Flatten the balls with a cookie stamp dipped in sugar or with the tines of a fork. Bake the cookies on the middle-level rack of the oven for 8 to 10 minutes, or until very lightly golden in color (watch these carefully as they can burn easily).

Transfer the cookies to cooling racks (I use double-size racks for big batches), then store them airtight for up to 10 days.

SOUR CREAM SUGAR COOKIES

MAKES ABOUT 4 DOZEN

Soft, thick, and buttery.

6½ cups all-purpose flour (preferably unbleached)
2 teaspoons baking soda
1 teaspoon baking powder
1 teaspoon salt
1 cup unsalted sweet butter, softened at room temperature

3 cups granulated sugar
1 extra-large egg, at room temperature
2 extra-large egg yolks, at room temperature
2 tablespoons pure vanilla extract
1 cup sour cream, at room temperature

Sift together the flour, baking soda, baking powder, and salt onto a sheet of waxed paper; set aside.

In the large bowl of an electric mixer, cream the butter on moderately high speed for 2 minutes, or until light. Beat in 2 cups sugar, a cup at a time, beating for 1 to 2 minutes on moderately high speed. Blend in the whole egg and egg yolks, one at a time. Beat in the vanilla extract.

On low speed, beat in half of the sifted flour mixture, all of the sour cream, and finish with the rest of the sifted mixture. Scrape down the sides of the bowl with a sturdy rubber spatula after each addition.

Chill the dough, covered in a big length of waxed paper, until firm enough to handle, about 6 hours, or (preferably) overnight.

Preheat oven to 400° F. Roll out portions of the dough (it is easiest to divide this dough into thirds) on a lightly floured wooden board to a thickness of about ⅓ inch. With a 3-inch cookie cutter of your choice—I am partial to a star, bell, round (plain and scalloped), or diamond shape—cut out the cookies. Place them at least 2½ inches apart on parchment paper–lined cookie sheets. Dust the tops with granulated sugar. Bake each sheet of cookies on the middle-level rack of the oven for 10 to 12 minutes, or until they are just firm to the touch.

With a wide metal spatula, transfer the cookies to a cooling rack; when they have reached room temperature, store them airtight in a tin for up to 1 week.

Gingersnaps

CRISPY GINGERSNAPS   MAKES ABOUT 6 DOZEN

Both Crispy Gingersnaps and Molasses Gingersnaps provide spicy conclusions to a meal when fresh seasonal fruit—such as a versatile mixed berry "salad"—appears, or when a lively citrusy mousse or clean and clear tasting sorbet is featured. Crispy Gingersnaps are plain and look highly dramatic if you present them in a perfect overlapping design on a large, fine-mesh round sifter (the kind that looks like a big drum), or in a shallow lacquered box. For either, put in a spiffy bundle of ginger.

4 cups all-purpose flour (preferably unbleached)
1 tablespoon plus 1 teaspoon baking soda
¾ teaspoon salt
2 tablespoons ground ginger (preferably dried Jamaican ginger), freshly ground on the small holes of a hand grater

1½ teaspoons ground cinnamon
1½ cups solid shortening
3 cups granulated sugar
2 extra-large eggs, at room temperature
½ cup light molasses

Sift together the first 5 ingredients onto a sheet of waxed paper; set aside.

In the large bowl of an electric mixer, cream the shortening until light, about 3 minutes on moderately high speed. Add 2 cups sugar in two additions, beating for 2 minutes after each portion is added. Beat in the eggs, one at a time. Blend in the light molasses and beat for 1 minute; scrape down the sides of the bowl to keep the mixture even.

Add the sifted mixture in three parts, beating on low speed to incorporate the flour; beat for about 1 minute after each amount of flour is added. Cover the bowl and chill the dough in the refrigerator for about 5 hours, or until firm.

To bake the cookies, preheat oven to 350° F. Roll level tablespoons of dough into balls between the palms of your hands. Roll the balls lightly in the granulated sugar. Place the balls 2½ to 3 inches apart on parchment paper–lined cookie sheets. Bake the gingersnaps on the middle-level rack of the oven, a sheet at a time, for 12 to 14 minutes, or until they are firm to the touch.

Transfer the cookies to a wire cooling rack; when thoroughly cooled, store them airtight for up to 1 week.

MOLASSES GINGERSNAPS   MAKES ABOUT 6 DOZEN

Dark molasses is a rich liquid flavoring, a boiled by-product of cane sugar. I keep three kinds on hand: dark sulphured (used below), light unsulphured, and blackstrap. These cookies are earthier tasting than those made up by the preceding recipe and would feel right at home on a rough-hewn wooden tray or in a not-too-sleek woven basket.

4 cups all-purpose flour (preferably unbleached)
1 tablespoon plus 1 teaspoon baking soda
½ teaspoon salt
2 tablespoons ground ginger (preferably dried Jamaican ginger), freshly ground on the small holes of a hand grater
1 teaspoon ground cinnamon
1 teaspoon freshly ground nutmeg
¼ teaspoon ground cloves
2 large eggs, at room temperature
2 cups firmly packed light brown sugar
½ cup dark molasses
1½ cups vegetable oil
about 1 cup granulated sugar

Sift together the first 7 ingredients onto a sheet of waxed paper; set aside.

In the large bowl of an electric mixer, beat the eggs with the light brown sugar for 2 minutes on moderately high speed. Add the molasses and beat for 1 minute. With the machine on moderate speed, add the vegetable oil in a thin, steady stream. From time to time, scrape down the sides of the bowl to ensure an even mix. Beat the mixture for 1 minute on high speed.

On low speed, add the sifted flour mixture in three additions, blending just until the flour particles have been absorbed.

Cover the bowl and refrigerate the dough for at least 5 hours (or overnight, if you like) so that it can be rolled into balls.

Preheat oven to 375° F. Roll tablespoon-size balls of dough between your palms, roll them around in the granulated sugar, and place them 3 inches apart on parchment paper–lined cookie sheets. Bake each sheet of cookies on the middle-level rack of the oven for about 11 to 13 minutes, or until firm to the touch.

With a wide spatula transfer the cookies to cooling racks; store airtight for up to 1 week.

Oatmeal Cookies

OATMEAL AND DATE COOKIES   MAKES ABOUT 6 DOZEN

Where would the laid-back, kindly, old-fashioned cookie jar be without the invention of oatmeal cookies? A jar stuffed with a good and dense kind makes solitude pleasurable and children happy. Dates in the batter give this cookie a good "chew."

4 cups all-purpose flour (preferably unbleached)
1 tablespoon baking powder
2 teaspoons baking soda
1¼ teaspoons salt
2 teaspoons ground cinnamon
1 teaspoon freshly ground nutmeg
½ teaspoon ground cloves

2 cups unsalted sweet butter, softened at room temperature
3 cups firmly packed light brown sugar
4 large eggs, at room temperature
1 tablespoon pure vanilla extract
2 tablespoons buttermilk or sour milk
3 cups "quick-cooking" oatmeal
2 cups diced plump dates

Sift together the first 7 ingredients onto a sheet of waxed paper; set aside. Preheat oven to 375° F.

In the large bowl of an electric mixer, cream the butter on moderately high speed for 2 minutes. On moderate speed, add the sugar in three additions, mixing for about 1 minute after each amount is added. Add the eggs, one at a time, mixing for 1 minute after each is added. Scrape down the sides of the bowl now and again to keep the mixture even. Blend in the vanilla extract and buttermilk (or sour milk).

On low speed, add the sifted ingredients in two additions, mixing just until the flour particles have been incorporated. By hand, stir in the oatmeal and dates.

Drop rounded tablespoon mounds (keep them neat and even) of dough 3 inches apart on parchment paper–lined cookie sheets. Bake the cookies, a sheet at a time, on the middle-level rack of the oven for about 12 minutes, or until they are firm to the touch (just) and an overall light tan color.

With a wide spatula carefully remove the cookies to a large cooling rack. When cool, store them airtight for up to 1 week.

MOLASSES-OATMEAL SAUCERS   MAKES ABOUT 4 DOZEN

A hefty, satisfying cookie, jam-packed with coconut, raisins, and a full 3 cups of oatmeal.

1½ cups plus 1 tablespoon all-purpose
  flour (preferably unbleached)
¾ teaspoon baking soda
½ teaspoon baking powder
½ teaspoon salt
1 teaspoon ground cinnamon
¼ teaspoon ground allspice
¼ teaspoon ground cloves
6 tablespoons unsalted sweet butter,
  softened at room temperature
6 tablespoons solid shortening

1 cup granulated sugar
2 extra-large eggs, at room temperature
3 tablespoons plus 1 teaspoon dark
  molasses
3 tablespoons buttermilk, at room temperature
3 cups "quick-cooking" oatmeal
1 cup sweetened shredded coconut
1 cup dark seedless raisins, plumped in
  boiling water to cover, drained
  well, and dried on paper toweling

Sift together the first 7 ingredients onto a sheet of waxed paper; set aside. Preheat oven to 350° F.

In the large bowl of an electric mixer, cream the butter and shortening together on moderately high speed for 3 minutes. Beat in the sugar in two additions, beating for about 1 minute after each portion is added. Beat in the eggs, one at a time. Beat in the molasses and buttermilk.

On low speed, add the sifted ingredients in two additions, mixing just until combined with the creamed mixture. By hand, stir in the oatmeal, coconut, and raisins.

Drop the dough by rounded tablespoons 3 inches apart on parchment paper–lined cookie sheets. Bake the cookies, a sheet at a time, on the middle-level rack of the oven for about 15 minutes, or until they are firm to the touch.

Transfer the cookies to wire cooling racks; store airtight for up to 1 week.

NOTE: You could sacrifice ½ cup each of coconut and raisins, and stir in a cup of chopped walnuts if you like a complicated-tasting oatmeal cookie. Sometimes I do.

OATMEAL WAFERS

MAKES ABOUT 6 DOZEN

Mostly oatmeal, thin and wispy, and like a confection.

5½ cups "quick-cooking" oatmeal
6 tablespoons all-purpose flour (preferably unbleached)
¾ teaspoon salt
5 cups firmly packed light brown sugar

2 cups unsalted sweet butter, melted
  and cooled to tepid
2 large eggs, lightly beaten, at room
  temperature
2¼ teaspoons pure vanilla extract

Preheat oven to 375° F. Pour the oatmeal into a very large mixing bowl. Stir in the flour, salt, and brown sugar. Pour in the melted butter and mix.

In a small bowl, blend together the eggs and vanilla extract. Blend this into the oatmeal mixture.

Using 2 tablespoons, scoop up a tablespoon of the dough and release it with the second tablespoon onto a parchment paper–lined cookie sheet: 6 tablespoons, or mounds, of dough will fit on 1 cookie sheet, so space each tablespoon far apart from the next (I place them in 3 rows of 2 to a row). Do not place them any closer because the wafers will run into each other.

Bake the wafers, a sheet at a time, on the middle-level rack of the oven for 7 to 8 minutes. The centers must be cooked through and not feel tacky to the touch, but be careful, as the cookies go from a gentle brown color to burnt quite fast.

Remove the sheet from the oven (put in the next one to bake) and let it stand for about 5 minutes. Then carefully remove the cookies with a wide metal spatula to cooling racks. Store these delicate wafers in not-too-deep containers—piling up the cookies encourages breaking; these keep for up to 3 days.

MOLASSES AND SPICE COOKIES   MAKES ABOUT 5½ DOZEN

A noteworthy gift presentation is to find one of those plain medium-gray colored biscuit tins (an old one), line it with fabric, and fill it with a batch of these hearty cookies.

½ cup solid shortening
½ cup unsalted sweet butter
1 cup granulated sugar
1 cup light molasses
5½ cups all-purpose flour (preferably
    unbleached)

1½ teaspoons baking soda
1 teaspoon ground cinnamon
1 teaspoon ground ginger
1 teaspoon ground allspice
¼ teaspoon ground cloves
2 large eggs, at room temperature

Place the shortening, butter, sugar, and molasses in a heavy 6-cup saucepan. Warm the mixture over a low heat to dissolve the sugar, then bring to a boil. Remove from the heat to cool.

Sift together the next 6 ingredients onto a sheet of waxed paper; set aside.

In a small bowl, beat the eggs for 1 minute, then blend them into the cooled molasses mixture.

Slide the sifted mixture into a large bowl. Make a well in the center. Pour in all of the liquid mixture and stir to make a dough. Chill the dough in two portions wrapped in sheets of waxed paper; this will take about 5 hours. You may wish to store the dough in the refrigerator for up to 3 days before baking; if you do, double wrap the chilled dough first in sheets of plastic wrap, then in aluminum foil.

Preheat oven to 375° F. On a lightly floured board, roll out a portion of dough to a thickness of ¼ inch. Cut out cookies with a 3-inch cutter and place them at least 2 inches apart on parchment paper–lined cookie sheets. Bake the cookies, a sheet at a time, on the middle-level rack of the oven for 10 minutes, or until they are just firm to the touch.

Using a wide spatula place the baked cookies on a wire cooling rack. Store the cooled cookies airtight for up to 1 week.

WHOLE-WHEAT, COCONUT, AND RAISIN COOKIES

MAKES ABOUT 10 DOZEN

These are cookies of extravagant earthiness. Fans of humble, plump cookies most assuredly will love to sink their teeth in these.

5 cups sifted all-purpose flour (prefera-
    bly unbleached)
5 cups whole-wheat flour, fork-stirred
    to aerate it before measuring
1 tablespoon plus 1 teaspoon baking
    soda
¼ teaspoon baking powder
1 teaspoon salt
2 teaspoons ground cinnamon
1 teaspoon ground allspice
1 teaspoon freshly ground nutmeg
½ teaspoon ground cloves
½ teaspoon ground ginger
2 cups unsalted sweet butter, softened
    at room temperature

1 cup solid shortening
3 cups granulated sugar
2 cups firmly packed light brown sugar
1 tablespoon pure vanilla extract
8 large eggs, at room temperature
3 cups dark seedless raisins, plumped
    in boiling water to cover for 10
    minutes, then drained and dried
    on a double thickness of paper
    toweling
2½ cups sweetened shredded coconut
2 tablespoons light cream

Sift together the first 10 ingredients onto a very large sheet of waxed paper; set aside. Preheat oven to 350° F.

In the largest bowl of an electric mixer (this batter will fill the bowl to the brim), cream the butter with the shortening on moderately high speed for 5 minutes, or until light. Add all of the granulated sugar and continue creaming on moderate speed for 4 minutes; add all of the light brown sugar and cream for 3 minutes longer. Blend in the vanilla extract. Add the eggs on low speed, two at a time, beating to incorporate them before the next two are added.

On low speed, add the sifted dry ingredients in five portions, beating slowly to blend in the flour particles. Scrape down the sides of the bowl with a rubber spatula often. Remove the bowl from the mixer stand and scrape the batter into a bigger bowl. By hand, stir in the raisins, coconut, and light cream.

Drop tablespoon mounds of dough about 2 inches apart on parchment paper–lined cookie sheets. Bake 2 sheets of cookies on the upper- and lower-level racks of the oven for 12 to 15 minutes, or until just firm to the touch. Reverse the sheets from bottom to top and top to bottom after 6 minutes of baking time.

With a metal spatula transfer the cookies to wire racks. Store airtight when cool. These cookies stay fresh up to 1 week.

NOTE: Without betraying the goodness of the ingredient combination, roasted and unsalted sunflower seeds and chopped Brazil nuts, pecans, or walnuts can be tossed in. Just decrease portions of coconut and raisins and make up the volume with the nuts, seeds, or both.

PEANUT BUTTER COOKIES MAKES ABOUT 4 DOZEN

These crisp pillow-shaped cookies beg for some American-made container to hold them in. If the cookies are wrapped individually, then a wireware egg basket (with handle) makes a beautiful "bucket of cookies." Otherwise, some of those new gingham-patterned tins available at fashionable houseware stores gives a similar "country market" feeling to the gift. Peanut butter that is lightly salted and creamy, made from unblanched roasted Valencia peanuts, is the kind to use in this recipe. The peanut skins, bran, and germ are all included, which creates a cookie of particular richness and excellence.

2½ cups all-purpose flour (preferably unbleached)
1½ teaspoons baking soda
¼ teaspoon salt
1 cup unsalted sweet butter, softened at room temperature
1 cup granulated sugar

½ cup firmly packed light brown sugar
1 cup smooth, preservative-free peanut butter (available at health-food stores)
2 large eggs, at room temperature
2 teaspoons pure vanilla extract

Sift together the flour, baking soda, and salt onto a sheet of waxed paper; set aside. Preheat oven to 375° F.

In the large bowl of an electric mixer, cream the butter until light on moderately high speed, about 3 minutes. Add the granulated sugar and continue beating for 2 minutes. Add the brown sugar and beat for 2 minutes longer. Scrape down the sides of the bowl with a rubber spatula.

On moderately low speed, beat in the peanut butter along with the eggs. Scrape down the sides of the bowl again and beat on moderately high speed for 2 minutes. Blend in the vanilla extract.

On low speed, add the sifted flour mixture in two additions, beating just long enough for the batter to absorb the flour particles.

Drop the dough by even tablespoons 2 inches apart on parchment paper–lined cookie sheets. Dip the tines of a fork in a little flour, then press a crisscross pattern of lines in the center of each cookie to flatten it somewhat. Bake the cookies, a sheet at a time, on the middle-level rack of the oven for about 10 minutes, or until firm to the touch.

With a metal spatula remove the cookies to a wire rack. Store the cooled cookies airtight.

COCONUT ROUNDS
MAKES ABOUT 5 DOZEN

These cookies could just as well be picked out of a wooden barrel in a country store, they are that old-fashioned. The rounds are plain, crisp, and slightly cakey in texture, and look charming when gently stacked up in an old round dry measure. If you are not going the antique cookware route, take a trip to the hardware store and buy several galvanized mini-pails of 1-quart capacity. Line them with fabric and toss in the cookies.

2¼ cups all-purpose flour (preferably unbleached)
¾ teaspoon baking soda
½ teaspoon salt
½ teaspoon freshly ground nutmeg
1 cup unsalted sweet butter, softened at room temperature

2 teaspoons pure vanilla extract
1 cup granulated sugar
2 extra-large egg yolks, at room temperature
2 cups sweetened shredded coconut

Sift together the flour, baking soda, salt, and nutmeg onto a sheet of waxed paper; set aside. Preheat oven to 325° F.

In the large bowl of an electric mixer, cream the butter on moderately high speed for 3 minutes. Add the vanilla and sugar, and continue creaming for 3 minutes. Beat in the egg yolks.

Scrape down the sides of the bowl with a rubber spatula, and continue beating for 30 seconds longer. On low speed, add the sifted dry ingredients in two portions, blending just until the flour particles have been absorbed. By hand, stir in 1¼ cups shredded coconut.

Drop even (and neat) tablespoons of dough 2 inches apart onto parchment paper–lined cookie sheets. Sprinkle the tops of the cookies with shredded coconut. Lightly press the coconut on the cookies with your fingertips to make it stick. Bake the cookies, a sheet at a time, on the middle-level rack of the oven for 16 to 20 minutes, or until firm to the touch and pale golden.

With a wide spatula remove the cookies to a wire rack to cool. Store airtight.

ORANGE–POPPY-SEED COOKIES MAKES ABOUT 4 DOZEN

Light and crunchy.

2½ cups all-purpose flour (preferably
   unbleached)
1 cup unsalted sweet butter, melted
   and cooled
¼ cup sifted confectioners' sugar

1 teaspoon baking powder
¼ cup poppy seed
2 teaspoons pure vanilla extract
2 tablespoons finely grated orange peel

Sift the flour onto a sheet of waxed paper; set aside.

In a large mixing bowl, stir together the remaining ingredients. Stir in the sifted flour in three portions.

Chill the dough, covered, in the refrigerator for 3 hours or until firm.

Preheat oven to 350° F. Take up heaping teaspoonfuls of dough and roll them into balls. Place the balls 2 inches apart on parchment paper–lined cookie sheets. Bake the cookies on the middle-level rack of the oven until firm and barely colored, about 12 to 15 minutes.

With a metal spatula transfer the cookies to a cooling rack. When cool, store them airtight for up to 1 week. Just before packing or serving, dust the tops with confectioners' sugar.

A Luxurious Sweet Spread

CHOCOLATE-CHESTNUT SPREAD WITH RUM   MAKES ABOUT 4 CUPS

What a splendid treat to have or give, this chocolate spread. Thin, plain butter cookies and wedges of crisp pear or apple, or a bowl of strawberries with their stems attached, are the perfect accompaniments. Divide the recipe among 4 small crocks of 1-cup capacity and cover the tops of the spread, once firm, with rounds of dark brown paper dipped in rum before sealing with the lids. This keeps the spread fresh for up to 3 weeks in the refrigerator.

½ pound bittersweet chocolate
4 tablespoons light cream
½ cup granulated sugar
1 15½-ounce can unsweetened chestnut puree

½ cup cool, not cold, unsalted sweet butter
3 ounces cream cheese, cool not cold
4 tablespoons dark rum
2 teaspoons pure vanilla extract

Place the chocolate, cream, and sugar in the top of a double boiler set over barely simmering water. Heat the mixture until the chocolate and sugar melt down. Remove the top of the double boiler from the heat, wipe dry the bottom and sides with a cloth, and pour the melted mixture into a measuring cup; set aside.

Place the chestnut puree, butter, and cream cheese in the bowl of a food processor fitted with a steel blade. Cover and process the mixture until it is evenly pureed and very smooth. Scrape down the sides of the bowl with a rubber spatula. At first, the unprocessed lumps of butter and cream cheese ball up around the blade, but after several seconds the balls will be incorporated. Scraping down the sides of the bowl helps to blend everything together.

Stir 2 big blobs of the chestnut puree mixture into the chocolate and refrigerate the chocolate mixture for 10 minutes so that when you incorporate it into the pureed mixture, the butter in the mixture won't melt down.

Quickly, but thoroughly, whisk together the chocolate and chestnut mixtures with the rum and vanilla extract.

Without haste, pour the blend into four 1-cup containers, cover, and refrigerate. If you are putting rum papers on the tops, chill the spread in the refrigerator for about 1 hour, or until the top is firm, place on the rum-soaked papers, and cover.

NOTE: A ½ cup finely chopped English walnuts, very lightly toasted, tastes delicious in the spread. Fold them in by hand after the rum and vanilla have been added.

Appendix

Resources for Spices

Wide World of Herbs
11 St. Catherine Street E
Montreal, Quebec
H2X IK# Canada

San Francisco Herb and Natural Food Co.
P.O. Box 40604
San Francisco, California 94140

Green Mountain Herbs
P.O. Box 2369
Boulder, Colorado 80302

Cambridge Coffee, Tea and Spice House
1765 Massachusetts Avenue
Cambridge, Massachusetts 02138

Maid of Scandinavia
3244 Raleigh Avenue
Minneapolis, Minnesota 55416

Purity Maid
480 Johnson Avenue
Brooklyn, New York 11237

Zabar's
2245 Broadway
New York, New York 10024

The Spice Market
94 Reade Street
New York, New York 10013

Mr. Spiceman
615 Palmer Road
Yonkers, New York 10701

The Spice Corner
904 South 9th Street
Philadelphia, Pennsylvania 19147

Specialty Spice Shop
2757 152nd Avenue, NE
Redmond, Washington 98052

Specialty Spice House
Pike Place Market
Seattle, Washington 98105

The Spice Houses
1102 North Third
Milwaukee, Wisconsin 53203

Index